WORLD
Geography Activity Book

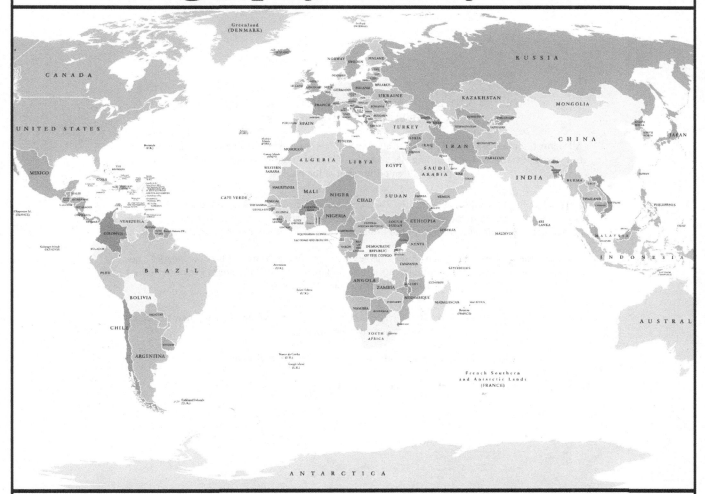

Maps, Facts, Flags, Activities:
Learn About the Countries of the World

Editor: Julie Grady

Earth, the third planet from the sun, has a total surface area of approximately 197 million square miles (509.6 million square km), of which about 29 percent is land (57.510 million square miles/148.940 million square kilometers). This landmass is divided into seven continents and 197 countries, each with its own unique history, cultures, and landscapes. The total population of Earth is 8.045 billion as of 2023. The seven continents are:

Africa — The only continent that lies in all four hemispheres, it is the second-largest and second-most-populous continent (behind Asia) with an area of approximately 30.37 million square kilometers (or 11.7 million square miles) and is home to 54 countries. From the vast Sahara desert to the dense rainforests of Central Africa, this continent boasts a wide range of climates and ecosystems. Africa is known for its rich cultural heritage, wildlife, and historic landmarks like the Pyramids of Egypt.

Africa is divided into five regions:

Northern Africa, which includes Algeria, Egypt, Libya, Morocco, Tunisia, Sudan, and Western Sahara.

Western Africa, which includes Benin, Burkina Faso, Cabo Verde, Côte d'Ivoire, Gambia, Ghana, Guinea, Guinea-Bissau, Liberia, Mali, Mauritania, Niger, Nigeria, Senegal, Sierra Leone, and Togo.

Central Africa, which includes Angola, Cameroon, Central African Republic, Chad, Democratic Republic of Congo, Equatorial Guinea, Gabon, Republic of Congo, and São Tomé & Príncipe.

Eastern Africa, which includes Burundi, Comoros, Djibouti, Eritrea, Ethiopia, Kenya, Madagascar, Malawi, Mauritius, Mozambique, Rwanda, Seychelles, Somalia, South Sudan, Tanzania, Uganda, Zambia, and Zimbabwe.

Southern Africa, which includes Botswana, Eswatini, Lesotho, Namibia, and South Africa.

While there are over 1,000 languages spoken across Africa, some of the most widely spoken include Arabic, Swahili, Hausa, Yoruba, French, Igbo, and Fula. Christianity, Islam, and traditional African religions are the most commonly practiced religions on the continent.

...

Asia — The Earth's largest and most populous continent. Covering about 44.58 million square kilometers, it is made up of 49 recognized sovereign states, the de facto state of Taiwan, and two special administrative regions (Hong Kong and Macau). Three countries (Russia, Turkey, and Kazakhstan) are transcontinental, with territory in both the Asian and European continents. The total population is about 4.6 billion (as of 2020). Asia has a variety of climates, from the cold mountains of the Himalayas to the tropical rainforests of Southeast Asia. Asia boasts rich histories, diverse cultures, and wonders like the Great Wall of China.

Asia is divided into six regions:

North Asia, which includes Russia, Mongolia, and Kazakhstan.

West Asia (often called the Middle East), which includes Armenia, Azerbaijan, Bahrain, Cyprus, Georgia, Iraq, Israel, Jordan, Kuwait, Lebanon, Oman, Palestine, Qatar, Saudi Arabia, Syria, Turkey, United Arab Emirates, and Yemen.

Central Asia, which includes Kazakhstan, Kyrgyzstan, Tajikistan, Turkmenistan, and Uzbekistan.

East Asia, which includes China, Japan, Mongolia, North Korea, South Korea, and Taiwan.

South Asia, which includes Afghanistan, Bangladesh, Bhutan, India, Iran, Maldives, Nepal, Pakistan, and Sri Lanka.

Southeast Asia, which includes Brunei, Cambodia, Timor-Leste, Indonesia, Laos, Malaysia, Myanmar, Philippines, Singapore, Thailand, and Vietnam.

While there are over 2,300 languages spoken across Asia, some of the most widely spoken include Mandarin Chinese, Hindi, Bengali, Russian, Japanese, Korean, and Arabic. Major religions practiced on the continent include Buddhism, Hinduism, Islam, and Christianity.

•••

Australia (and Oceania) — Australia, the smallest of the continents, is often referred to along with Oceania. This unique area encompasses the continent of Australia, the islands of New Zealand, and the Pacific islands scattered across the vast Pacific Ocean. Covering an area of approximately 8.525 million square kilometers (or about 3.3 million square miles), the region is home to a variety of sovereign states and territories. As of 2020, the combined population of Australia and Oceania is approximately 42 million. Known for its unique wildlife, coral reefs, and indigenous cultures, it's a beautiful and mysterious place to explore.

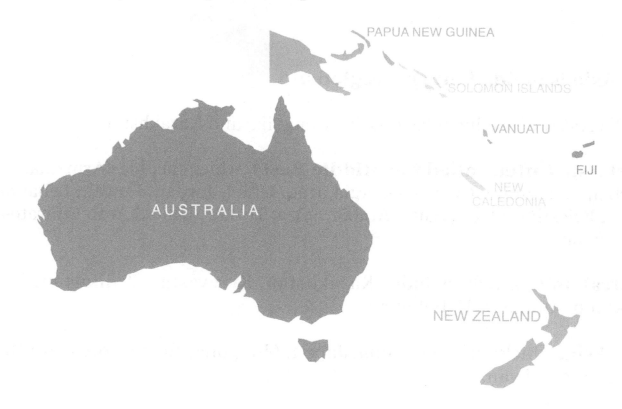

Australia and Oceania can be divided into three main regions:

Australia — The continent itself, known for its diverse landscapes, ranging from the arid deserts of the Outback to the bustling urban areas of Sydney and Melbourne.

Melanesia — Includes Papua New Guinea, Fiji, Solomon Islands, Vanuatu, and New Caledonia (France).

Polynesia and Micronesia — Encompassing the nations of Samoa, Tonga, Kiribati, Tuvalu, Micronesia, Marshall Islands, Nauru, and Palau, this area is spread out over thousands of miles of the Pacific Ocean.

New Zealand — Though part of Polynesia by its Maori heritage, it often stands distinct due to its significant cultural and environmental differences.

Languages in Australia and Oceania are diverse. English is the predominant language in Australia and New Zealand. However, across Oceania, over 1,100 languages are spoken, especially in Papua New Guinea, which alone has more than 800 recognized languages. Some of the commonly spoken languages in the Pacific islands include Fijian, Samoan, and Tongan. In addition to English, Australia recognizes many indigenous languages, with Aboriginal and Torres Strait Islander peoples preserving their linguistic heritage.

Christianity is the most practiced religion in the region, but indigenous beliefs and customs play a significant role, especially in the Pacific islands and among the Aboriginal and Torres Strait Islander communities of Australia.

•••

Europe — Situated entirely in the Northern Hemisphere, Europe is the second smallest continent covering approximately 3.93 million square miles (or 10.18 million square kilometers). It consists of 51 countries, with seven of these spanning both Europe and Asia. The total population is about 750 million (as of 2020). Europe is celebrated for its rich history, art, and culture. From the romantic streets of Paris to the ancient ruins of Greece, there's something for everyone.

Europe is divided into the following regions:

Western Europe, which includes Austria, Belgium, France, Germany, Liechtenstein, Luxembourg, Monaco, Netherlands, and Switzerland

Eastern Europe, which includes Belarus, Bulgaria, Czech Republic, Hungary, Poland, Moldova, Romania, Russia, Slovakia, and Ukraine

Northern Europe, which includes Denmark, Estonia, Finland, Iceland, Ireland, Latvia, Lithuania, Norway, Sweden, and United Kingdom

Southern Europe, which includes Albania, Andorra, Bosnia and Herzegovina, Croatia, Greece, Italy, Malta, Montenegro, North Macedonia, Portugal, San Marino, Serbia, Slovenia, Spain, and Vatican City

The countries of Russia, Turkey, Kazakhstan, Azerbaijan, Georgia, Armenia, and Cyprus have territory in both Asia and Europe.

Europe is a continent of diversity. There are twenty-four official languages and as many as 200 other languages spoken across the countries of Europe. While Christianity is the dominant religion, others such as Judaism and Islam are common and about 20 percent of the population does not identify with any religion.

•••

The Americas — Made up of North and South America, which together form two of the seven continents and make up the majority of the Western Hemisphere. With a combined area of approximately 42.549 million square kilometers (or 16.428 million square miles), the Americas consist of 35 recognized sovereign states, along with 13 dependent territories and

Alaska
(U.S.)

Greenland
(DENMARK)

C A N A D A

U N I T E D   S T A T E S

M E X I C O

THE BAHAMAS

Turks and Caicos
Islands (U.K.)

CUBA

Puerto Rico
(U.S.)

JAMAICA

ANTIGUA AND BARBUDA

BELIZE

HAITI

DOMINICAN
REPUBLIC

ST. KITTS
& NEVIS

Guadeloupe (FR.)

DOMINICA
Martinique (FR.)
ST. LUCIA

GUATEMALA

HONDURAS

ST. VINCENT AND
THE GRENADINES

BARBADOS

EL SALVADOR

NICARAGUA

GRENADA

TRINIDAD AND
TOBAGO

COSTA RICA

PANAMA

VENEZUELA

COLOMBIA

GUYANA

SURI-
NAME

Fr.
Guiana
(FR.)

Galapagos Islands
(ECUADOR)

ECUADOR

B R A Z I L

PERU

BOLIVIA

PARAGUAY

CHILE

URUGUAY

ARGENTINA

Falkland Islands
(U.K.)

0   1000 km
0   1000 mi

Greenland, an autonomous territory within the Kingdom of Denmark. The total population is 1.02 billion (as of 2020).

The Americas can be divided into four regions:

North America, which includes Canada, the United States, and Mexico.

The Caribbean, which includes Antigua and Barbuda, Bahamas, Barbados, Cuba, Dominica, Dominican Republic, Grenada, Haiti, Jamaica, Saint Lucia, Saint Kitts and Nevis, Saint Vincent and the Grenadines, Trinidad and Tobago, as well as the overseas territories of several European countries.

Central America, which includes Belize, Costa Rica, El Salvador, Guatemala, Honduras, Nicaragua, and Panama.

South America, which includes Argentina, Bolivia, Brazil, Chile, Colombia, Ecuador, Guyana, Paraguay, Peru, Suriname, Uruguay, and Venezuela.

While there are hundreds of languages spoken across the Americas, some of the most widely spoken include English, Spanish, Portuguese, French, and various indigenous languages. The main religion practiced on the continents is Christianity including Catholicism and Protestantism as well as a variety of indigenous religions, which reflect the diversity of the population. From the Andes mountains to the Amazon rainforest, it's a continent rich in history, culture, and natural wonders.

...

Antarctica — The southernmost continent, Antarctica, is the fifth-largest of the world's continents. Almost entirely covered by ice, it doesn't have any countries, but it is visited by scientists from around the world. It's a land of extremes: it's the coldest, driest, and windiest continent!

Our world is an enchanting mosaic of landscapes, languages, and cultures. From the bustling streets of Asian cities to the quiet vastness of the African savannah, there's a world waiting to be discovered. As you explore the pages of this book, remember that our planet is a treasure to be cherished and protected.

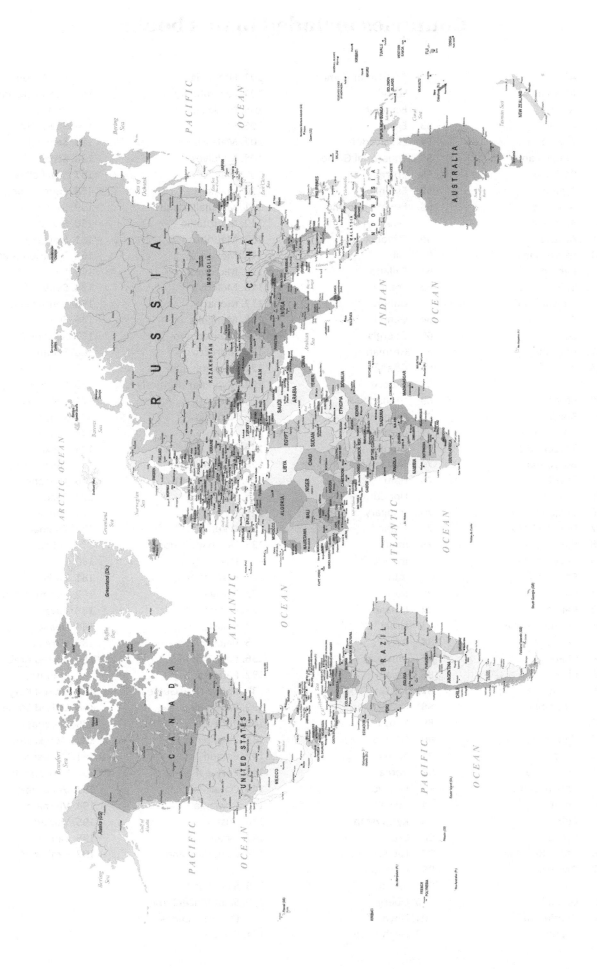

Countries included in this book:

1. Afghanistan
2. Albania
3. Algeria
4. Andorra
5. Angola
6. Antigua and Barbuda
7. Argentina
8. Armenia
9. Australia
10. Austria
11. Azerbaijan
12. Bahamas
13. Bahrain
14. Bangladesh
15. Barbados
16. Belarus
17. Belgium
18. Belize
19. Benin
20. Bhutan
21. Bolivia
22. Bosnia and Herzegovina
23. Botswana
24. Brazil
25. Brunei
26. Bulgaria
27. Burkina Faso
28. Burundi
29. Cabo Verde
30. Cambodia
31. Cameroon
32. Canada
33. Central African Republic
34. Chad
35. Chile
36. China
37. Colombia
38. Comoros
39. Congo
40. Congo
41. Costa Rica
42. Côte d'Ivoire
43. Croatia
44. Cuba
45. Cyprus
46. Czech Republic
47. Denmark
48. Djibouti
49. Dominica
50. Dominican Republic
51. East Timor (Timor-Leste)
52. Ecuador
53. Egypt
54. El Salvador
55. Equatorial Guinea
56. Eritrea
57. Estonia
58. Eswatini (formerly Swaziland)
59. Ethiopia
60. Fiji
61. Finland
62. France
63. Gabon
64. Gambia
65. Georgia
66. Germany
67. Ghana
68. Greece
69. Grenada
70. Guatemala
71. Guinea
72. Guinea
73. Guyana
74. Haiti
75. Honduras
76. Hungary
77. Iceland
78. India
79. Indonesia
80. Iran
81. Iraq
82. Ireland
83. Israel
84. Italy
85. Jamaica
86. Japan
87. Jordan
88. Kazakhstan
89. Kenya
90. Kiribati
91. Korea
92. Korea
93. Kosovo
94. Kuwait
95. Kyrgyzstan
96. Laos
97. Latvia
98. Lebanon
99. Lesotho
100. Liberia
101. Libya
102. Liechtenstein
103. Lithuania
104. Luxembourg
105. Madagascar
106. Malawi
107. Malaysia
108. Maldives
109. Mali
110. Malta
111. Marshall Islands
112. Mauritania
113. Mauritius
114. Mexico
115. Micronesia
116. Moldova
117. Monaco
118. Mongolia
119. Montenegro
120. Morocco
121. Mozambique
122. Myanmar (formerly Burma)
123. Namibia
124. Nauru
125. Nepal
126. Netherlands
127. New Zealand
128. Nicaragua
129. Niger
130. Nigeria
131. North Macedonia (formerly Macedonia)
132. Norway
133. Oman
134. Pakistan
135. Palau
136. Palestine
137. Panama
138. Papua New Guinea
139. Paraguay
140. Peru
141. Philippines
142. Poland
143. Portugal
144. Qatar
145. Romania
146. Russia
147. Rwanda
148. Saint Kitts and Nevis
149. Saint Lucia
150. Saint Vincent and the Grenadines
151. Samoa
152. San Marino
153. Sao Tome and Principe
154. Saudi Arabia
155. Senegal
156. Serbia
157. Seychelles
158. Sierra Leone
159. Singapore
160. Slovakia
161. Slovenia
162. Solomon Islands
163. Somalia
164. South Africa
165. South Sudan
166. Spain
167. Sri Lanka
168. Sudan
169. Suriname
170. Sweden
171. Switzerland
172. Syria
173. Taiwan
174. Tajikistan
175. Tanzania
176. Thailand
177. Togo
178. Tonga
179. Trinidad and Tobago
180. Tunisia
181. Turkey
182. Turkmenistan
183. Tuvalu
184. Uganda
185. Ukraine
186. United Arab Emirates
187. United Kingdom
188. United States
189. Uruguay
190. Uzbekistan
191. Vanuatu
192. Vatican City
193. Venezuela
194. Vietnam
195. Yemen
196. Zambia
197. Zimbabwe

AFGHANISTAN

National Motto: There is no god but God;
Muhammad is the messenger of God.

Capital: Kabul
Area: 252,071 square miles
(652,864 square kilometers)
Major Cities: Herat, Mazar-i-Sharif Jalalabad,
Kandahar
Population: 40.1 million
Bordering Countries:
Pakistan, Iran, Turkmenistan,
Uzbekistan, Tajikistan, China
Languages: Dari (Farsi),
Pashto
Major Landmarks: Babur's
Gardens, Herat Citadel,
Minaret of Jam, Band-e-Amir
National Park
Famous Afghans: Ahmad
Zahir (musician), Khaled
Hosseini (author), Ashraf
Ghani (politician)

National Symbol

Snow Leopard

Find the Words

F	X	D	K	P	Z	I	J	G	V	S	A
R	U	M	H	E	R	A	T	H	N	F	H
K	A	N	D	A	H	A	R	I	A	D	P
A	A	J	S	G	A	H	A	B	N	B	A
M	F	K	A	T	V	T	G	A	V	X	N
L	G	E	B	L	N	K	M	Q	A	O	J
M	H	A	N	U	A	L	U	I	T	T	S
G	A	B	O	E	E	L	K	N	K	V	H
D	N	M	P	H	J	I	A	A	D	B	I
N	S	W	G	D	U	R	G	B	B	U	R
T	O	R	A	B	O	R	A	H	A	U	Z
N	N	R	X	U	M	I	L	O	W	D	L

AFGHANS   KANDAHAR
HELMAND   KUNDUZ
HERAT   MOUNTAINS
JALALABAD   PANJSHIR
KABUL   TORA BORA

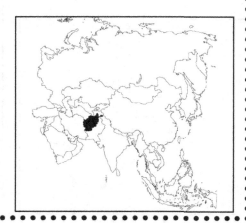

ALBANIA

National Motto: You, Albania, give me honor, give me the name Albanian

Capital: Tirana

Area: 11,100 square miles (28,748 square kilometers)

Major Cities: Durres, Elbasen, Vlore

Population: 4,802,740

Bordering Countries: Montenegro, Kosovo, North Macedonia, Greece

Language: Albanian

Major Landmarks: Osum Gorge, Langarica Canyon, Lake Ohrid

Famous Albanians: Frederik Ndoci (artist), Fadil Berisha (photographer)

Find the Words

```
F L B G R U P B E A M H
V G A J R E I G X N O E
U S N K R Y R E E P T B
Y U D O E O F S Z E H A
M A L U G O A U V P E L
Y V L M R B H K A Q R K
B R U B L R L R C G T A
P S M E A C E R I E E N
O T I G U N Z S Y D R S
U L X J X I I D V I E Q
T I R A N A Y A P G S V
R L A N G A R I C A A S
```

ALBANIA
BALKANS
DURRES
ELBASEN
LAKE OHRID

LANGARICA
MOTHER TERESA
OSUM GORGE
TIRANA
VLORE

National Symbol

Eagle

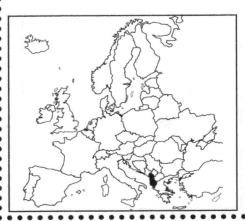

ALGERIA

National Motto: By the People and for the People

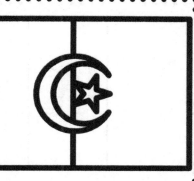

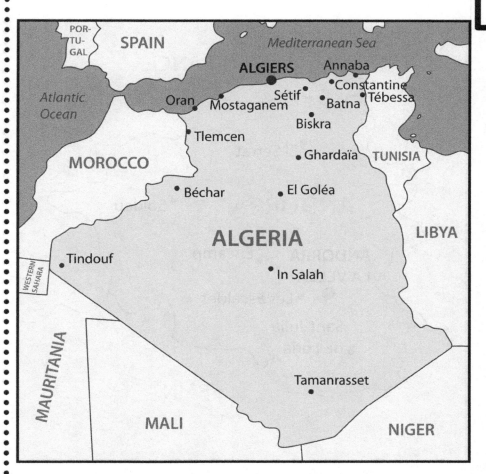

Capital: Algiers
Area: 919,595 square miles (2,381,741 square kilometers)
Major Cities: Algiers, Oran, Constantine, Annaba
Population: 44.6 million
Bordering Countries: Tunisia, Libya, Niger, Mali, Mauritania, Morocco, Western Sahara
Languages: Arabic, French, Tamazight (Berber)
Major Landmarks: Kasbah of Algiers, Djemila, Fort Santa Cruz, Pic des Singes, Ahaggar National Park
Famous Algerians: Albert Camus (author), Rachid Boudjedra (author), Yves Saint Laurent (fashion designer)

National Symbol

Fennec Fox

Find the Words

O	L	J	E	J	V	C	T	X	X	R	S
U	C	N	B	T	F	R	C	Y	F	R	P
C	Y	X	V	E	E	U	V	I	E	I	P
Z	L	V	O	S	R	F	R	I	I	F	S
O	I	L	E	R	Q	B	G	N	Q	A	A
T	G	D	F	Y	A	L	E	Q	Q	R	H
W	P	M	Y	V	A	N	R	R	Y	A	A
X	H	J	F	W	Z	I	I	O	S	B	R
M	Q	O	Q	T	T	F	I	S	A	I	A
A	L	G	E	R	I	A	P	S	L	C	N
C	T	A	J	L	U	A	T	R	N	A	E
K	A	S	B	A	H	W	B	S	W	G	M

ALGERIA   ISLAM
ALGIERS   KASBAH
ARABIC   OIL
BERBERS   ORAN
DESERT   SAHARA

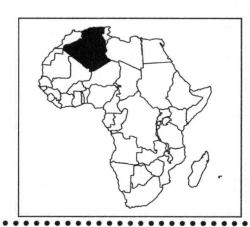

ANDORRA

National Motto: Strength United Is Stronger

Capital: Andorra La Vella

Area: 181 square miles (470 square kilometers)

Major Cities: Escaldes-Engordany, Encamp

Population: 77,265

Bordering Countries: Spain, France

Language: Catalan

Major Landmarks: Casa de la Vall, Centro Historico

Famous Andorrans: Antoni Bernadó (Olympic athlete), Marc Vales (soccer player)

FRANCE

• El Serrat

ANDORRA

• Soldeu

ANDORRA LA VELLA
• Encamp
• Les Escaldes

Sant Julià
• de Lòria

SPAIN

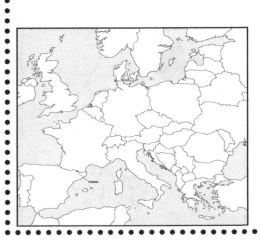

Find the Words

```
M C P M O U N T A I N S
Y A R W M C I A A F G Y
G S I Y C A N P O Q T Z
A A N R A T D Y R A U B
N D C O N A E R D U C O
D E I M I L P E I Y D B
O L P E L A E N N D X P
R A A R L N N E O D G Z
R V L O O D D E V N S Z
A A I L I F E S I L N Z
W L T F O L N V E R T F
V L Y X V B T C B I I D
```

ANDORRA	MOUNTAINS
CANILLO	ORDINO
CASA DE LA VALL	PRINCIPALITY
CATALAN	PYRENEES
INDEPENDENT	ROMERO

National Symbol

Brown Bear

ANGOLA

National Motto: Virtue Is Stronger When United

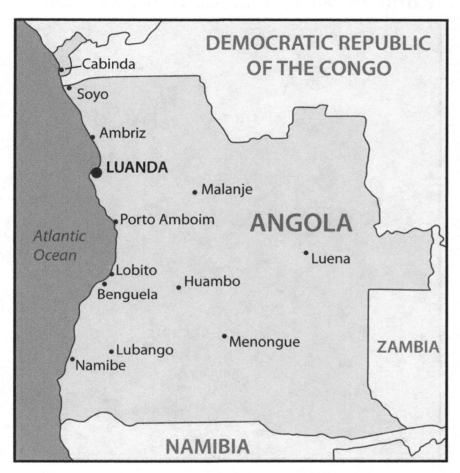

Capital: Luanda
Area: 481,354 square miles (1,246,700 square kilometers)
Major Cities: Luanda, Huambo, Lubango, Malanje
Population: 34.5 million
Bordering Countries: Republic of the Congo, Democratic Republic of the Congo, Zambia, Namibia
Languages: Portuguese, Umbundu, Kimbundu, and Kikongo
Major Landmarks: Fortaleza de São Miguel, Kalandula Falls, Iona National Park
Famous Angolans: Agostinho Neto (president), Isabel dos Santos (entrepreneur)

National Symbol

Giant Sable Antelope

Find the Words

```
B C T N B C E C N X T M
I K G C W I L D L I F E
K B W R S A T B K E F A
D A P A Z A Q M S F D J
I N H G N I V E Z N H S
A G R O D Z U A A U O Z
M O L S I G A U N R I A
O L E Q U L L R S N D G
N A H T A U K U I D A R
D B R A O O A R C V A D
S O A M U X I M A W E O
P E Y U V V T T V B C R
```

ANGOLA
DIAMONDS
KWANZA RIVER
LUANDA
MUXIMA
OIL
PORTUGUESE
SAVANNA
WAR
WILDLIFE

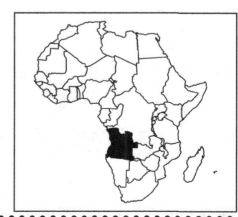

ANTIGUA AND BARBUDA

National Motto: Each Endeavoring, All Achieving

Capital: St. John's

Area: 171 sq mi (442 sq km)

Major Cities: St. John's

Population: 97,929

Bordering Countries: Maritime borders with Saint Kitts and Nevis, Montserrat

Language: English

Major Landmarks: Nelson's Dockyard, Shirley Heights, St. John's Cathedral

Famous Atiguans and Barabudans: Viv Richards (cricketer), Andy Roberts (cricketer), Jamaica Kincaid (author)

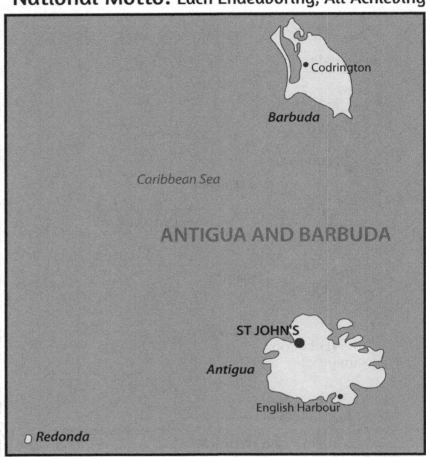

Codrington

Barbuda

Caribbean Sea

ANTIGUA AND BARBUDA

ST JOHN'S

Antigua

English Harbour

Redonda

Find the Words

```
J J L H D O C K Y A R D
D U M J R L K Z K M L G
B E S A I L I N G A B B
A C B C B P S H V D G A
R W A W R E O I E N G T
B A H R H I N R O Z V L
U W N C I R C S V T U A
D I A T A B L K W V I N
A E X C I E B B E H E T
B K B T N G D E L T N I
D Z Q Q F D U E A Y N C
R V W X N Z R A X N B K
```

ANTIGUA
ATLANTIC
BARBUDA
BEACHES
CARIBBEAN

CARNIVAL
CRICKET
DOCKYARD
NELSON
SAILING

National Symbol

Magnificent Frigatebird

ARGENTINA

National Motto: In Union and Liberty

Capital: Buenos Aires

Area: 11,073,500 sq mi (2,780,400 sq km)

Major Cities: Buenos Aires, Rosario, Mendoza

Population: 45.2 million

Bordering Countries: Bolivia, Brazil, Chile, Paraguay, Uruguay

Language: Spanish

Major Landmarks: Iguazu Falls, Perito Moreno Glacier, Buenos Aires' Obelisco, Casa Rosada

Famous Argentinians: Lionel Messi (footballer), Diego Maradona (footballer), Pope Francis

National Symbol

Rufous Hornero

Find the Words

```
T F W H P A M P A S A G
B T O P R R L P C M N X
Y U N T A Y X S A E D G
I B E T S I D I J S E A
V S I N F G N D C S S U
W V N R O O T E W I I C
E W V V G S B A F H T H
Q P B A A L A E N U P O
J D T R A N V I K G N S
E A C M I W H W R U O C
P E A C L W H J A E L Z
M A R A D O N A M W S A
```

ANDES
BUENOS AIRES
EVITA
GAUCHOS
MALBEC

MARADONA
MESSI
PAMPAS
PATAGONIA
TANGO

ARMENIA

National Motto: One Nation, One Culture

Capital: Yerevan

Area: 11,484 square miles (29,743 square kilometers)

Major Cities: Gyumri, Vanadzor

Population: 2,970,404

Bordering Countries: Georgia, Azerbaijan, Iran, Turkey

Language: Armenian

Major Landmarks: Geghard Monastery, Tatev Monastery, Khor Virab

Famous Armenians: Levon Aronian (chess player), Sirusho (singer)

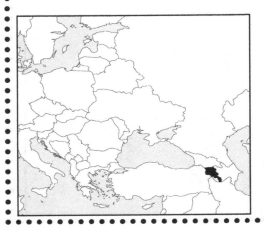

Find the Words

```
A K G A R M A V I R J B
R H G Y Z T F A S Y S J
M O W P U U H T G E Q N
E R J D O M A Z I H A K
N V V Q I G R R L V L J
I I F A A A E I E V H D
A R J R N T S R P I A U
N A A C S A E P U I T D
G B H A T Y D L O P K I
D L N J D L G Z B R R L
H O L Q I B D U O Y A M
M O T T O M A N S R D T
```

ARAGATS   KHOR VIRAB
ARMAVIR   MONASTERIES
ARMENIAN   OTTOMANS
DIASPORA   VANADZOR
GYUMRI   YEREVAN

National Symbol

Eagle

AUSTRALIA

National Motto: No official motto

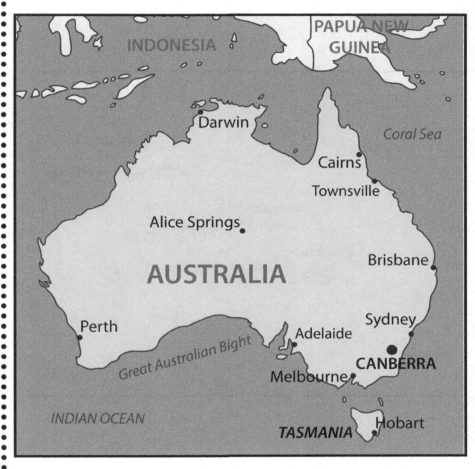

Capital: Canberra

Area: 2.969 million square miles (7.692 million square kilometers)

Major Cities: Sydney, Melbourne, Brisbane, Perth, Adelaide

Population: 25.69 million

Bordering Countries: Maritime borders with East Timor, Indonesia, New Zealand, Papua New Guinea, Solomon Islands, and New Caledonia

Language: English

Major Landmarks: Sydney Opera House, Great Barrier Reef, Uluru (Ayers Rock), The Twelve Apostles

Famous Australians: Hugh Jackman (actor), Steve Irwin (conservationist), Cate Blanchett (actress)

National Symbol

Kangaroo

Find the Words

```
D O S Y D N E Y P V O Z
K I V N A E B E E O M I
K D C W U W X C R M E D
O O Y Z S K L A T L L B
G R A G T A G Q H D B R
K J B L R N D H E B O I
O P E R A H O U S E U S
T J S K L B P F Z U R B
L F D I I N E L T C N A
Q H N M A M H A R R E N
C O R A L S E A R K Y E
V B A I C A N B E R R A
```

AUSTRALIA   KOALA BEAR
BRISBANE   MELBOURNE
CANBERRA   OPERA HOUSE
CORAL SEA   PERTH
KANGAROO   SYDNEY

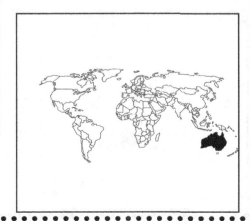

AUSTRIA

National Motto: No official motto

Capital: Vienna

Area: 32,386 square miles (83,879 square kilometers)

Major Cities: Vienna, Salzburg, Graz

Population: 9,006,398

Bordering Countries: Czech Republic, Germany, Slovakia, Hungary, Slovenia, Italy, Switzerland, Liechterstein

Language: German

Major Landmarks: Clock Tower, Hallstatt Old Town, Hofburg Palace

Famous Austrians: Joseph Haydn (composer), Karl Popper (philosopher)

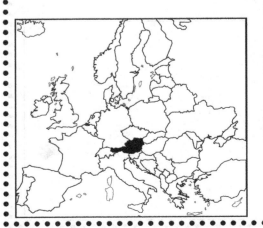

Find the Words

```
Q B V P E Z Q P E R O U
A O L D T O W N E E E U
L B A I G Z Z W K S A J
P H D U A F O Q R A S G
S K A R S T J I L L I E
J M G L K T G X Y Z D R
D W B C L R R A S B R M
H Q O X U S W I H U K A
J L J B G F T U A R L N
C W F V S I T A A G A S
D O X C X V S W T I G A
H Q V I E N N A J T Q M
```

ALPS	HALLSTATT
AUSTRIA	HOFBURG
CLOCK TOWER	OLD TOWN
GERMAN	SALZBURG
GRAZ	VIENNA

National Symbol

Austrian Black and Tan Hound

AZERBAIJAN

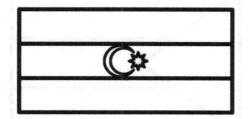

National Motto: No official motto (unofficial The Land Of Fire)

Capital: Baku
Area: 30,750 square miles (79,640 square kilometers)
Major Cities: Ganja, Mingecevir, Nakhchivan
Population: 10,139,177
Bordering Countries: Russia, Iran, Armenia, Georgia
Language: Azerbaijani
Major Landmarks: Baku Old City, Flame Towers, Gobustan National Park, Heydar Aliyev Center, Maiden Tower
Famous Azerbaijanis: Heydar Aliyev (politician), Garry Kasparov (chess player), Nizami Ganjavi (poet), Rashid Behbudov (singer)

National Symbol

Karabakh Horse

Find the Words

N	I	A	T	N	U	O	F	K	N
A	Z	E	R	B	A	I	J	A	N
G	Q	A	J	N	A	G	V	W	N
A	C	B	A	K	U	I	V	E	A
N	S	O	K	H	H	Y	S	M	R
J	F	V	U	C	X	R	P	A	A
A	A	C	H	N	E	G	S	L	K
V	K	K	Q	W	T	B	L	F	N
I	A	K	O	I	A	R	U	L	A
N	G	T	J	C	E	I	Y	X	L

AZERBAIJAN   GANJA
BAKU   GANJAVI
COUNTRY   LANKARAN
FLAME   NAKHCHIVAN
FOUNTAIN   TOWERS

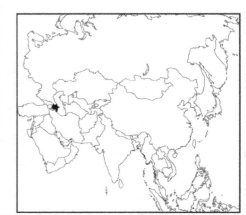

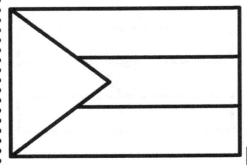

BAHAMAS

National Motto: Forward, Upward, Onward Together

Capital: Nassau

Area: 5,358 sq mi (13,878 sq km)

Major Cities: Nassau, Freeport

Population: 393,244

Bordering Countries: Maritime borders with Cuba, Haiti, United States, Turks and Caicos Islands

Language: English

Major Landmarks: Atlantis Paradise Island, Blue Lagoon Island, Andros Island

Famous Bahamians: Sidney Poitier (actor), Lynden Pindling (first Prime Minister), Buddy Hield (basketball player)

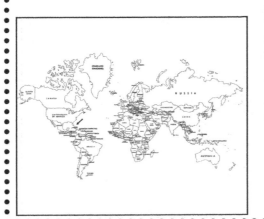

Find the Words

```
F U P C C M C S Y D V O
P N K I G O O Q N W O W
F B A Q R R N A Q N K N
O A G S D A L C A I A L
X H R N S S T K H S T V
J A A Y I A N E L O L S
U M U Z T I U Y S K A Y
D A R K J L H C T Y N U
Z S Y Y Q G W G Q F T X
A F L A M I N G O H I G
B I M I N I I Y U T C M
H B L T O L C A P S I A
```

ANDROS
ATLANTIC
BAHAMAS
BIMINI
CONCH
FLAMINGO
ISLAND
JINKANOO
NASSAU
PIRATES

National Symbol

Flamingo

BAHRAIN

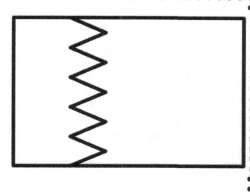

National Motto: No official motto (unofficial: Our Bahrain)

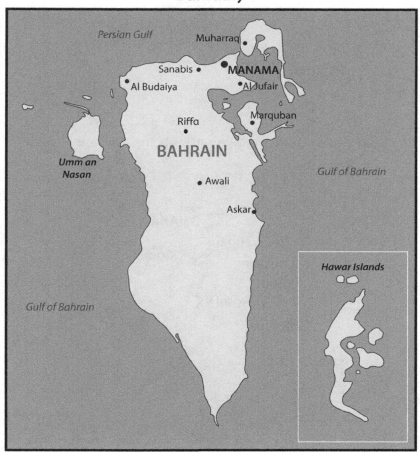

Capital: Manama

Area: 300 square miles (780 square kilometers)

Major Cities: Riffa, Muharraq

Population: 1.463 million

Bordering Countries: Maritime borders with Iran, Qatar, Saudi Arabia

Language: Arabic

Major Landmarks: Bahrain Fort, National Museum, Al-Fateh Grand Mosque, Tree of Life

Famous Bahrainis: Sheikh Isa bin Salman Al Khalifa (politician), Zainab Al-Eqabi (activist), Faisal Abdulaziz Al Mutawa (athlete)

National Symbol

Arabian Camel

Find the Words

A	F	N	H	B	M	C	I	Q	G
G	L	H	U	I	I	M	S	T	N
R	O	F	N	B	U	Y	A	C	I
A	C	B	A	E	P	X	T	A	A
N	I	R	S	T	L	E	O	M	R
D	A	U	D	D	E	N	W	A	H
E	M	F	J	I	S	H	N	N	A
N	A	T	I	O	N	A	L	A	B
Q	V	D	D	I	H	L	A	M	X
N	B	Z	X	E	U	Q	S	O	M

AL FATEH	ISA TOWN
AL HIDD	MANAMA
ARABIC	MOSQUE
BAHRAIN	MUSEUM
GRAND	NATIONAL

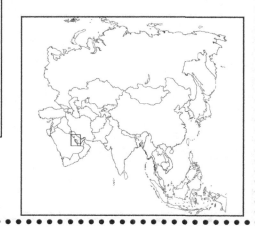

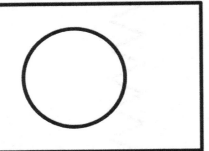

BANGLADESH

National Motto: Victory to Bengal

Capital: Dhaka

Area: 56,980 square miles
(147,570 square kilometers)

Major Cities:
Chittagong, Khulna, Rajshahi

Population: 169.4 million

Bordering Countries:
India, Myanmar

Language: Bengali

Major Landmarks:
Sundarbans National Park,
Cox's Bazar Beach, Lalbagh
Fort, Sixty Dome Mosque

Famous Bangladeshi:
Sheikh Mujibur Rahman
(politician), Rabindranath
Tagore (poet), Muhammad
Yunus (economist)

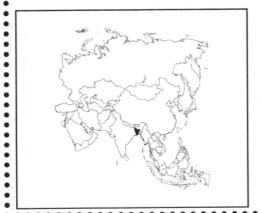

Find the Words

```
B D C S B A P I T J B Z
B A R O N O H Q A E E N
K T R L M A L A R S N K
W P U I H I N K O S G J
D H P S S B L H G O A H
K D J R A A W L C R L Y
L A C P C T L J A E I N
R G C H I T T A G O N G
N D T S Y L H E T N P B
Q W D D H A K A I N K P
P O U H N F O I T V R W
L D F L J H O D G Y K Z
```

BARISAL   JESSORE
BENGALI   KHULNA
CHITTAGONG   PABNA
COMILLA   RAJSHAHI
DHAKA   SYLHET

National Symbol

Bengal Tiger

BARBADOS

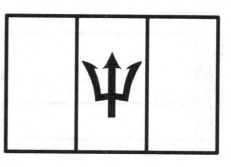

National Motto: Pride and Industry

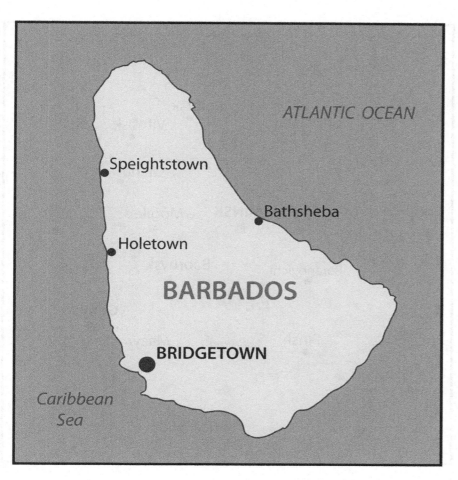

Capital: Bridgetown
Area: 166 sq mi (430 sq km)
Major Cities: Bridgetown, Speightstown
Population: 287,375
Bordering Countries: Maritime borders with Saint Vincent and the Grenadines, Saint Lucia
Language: English
Major Landmarks: Harrison's Cave, Carlisle Bay, Mount Gay Rum Distillery
Famous Barbadians: Rihanna (singer), Sir Garfield Sobers (cricketer), Mia Mottley (current Prime Minister)

National Symbol

Pelican

Find the Words

S	F	L	Y	I	N	G	F	I	S	H	S
N	P	X	B	T	O	E	R	J	M	E	B
D	B	E	K	A	B	Q	E	P	I	C	R
S	A	H	I	Q	R	N	Z	D	M	A	I
C	T	J	G	G	A	B	N	N	R	V	D
H	H	C	N	J	H	I	A	E	H	E	G
S	S	U	A	R	T	T	V	D	Q	S	E
T	H	B	O	S	L	O	S	I	O	S	T
R	E	P	E	E	P	D	K	T	G	S	O
Q	B	W	H	O	F	S	I	L	O	E	W
Z	A	I	R	D	N	G	B	G	Z	W	N
E	J	C	R	I	H	A	N	N	A	O	N

BAJAN
BARBADOS
BATHSHEBA
BRIDGETOWN
CAVES
CROP OVER
FLYING FISH
RIHANNA
SPEIGHTSTOWN
WEST INDIES

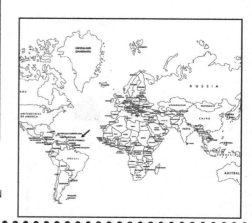

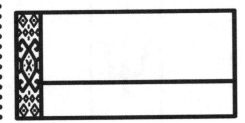

BELARUS

National Motto: Long Live Belarus!

Capital: Minsk

Area: 80,200 square miles (207,600 square kilometers)

Major Cities: Grodno, Gomel, Mogilev

Population: 9,449,323

Bordering Countries: Poland, Lithuania, Latvia, Russia, Ukraine

Language: Belarusian, Russian

Major Landmarks: Kosava Castle, Brest Fortress, Bialowieza Forest

Famous Belarusians: Marc Chagall (artist), Lev Vygotsky (psychologist)

Find the Words

```
E R G M X K E N E D O U
X U O E O S O L W N H X
B S M B L G T S D B B K
E S E G R S I O A E L M
L I L D A E R L K V X C
A A I C D G S Y E L A K
R N K O S M G T L R U Z
U R L A N D L O C K E D
S Q Y E I H M M C U Z N
I U R A D Z I W I L L L
A T H B F D I J Q U D U
N P N B C O W Z Q N K U
```

BELARUSIAN   KOSAVA
BREST   LANDLOCKED
CASTLE   MOGILER
GOMEL   RADZIWILL
GRODNO   RUSSIAN

National Symbol

European Bison

BELGIUM

National Motto: Unity makes strength

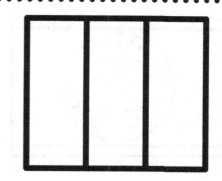

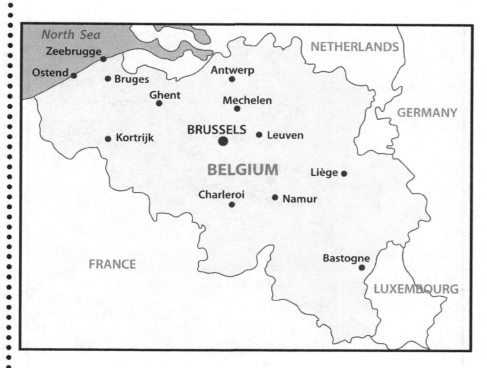

Capital: Brussels

Area: 11,849 square miles (30,689 square kilometers)

Major Cities: Brussels, Bruges, Antwerp

Population: 11,589,623

Bordering Countries: Netherlands, Germany, Luxembourg, France

Language: Dutch, French, German

Major Landmarks: Grand Palace, Canal du Centre

Famous Belgians: Charlemagne (king), Jean-Claude Van Damme (martial arts)

National Symbol

Lion

Find the Words

V	C	P	B	R	U	S	S	E	L	S	E
L	H	K	B	D	A	F	V	E	I	R	Z
Z	O	I	F	I	R	N	Q	Y	U	W	V
T	C	N	C	A	L	Y	T	T	O	S	K
P	O	G	W	H	O	I	C	W	E	C	N
K	L	D	X	K	G	E	N	L	E	S	R
H	A	O	R	I	T	B	R	G	L	R	P
W	T	M	E	I	Y	A	Y	A	U	K	P
S	E	F	H	N	H	X	N	X	I	A	K
G	P	C	O	C	E	A	N	L	O	L	L
I	R	L	E	E	C	B	R	U	G	E	S
A	G	R	A	N	D	P	A	L	A	C	E

ANTWERP   CANALS
ARCHITECTURE   CHARLES V
BILINGUAL   CHOCOLATE
BRUGES   GRAND PALACE
BRUSSELS   KINGDOM

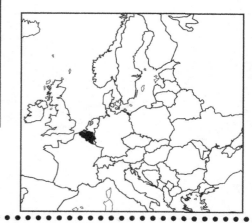

BELIZE

National Motto: Under the shade I flourish

Capital: Belmopan

Area: 8,867 sq mi (22,966 sq km)

Major Cities: Belize City, San Ignacio, Orange Walk, Belmopan

Population: 397,628

Bordering Countries: Guatemala, Mexico

Languages: English, Spanish, Creole

Major Landmarks: Great Blue Hole, Caracol Mayan Ruins, Xunantunich

Famous Belizeans: George Cadle Price (first Prime Minister), Marion Jones (athlete), Shyne (rapper)

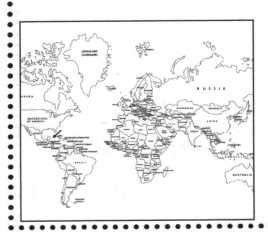

Find the Words

```
K B S U E N G L I S H Y
A R E A J E E W K K U F
D A M L K R A R S T E I
I I P Q I S C N F E W G
V N M E P Z I A R N D F
I F Q Z L U E R C G Y F
N O W Z R P E C M A W Z
G R Q R S I F C I Y O M
C E K M R X A T A T J A
U S W R Z Y P F H V Y Y
G T A J A G U A R C E A
L B G G I S D P S V G S
```

BARRIER REEF
BELIZE CITY
CACAO
CAVES
DIVING

ENGLISH
JAGUAR
MAYA
RAINFOREST
RUINS

National Symbol

Baird's Tapir

BENIN

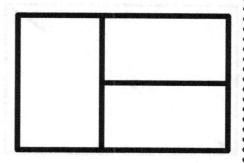

National Motto: Fellowship, Justice, Labor

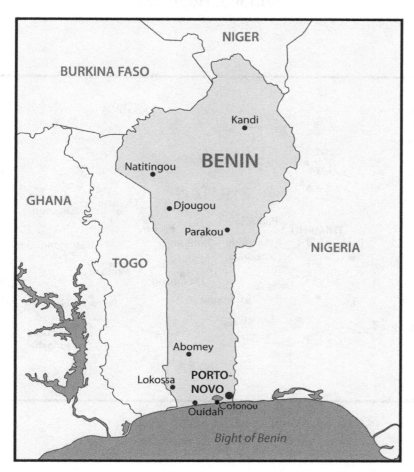

Capital: Porto-Novo

Area: 43,484 square miles (112,622 square kilometers)

Major Cities: Porto-Novo, Cotonou, Parakou

Population: 13 million

Bordering Countries: Burkina Faso, Niger, Nigeria, Togo

Languages: French, Fon, Yom, Yoruba

Major Landmarks: Kota Falls, Tanongou Falls, Abomey Palaces

Famous Beninese: Mathieu Kérékou (president), Angelique Kidjo (singer)

National Symbol

Leopard

Find the Words

```
Z W X H T B M M V P Y N
B A E U N X S U N E U W
X B A S G D O V M G P F
R O G I T N Q O P R Z C
B M A A O A H M A C A E
E E R T N A F Z E B G Q
N Y O N D V R R M N B O
I C N O K R I O I D D U
N P D D Q V S E G C H I
E P O R T N O V O U A D
S N O Y O R U B A G K A
E G J U T A R Z V N K H
```

ABOMEY
BENINESE
COTONOU
DAHOMEY
GANVIE

OUIDAH
PORT NOVO
SOMBA
WEST AFRICA
YORUBA

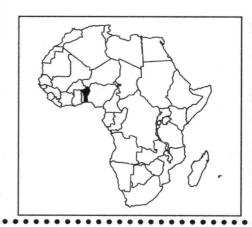

BHUTAN

National Motto: No official motto (unofficial: Gross National Happiness)

Capital: Thimphu

Area: 14,824 square miles (38,394 square kilometers)

Major Cities: Paro, Punakha, Trongsa

Population: 777,486

Bordering Countries: China, India

Languages: Dzongkha (Bhutanese), English

Major Landmarks: Taktsang Monastery, Punakha Dzong, Tashichho Dzong, Dochula Pass

Famous Bhutanese: Jigme Singye Wangchuck (king), Tshering Tobgay (politician), Tshewang Dendup (actor)

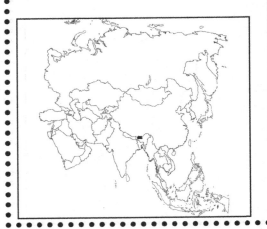

Find the Words

```
J  I  V  C  T  W  U  U  Q  V  Z  D
E  T  D  Z  O  N  G  K  H  A  R  K
S  B  R  S  Q  V  J  C  O  A  V  Y
A  U  C  O  B  P  U  J  K  A  E  R
M  M  X  D  N  M  U  A  E  L  S  E
D  T  V  Y  L  G  J  N  L  D  F  Q
R  H  B  T  G  O  S  A  A  Y  X  M
U  A  L  N  R  A  V  A  B  K  M  D
P  N  D  A  Q  A  S  F  S  Z  H  O
D  G  P  W  A  B  Z  A  A  J  Z  A
F  G  L  H  C  Q  P  K  X  Z  Z  R
T  H  I  M  P  H  U  J  I  H  C  N
```

BUMTHANG   PARO
DZONGKHA   PUNAKHA
GASA   SAMDRUP
HAA VALLEY   THIMPHU
JAKAR   TRONGSA

National Symbol

Takin

BOLIVIA

National Motto: Unity Makes Strength

Capitals: Sucre (constitutional), La Paz (administrative)

Area: 424,164 sq mi (1,098,581 sq km)

Major Cities: La Paz, Santa Cruz de la Sierra, Cochabamba, Sucre

Population: 11.67 million

Bordering Countries: Argentina, Brazil, Chile, Paraguay, Peru

Languages: Spanish, Quechua, Aymara

Major Landmarks: Salar de Uyuni, Lake Titicaca, Tiwanaku ruins

Famous Bolivians: Evo Morales (former President), Jaime Escalante (educator), Marcelo Martins (footballer)

National Symbol

Andean Condor

Find the Words

```
B  O  L  I  V  I  A  A  D  Z  C  X
L  L  A  M  A  I  C  W  A  F  L  P
A  L  Q  A  M  A  C  P  D  D  T  D
V  Y  B  A  C  V  A  A  A  G  B  M
Q  C  M  I  R  L  I  L  H  J  F  W
T  U  T  A  R  W  M  T  N  H  D  P
R  I  E  A  R  W  Y  I  P  H  N  O
T  V  L  C  W  A  E  P  S  X  Q  T
H  A  I  I  H  X  I  L  L  E  A  O
S  H  M  L  X  U  W  A  S  B  S  S
H  X  H  R  W  U  A  N  R  D  S  I
Q  U  I  N  O  A  G  O  J  O  V  K
```

ALTIPLANO	POTOSI
AYMARA	QUECHUA
BOLIVIA	QUINOA
LA PAZ	SALAR
LLAMA	TITICACA

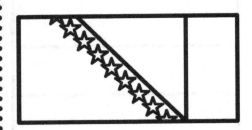

BOSNIA AND HERZEGOVINA

National Motto: No official motto

Capital: Sarajevo

Area: 19,767 square miles (51,200 square kilometers)

Major Cities: Sarajevo, Banja Luka, Tuzla

Population: 3,280,819

Bordering Countries: Croatia, Serbia, Montenegro

Language: Croatian, Bosnian, Serbian

Major Landmarks: Old Bridge, Kravica Waterfall, Stari Most

Famous Bosnians: Goran Bregović (musician), Ivo Andric (writer)

Find the Words

```
V T U Z L A J O B H M J
H E R Z E G O V I N A S
K S B O Q G O T A T P S
H T A J L D Q I S L R A
L A I B W D N G A L A R
Q R N K A S B C E C O A
D I X M O L I R I U O J
E M T B W R K V I H Y E
W O J D A I A A Q D F V
I S N N Q R J C N X G O
X T I Y K B H K P S O E
C D P D K T R A V N I K
```

BALKANS   OLD BRIDGE
BOSNIA   SARAJEVO
DINARIC ALPS   STARI MOST
HERZEGOVINA   TRAVNIK
KRAVICA   TUZLA

National Symbol

Golden Eagle

BOTSWANA

National Motto: Rain

Capital: Gaborone

Area: 224,606 square miles (581,726 square kilometers)

Major Cities: Gaborone, Francistown, Maun

Population: 2.588 million

Bordering Countries: Namibia, Zambia, Zimbabwe, South Africa

Languages: Setswana and English

Major Landmarks: Chobe National Park, Tsodilo Hills, Kalahari Desert

Famous Motswana: Ian Khama (president), Thomas Mogotlan (actor)

National Symbol

Zebra

Find the Words

```
K L K S V L O H O B D K
A A U N E N V G Y N P G
L W O C U R N C O V H A
A L U A W A O M U F R L
H M M O V I A W Z S C E
A M E A F I L O E E H H
R F K P D H N D U F O I
I O B I D Q K C L C B L
K S E T S W A N A I E L
G Y J D O V G P H J F P
X K G A B O R O N E G E
I D Q R V C P R L P O V
```

CHOBE   MAUN
DIAMOND   OKAVANGO
GABORONE   SEROWE
KALAHARI   SETSWANA
KGALE HILL   WILDLIFE

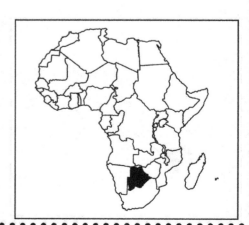

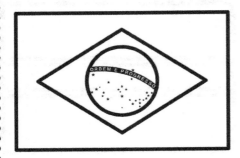

BRAZIL

National Motto: Order and Progress

Capital: Brasilia

Area: 3,287,957 sq mi (8,515,767 sq km)

Major Cities: São Paulo, Rio de Janeiro, Brasília, Salvador

Population: 212.56 million

Bordering Countries: Argentina, Bolivia, Colombia, French Guiana (France), Guyana, Paraguay, Peru, Suriname, Uruguay, Venezuela

Language: Portuguese

Major Landmarks: Christ the Redeemer, Amazon Rainforest, Iguazu Falls, Sugarloaf Mountain

Famous Brazilians: Pelé (footballer), Ayrton Senna (Formula One driver), Paulo Coelho (author)

Find the Words

```
S O N J G P E A H Q U T
A P Q G E Q B V A A Q D
O I A T H M C I E M C K
P F G N A C L F U A Q B
A Y F S T I B Z H Z V W
U R I O S A A R M O C L
L O Z A K U N H A N F O
O Q R T G D E A O Z S S
D B E I Q B V A L F I T
C P O R T U G U E S E L
O B Q C L P F J N T K R
L D S M X S O C C E R Z
```

AMAZON
BRASILIA
BRAZIL
IGUAZU
PANTANAL

PORTUGUESE
RIO
SAMBA
SAO PAULO
SOCCER

National Symbol

Jaguar

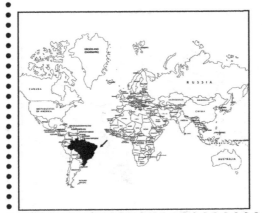

BRUNEI

National Motto: Always in service with God's guidance

South China Sea

Muara

BANDAR SERI BEGAWAN

Tutong

Seria

Kuala Belait

BRUNEI

Sukang

MALAYSIA

Capital: Bandar Seri Begawan

Area: 2,226 square miles (5,765 square kilometers)

Major Cities: Seria, Kuala Belait, Tutong

Population: 445,373

Bordering Countries: Malaysia

Languages: Malay, English

Major Landmarks: Sultan Omar Ali Saifuddin Mosque, Kampong Ayer, Royal Regalia Museum, Ulu Temburong National Park

Famous Bruneians: Hassanal Bolkiah (sultan), Pengiran Babu Raja (athlete)

National Symbol

White-bellied Sea Eagle

Find the Words

N	A	W	A	G	E	B	R	B	R
N	H	B	A	N	G	A	R	A	H
E	N	Y	A	L	A	M	M	N	A
D	N	J	K	A	U	O	U	D	I
Z	E	G	R	R	N	T	I	A	R
X	N	A	L	A	U	A	E	R	E
X	U	C	T	I	M	M	N	S	S
M	K	L	C	D	S	U	U	E	D
X	U	T	X	H	F	H	R	R	I
S	S	M	X	H	I	B	B	I	Y

BANDAR SERI	MALAY
BANGAR	MUARA
BEGAWAN	SERIA
BRUNEI	SULTAN OMAR
ENGLISH	TAMU

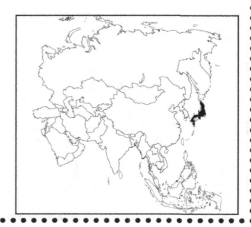

BULGARIA

National Motto: Unity Makes Strength

Capital: Sofia

Area: 42,855 square miles (110,879 square kilometers)

Major Cities: Plovdiv, Varna, Burgas

Population: 6,948,445

Bordering Countries: Greece, Macedonia, Romania, Serbia

Language: Bulgarian

Major Landmarks: Monastery of Saint Ivan of Rila, Sunny Beach, Aladzha Monastery

Famous Bulgarians: Nina Dobrev (actress), Grigor Dimitrov (tennis player)

ROMANIA
Vidin
Danube
Ruse
Dobrich
Pleven
SER.
BULGARIA
Varna
SOFIA
Sliven
Stara Zagora
Burgas
Black Sea
Blagoevgrad
Plovdiv
MACE.
Kardzhali
TURKEY
GREECE
Sea of Marmara
Aegean Sea

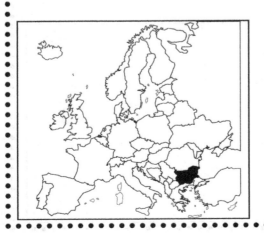

Find the Words

```
S Z U S M B F H H V W D
H U W V I Y R W O S E N
B S N K I L P K N B P P
L O T N V T H O U M S L
A F O Y Y C O N L L Q O
C I M O I B A S H Q V V
K A M O E D E J H L Z D
S D T G A U Y A W A R I
E S T F E X D G C I Q R
A B U R G A S Q H H V Q
W U L S A I N T I V A N
X L L V A R N A X E Z Q
```

BLACK SEA   SOFIA
BURGAS   STOICHKOV
DANUBE   SUNNY BEACH
PLOVDIR   VARNA
SAINT IVAN   VITOSHA

National Symbol

Lion

BURKINA FASO

National Motto: Unity, Progress, Justice

Capital: Ouagadougou
Area: 105,792 square miles (274,000 square kilometers)
Major Cities: Ouagadougou, Bobo-Dioulasso, Koudougou, Banfora
Population: 22.1 million
Bordering Countries: Mali, Niger, Benin, Côte d'Ivoire, Ghana, Togo
Languages: French, Mossi, Mooré, Dioula, Peul, Fulfuldé, Gourmantché
Major Landmarks: Ruins of Loropéni, Grand Mosque of Bobo-Dioulasso, Sindou Peaks, Douna Caves, Dô National Park
Famous Burkinabé: Thomas Sankara (president), Victor Démé (musician)

National Symbol

White Stallion

Find the Words

B	W	A	X	A	H	F	A	S	O	X	Q
U	L	N	E	P	I	H	N	U	U	Y	F
R	E	I	Y	W	D	J	M	W	X	M	M
K	F	K	D	O	U	N	A	C	A	V	E
I	M	R	J	B	N	O	E	X	O	E	O
N	L	U	E	U	A	V	Y	S	V	B	X
A	A	B	D	N	C	N	S	P	O	N	U
B	P	B	J	Q	C	A	F	B	J	Z	O
E	I	G	Z	J	L	H	S	O	D	S	D
U	O	G	U	O	D	U	O	K	R	N	N
N	M	V	I	T	H	C	L	I	E	A	I
I	S	D	G	G	G	L	F	P	W	L	S

BANFORA   DOUNA CAVE
BOBO   FASO
BURKINA   FRENCH
BURKINABE   KOUDOUGOU
DIOLASSO   SINDOU

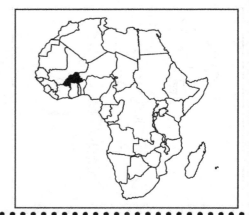

BURUNDI

National Motto: Unity, Work, Progress

Capitals: Gitega, Bujumbura

Area: 10,745 square miles (27,830 square kilometers)

Major Cities: Bujumbura, Gitega, Muyinga

Population: 12.55 million

Bordering Countries: Rwanda, Tanzania, Democratic Republic of Congo

Languages: Kirundi, French, English

Major Landmarks: Kibira National Park, Rusizi National Park, Karera Falls

Famous Burundian: Melchior Ndadaye (president), Gaël Bigirimana (athlete)

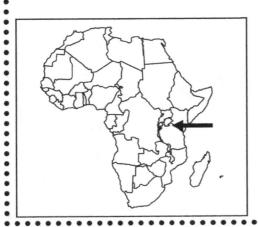

Find the Words

```
M C P Z U N Z V I A H E
F U R G K W M N B C S Y
K A S A G N I Y U M I B
U W O E S A H Q A G L K
W J B X E C L R A I G I
H Q L U N V U C Q T N R
W I I E R B I N B E E U
Z A R A M U K V Y G A N
D F G U W O N S A A C D
R K J Q H E U D H N I I
N U R U Y I G I I I T V
B I B U R U N D I A N J
```

BUJUMBURA	GITEGA
BURUNDI	KIRUNDI
BURUNDIAN	MUSEE VIVANT
ENGLISH	MUYINGA
FRENCH	RUYIGI

National Symbol

Leopard

CABO VERDE

National Motto: Unity, Work, Progress

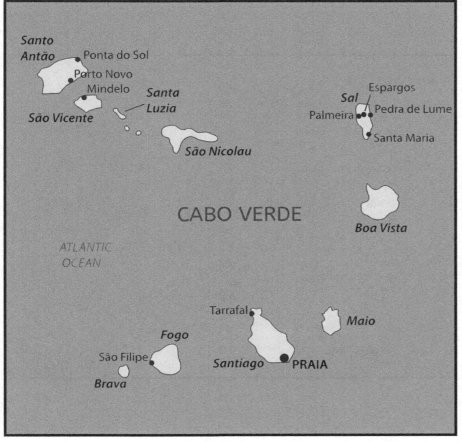

Capital: Praia

Area: 1,557 square miles (4,033 square kilometers)

Major Cities: Praia, Mindelo, Santa Maria

Population: 588,000

Bordering Countries: Maritime borders with Gambia, Guinea-Bissau, Mauritania, Senegal

Languages: Portuguese, Creole

Major Landmarks: Cidade Velha, Mount Fogo, Serra Malagueta Natural Park

Famous Cape Verdeans: Cesaria Evora (singer), Pedro Pires (president)

National Symbol

Grey-headed Kingfisher

Find the Words

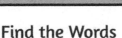

```
J P R B O A V I S T A A
T O G M W M B D E P H L
D R F N L T I L C L L S
C T W O D B O N E S E I
A U P B G E Z V D O Y P
P G R B R O E W N E I Q
E U A C Q D I A K C L N
V E I G A R C S H J H O
E S A D C L I P L O S Y
R E I H O T N R I A W L
D C U V G P N W O H N R
E S A N T A M A R I A D
```

BOA VISTA   MINDELO
CAPE VERDE   PORTUGUESE
CIDADE VELHA   PRAIA
CREOLE   SANTA MARIA
FOGO ISLAND   VOLCANOES

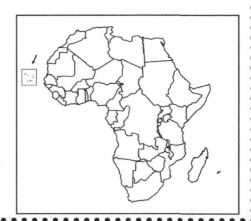

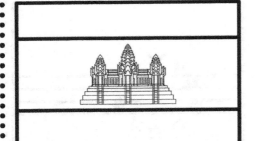

CAMBODIA

National Motto: Nation, Religion, King

Capital: Phnom Penh

Area: 69,898 square miles (181,035 square kilometers)

Major Cities: Siem Reap, Battambang

Population: 16.59 million

Bordering Countries: Thailand, Laos, Vietnam

Language: Khmer

Major Landmarks: Angkor Wat, Bayon Temple, Ta Prohm Temple, Royal Palace

Famous Cambodians: Norodom Sihamoni (king), Hun Sen (politician), Aki Ra (activist)

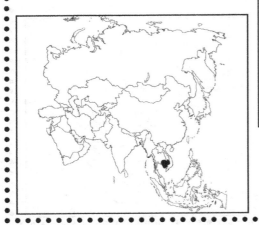

Find the Words

```
T O N L E S A P D S R M I
L G F B A T T A M B A N G
M E I S G N O R K H E A R
E L L I V K U O N A H I S
K D G B E Y A E M U I D E
V H O T E R P U P M V O U
O O M F W M J I O O H B Y
I R L E O X G U L L A M R
Z P Y N R R X H P P E A E
Q M H T G C E J O V R C A
X P R V M M Z Q T A P Y P
```

BATTAMBANG
CAMBODIA
KHMER
KRONG SIEM
PHNOM PENH

POL POT
PREAH VIHEAR
REAP
SIHANOUKVILLE
TONLE SAP

National Symbol

Kouprey

CAMEROON

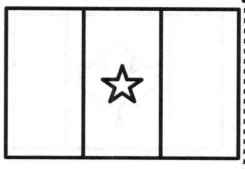

National Motto: Peace, Work, Fatherland

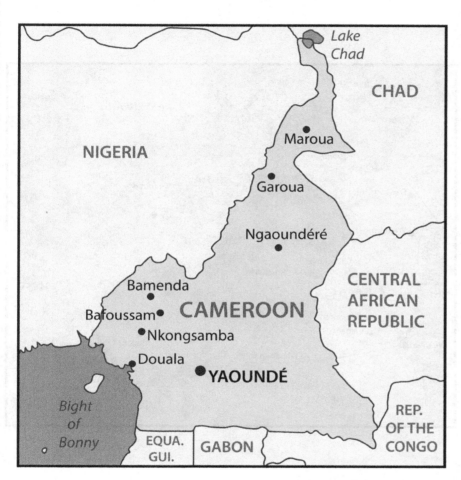

Capital: Yaoundé
Area: 183,569 square miles (475,442 square kilometers)
Major Cities: Douala, Yaoundé, Garoua
Population: 27.2 million
Bordering Countries: Nigeria, Chad, Central African Republic, Republic of the Congo, Gabon, Equatorial Guinea
Languages: French, English
Major Landmarks: Mount Cameroon, Waza National Park, Dja Faunal Reserve
Famous Cameroonians: Samuel Eto'o (soccer), Manu Dibango (musician), Paul Biya (president)

National Symbol

Lion

Find the Words

C	F	B	Y	A	O	U	N	D	E	M	L
K	A	A	L	R	E	T	O	O	A	N	V
R	E	M	F	P	C	K	H	S	A	O	C
W	R	E	E	I	I	F	S	L	L	O	J
V	L	N	C	R	P	U	A	A	E	R	B
I	I	D	L	T	O	U	B	I	N	E	M
M	B	A	M	F	O	O	K	B	K	M	S
T	E	N	A	D	I	Z	N	M	M	A	B
R	R	B	G	T	W	M	H	I	U	C	Y
G	T	R	S	O	I	E	J	B	A	X	Z
F	E	N	G	A	K	W	P	M	Q	N	V
I	E	D	O	G	A	P	A	L	M	F	S

BAFOUSSAM   DOUALA
BAMENDA   ETOO
BIMBIA   LA PAGODE
CAMEROON   LIBERTE
CAMEROONIANS   YAOUNDE

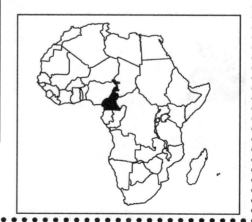

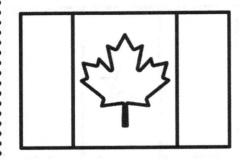

CANADA

National Motto: From Sea to Sea

Capital: Ottowa

Area: 3,854,083 sq mi (9,984,670 sq km)

Major Cities: Toronto, Montreal, Vancouver, Calgary

Population: 37.74 million

Bordering Countries: United States

Languages: English, French

Major Landmarks: Niagara Falls, Banff National Park, CN Tower, Old Quebec

Famous Canadians:
Justin Bieber (singer), Wayne Gretzky (ice hockey player), Margaret Atwood (author)

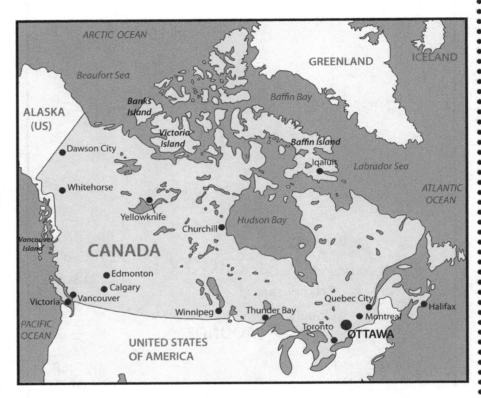

Find the Words

```
H F C I U E O E V I J S
A O J W L D N G Z T Z G
J I C P T I T N R T N U
Z F A K T Q U E B E C L
N M T U E K Y T M M D P
I D O O C Y I S X F H P
A P L O R R O C K I E S
G I U T R O M H E V R M
A N N T V S N S B A Q J
R U Y A H C O T N D I H
A I X W O O K D O D R M
O T J A M K I Z K J X A
```

HOCKEY   OTTAWA
INUIT   POUTINE
MAPLE   QUEBEC
MOOSE   ROCKIES
NIAGARA   TORONTO

National Symbol

Beaver

CENTRAL AFRICAN REPUBLIC

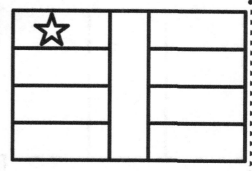

National Motto: Unity, Dignity, Work

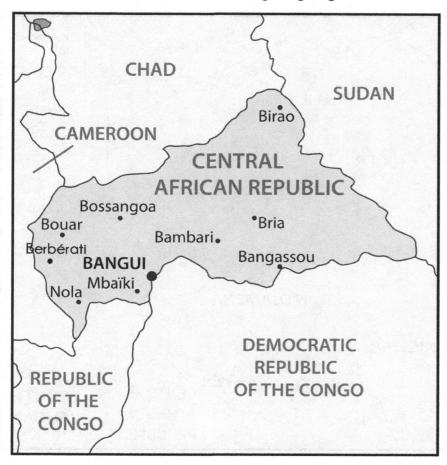

CHAD

SUDAN

CAMEROON

Birao

CENTRAL
AFRICAN REPUBLIC

Bossangoa

Bouar

•Bria

Bambari•

Berbérati

Bangassou

BANGUI

Nola   Mbaïki

REPUBLIC
OF THE
CONGO

DEMOCRATIC
REPUBLIC
OF THE CONGO

Capital: Bangui
Area: 240,535 square miles
(622,984 square kilometers)
Major Cities: Bangui,
Mbaiki, Berbérati
Population: 4,829,767
Bordering Countries:
Chad, Sudan, South Sudan,
Democratic Republic of
the Congo, Republic of the
Congo, Cameroon
Languages: Sango, French
Major Landmarks:
Dzanga-Sangha National Park, Boali Waterfalls,
Manovo-Gounda St Floris
National Park
Famous Central Africans:
Barthélemy Boganda (politician)

National Symbol

African Elephant

Find the Words

```
F J A F R I C A N N M P
I N R A D D A U O L R R
E T B E W C A R E I Z A
D I O B P F R P J A H U
D C E N A U M K O M U O
T E R X Y L B G E I I B
A N X D U P N L P K R N
P T O G B A P Y I Q A Z
S R N Z S E Z W Q C B H
S A T S N X W X U Y M V
B L O C V D F Z W R A Y
V B S H I U G N A B B P
```

AFRICAN	BOUAR
BAMBARI	CAR
BANGUI	CENTRAL
BANGUL	OUADDA
BOSSANGOA	REPUBLIC

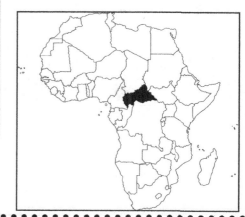

CHAD

National Motto: Unity, Work, Progress

Capital: N'Djamena

Area: 495,755 square miles (1,284,000 square kilometers)

Major Cities: N'Djamena, Abeche, Moundou, Sarh

Population: 17.18 million

Bordering Countries: Libya, Sudan, Central African Republic, Cameroon, Nigeria, Niger

Languages: Arabic, French

Major Landmarks: Zakouma National Park, Ennedi Plateau, Grand Mosque N'Djamena, Lake Chad

Famous Chadians: Idriss Déby (politician), Kaltouma Nadjina (sprinter)

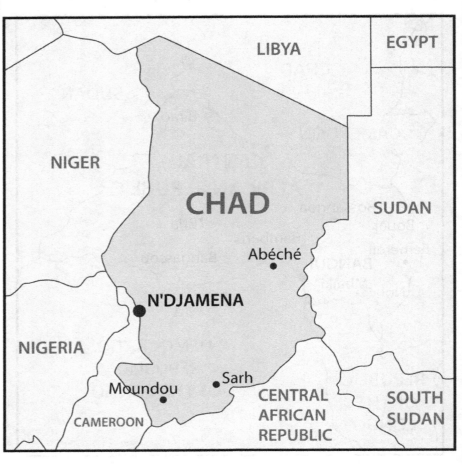

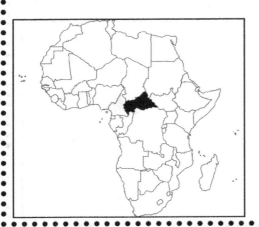

Find the Words

```
P Y C Q O O Q M L J Y A
L S F H Z I P V Z H N Z
O X C V A U X Y H E L C
E S H W G D X G M N S I
U R A O U N I A N G A B
Q Z D C L B J V C W Q A
S T I S E D F N M Q B R
O I A A N P H R I G S A
M J N R I X P X E X F D
D L S H G Y W G C N P L
N S U O D N U O M J C Q
A B E C H E N W Z B Z H
```

ABECHE MOSQUE
ARABIC MOUNDOU
CHAD NDJAMENA
CHADIANS OUNIANGA
FRENCH SARH

National Symbol

Lion

CHILE

National Motto: Through Reason Or By Force

Capital: Santiago
Area: 291,930 sq mi (756,102 sq km)
Major Cities: Santiago, Valparaíso, Concepción, Antofagasta
Population: 19.11 million
Bordering Countries: Argentina, Bolivia, Peru
Language: Spanish
Major Landmarks: Torres del Paine, Easter Island, Atacama Desert, Santiago's Sky Costanera
Famous Chileans: Pablo Neruda (poet), Arturo Vidal (footballer), Isabel Allende (author)

National Symbol

Huemul Deer

Find the Words

K	H	U	J	D	D	F	S	E	C	F	W
F	P	A	T	A	G	O	N	I	A	J	G
V	A	L	P	A	C	A	O	S	V	F	P
Q	I	M	O	A	I	R	G	A	A	F	X
N	N	N	Z	L	E	X	W	N	T	L	G
V	E	C	E	P	H	C	G	T	A	N	A
L	U	R	P	Y	I	Y	N	I	C	G	N
X	V	O	U	F	A	W	A	A	A	S	D
T	C	M	I	D	B	R	C	G	M	M	E
P	P	C	M	G	A	R	D	O	A	C	S
H	A	O	D	E	S	B	X	S	L	O	F
P	D	W	A	O	N	U	Q	C	D	G	P

ALPACA	NERUDA
ANDES	PACIFIC
ATACAMA	PATAGONIA
COPPER	SANTIAGO
MOAI	VINEYARDS

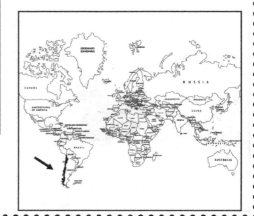

CHINA

National Motto: No official motto (unofficial: Serve the People)

Capital: Beijing
Area: 3,712,458 sq. mi. (9,615,222 sq. km.)
Major Cities: Shanghai, Xi'an, Chengdu
Population: 1.412 billion
Bordering Countries: Afghanistan, Bhutan, India, Kazakhstan, Kyrgyzstan, Laos, Myanmar, Mongolia, Nepal, North Korea, Pakistan, Russia, Tajikistan, Vietnam
Languages: Mandarin, Standard Chinese, Cantonese, Xiang
Major Landmarks: Great Wall, Forbidden City (Palace Museum), Terracotta Army, The Bund
Famous Chinese: Mao Zedong (politician), Confucius (philosopher), Yao Ming (athlete), Jackie Chan (actor)

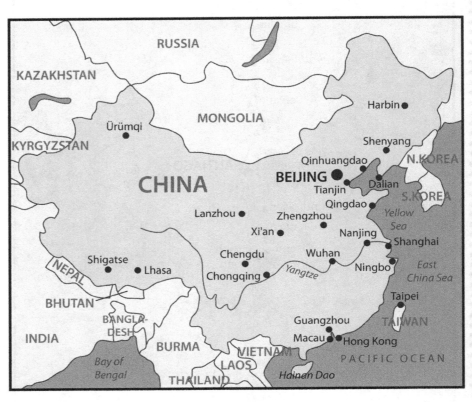

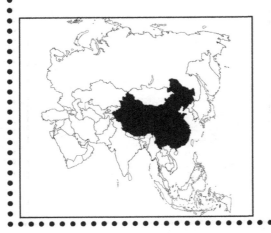

Find the Words

G	N	I	J	I	E	B	G	W	G
S	Q	U	A	R	E	N	R	G	A
S	P	H	V	O	B	U	E	N	C
C	H	I	N	E	S	E	A	O	H
E	R	A	N	C	G	P	T	K	I
Q	O	O	N	N	M	V	W	G	N
V	A	U	O	G	W	B	A	N	A
F	M	D	M	V	H	B	L	O	T
S	E	D	Q	X	N	A	L	H	U
Z	J	D	E	R	R	L	I	G	D

BEIJING   MAO
CHINA   RED
CHINESE   SHANGHAI
GREAT WALL   SQUARE
HONG KONG   ZEDONG

National Symbol

Giant Panda

COLOMBIA

National Motto: Freedom and Order

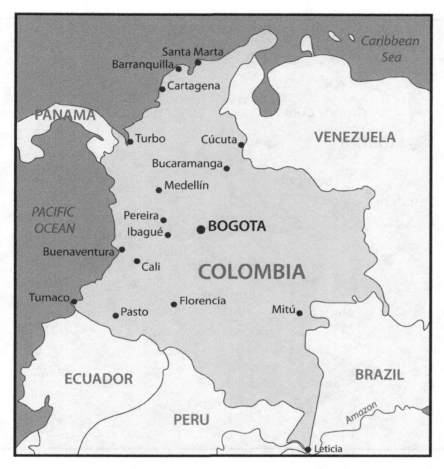

Capital: Bogota
Area: 440,831 sq mi
(1,141,748 sq km)
Major Cities: Bogotá,
Medellín, Cali, Barranquilla
Population: 50.88 million
Bordering Countries:
Brazil, Ecuador, Panama,
Peru, Venezuela
Language: Spanish
Major Landmarks: Ciudad
Perdida, Salt Cathedral of
Zipaquirá, Cartagena's Old
Town, Tayrona National Park
Famous Colombians:
Gabriel García Márquez
(author), Shakira (singer),
Sofía Vergara (actress)

National Symbol

Andean Condor

Find the Words

```
S I T C N J H G P R N U
F D S J A P I D K I A C
M P H U S R S G L U M F
B K A E P B T L S F A N
M V K M X Q E A H G Z H
A U I H K D E W G P O L
R W R U E E C S Q E N K
Q T A M F Z V U A A N F
U O H F Y S B X M L Y A
E N O P I O F O N B S X
Z C V Z B O G O T A I A
E M E R A L D S G D G A
```

AMAZON   EMERALDS
BOGOTA   MARQUEZ
CARTAGENA   MEDELLIN
COFFEE   SALSA
CUMBIA   SHAKIRA

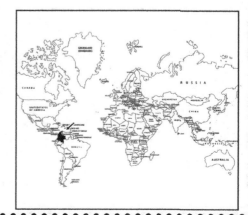

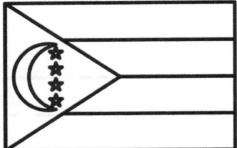

COMOROS

National Motto: Unity, Solidarity, Development

Capital: Moroni

Area: 863 square miles (2,235 square kilometers)

Major Cities: Moroni, Mutsamudu, Fomboni, Domoni

Population: 821,000

Bordering Countries: Maritime borders with Madagascar, Mayotte, Tanzania, Mozambique

Languages: Comorian, Arabic, French

Major Landmarks: Mount Karthala, Mitsamiouli Beach

Famous Comorians: Ahmed Abdallah (president), Jimmy Abdou (footballer)

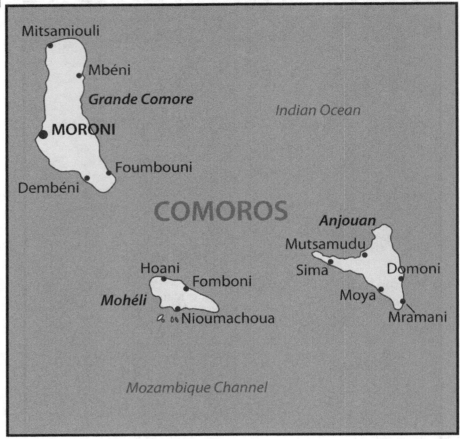

Mitsamiouli
Mbéni
Grande Comore
MORONI
Foumbouni
Dembéni
Indian Ocean
COMOROS
Anjouan
Mutsamudu
Sima
Domoni
Moya
Mramani
Hoani
Fomboni
Mohéli
Nioumachoua
Mozambique Channel

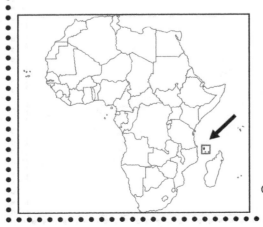

Find the Words

```
S U E M I L U U R W C G
H F S I S F I D B D A R
M C H O M O N I T J H A
L U V N T Z E V D E A N
R P T B N I Y I A O N D
P W H S L M Z S N O J E
I X H E A A O A I J O C
Z I H A G M C R G H U O
W O Z N L L U E O L A M
M E I Y O E Q D T N N O
R R H V V P S P U P I R
D C O M O R I A N F T E
```

ANJOUAN
CHOMONI
COMORIAN
GRANDE COMORE
MOHELI

MORONI
MUTSAMUDU
NGAZIDJA
VOLCANO
WHALES

National Symbol

African Civet

CONGO, DEMOCRATIC REPUBLIC OF THE

National Motto: Justice, Peace, Work

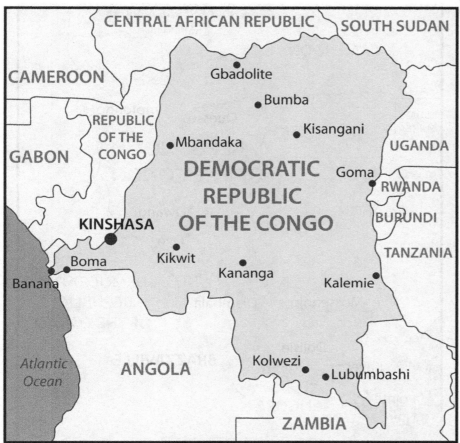

Capital: Kinshasa
Area: 905,355 square miles (2,344,858 square kilometers)
Major Cities: Kinshasa, Lubumbashi, Kisangani
Population: 95.89 million
Bordering Countries: Angola, Burundi, Central African Republic, Republic of the Congo, Rwanda, South Sudan, Tanzania, Uganda, Zambia
Languages: French, Kituba (Kikongo), Lingala, Swahili, Tshiluba
Major Landmarks: Mount Nyiragongo, Virunga National Park, Livingstone Falls
Famous Congolese: Patrice Lumumba (politician), Joseph Kabila (politician), Cédric Bakambu (soccer player)

National Symbol

Okapi

Find the Words

```
K V R K F E V Y E T R O
I I A L I R B S R E Y K
N R M C X S E H K N U E
S U O I A L A N V I C S
H N G L O Z X N C G A E
A G K G Y B H N G H M S
S A N R S V V T P A T E
A O S A B Y I N Y O N S
C I H S A B M U B U L I
S A A T C Q K Y P T F K
J E N O E S B B V T D A
U D I R N C O N G O J L
```

CONGO   KISANGANI
CONGOLESE   LUBUMBASHI
FRENCH   SABYINYO
GOMA   SESE SEKO
KINSHASA   VIRUNGA

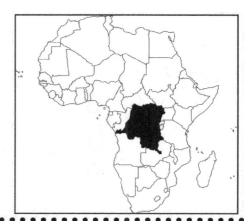

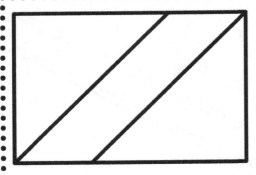

CONGO, REPUBLIC OF THE

National Motto: Unity, Work, Progress

Capital: Brazzaville
Area: 132,047 square miles (342,000 square kilometers)
Major Cities: Brazzaville, Pointe-Noire, Dolisie, Kayes
Population: 5.836 million
Bordering Countries: Angola, Cameroon, Central African Republic, Democratic Republic of the Congo, Gabon
Languages: French, Bantu, Kituba, and Lingala
Major Landmarks: Odzala-Kokoua National Park, Lesio-Louna Gorilla Reserve
Famous Congolese: Denis Sassou Nguesso (politician), Théophile Obenga (historian), Serge Ibaka (basketball player)

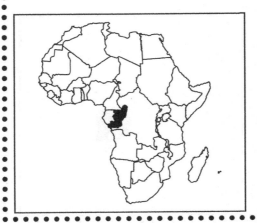

Find the Words

```
P P E C O N G O L E S E
E I O G E P P M Z R V E
L I M I R O B I C C U O
L M G N N N S G E Q D O
I P M A Q T C T S C D A
V F H T H D E O A N T M
A O E D D U M N A N W E
Z N C K T D A W O X N S
Z D U W N J O C M I K E
A O F A E O D K L B R K
R I R Z B U O G N O C E
B G W E Y E A L I B A K
```

BRAZZAVILLE
CONGO
CONGOLESE
GRAND MOSQUE
IMPFONDO
KABILA
OWANDO
POINTE NOIRE
PONT DU DJOUE
ST ANNE

National Symbol

Lion

COSTA RICA

National Motto: Pure Life

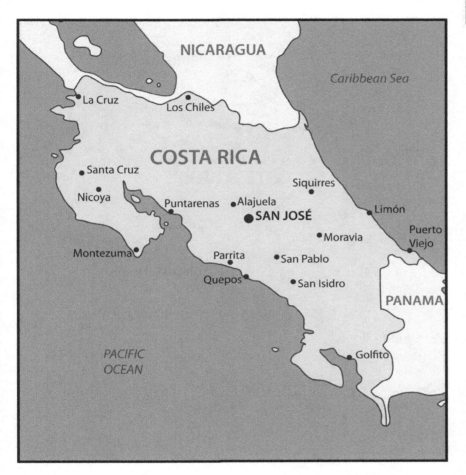

Capital: San José

Area: 19,730 sq mi (51,100 sq km)

Major Cities: San José, Alajuela, Cartago, Heredia

Population: 5.094 million

Bordering Countries: Nicaragua, Panama

Language: Spanish

Major Landmarks: Arenal Volcano, Manuel Antonio National Park, Monteverde Cloud Forest Reserve

Famous Costa Ricans: Keylor Navas (footballer), Óscar Arias Sánchez (former President and Nobel Peace Prize laureate), Claudia Poll (Olympic swimmer)

National Symbol

White-tailed Deer

Find the Words

```
X R I T W I L D L I F E
N S F O G T T I C O S U
S E F R X V O J G L X T
A S S T H V H Q A Z S G
N Z L U P I O N A E D W
J E O G K U E L R S L E
O Z T U V R R O C I J C
S M H E A M F A X A A Q
E K R R W N W R V H N W
Y B L O I Z F K I I A O
Q D K A T B E S U Y D Y
I I R Q U E T Z A L I A
```

ARENAL	SLOTH
PURA VIDA	TICOS
QUETZAL	TORTUGUERO
RAINFOREST	VOLCANO
SAN JOSE	WILDLIFE

CÔTE D'IVOIRE

National Motto: Unity, Discipline, Labor

Capital: Yamoussoukro

Area: 124,504 square miles (322,463 square kilometers)

Major Cities: Abidjan, Bouake, San-Pedro, Yamoussoukro

Population: 27.48 million

Bordering Countries: Mali, Burkina Faso, Ghana, Liberia, Guinea

Language: French

Major Landmarks: Basilica of Our Lady of Peace, St. Paul's Cathedral, Banco National Park, The Plateau, Treichville

Famous Ivorians: Didier Drogba (soccer player), Laurent Gbagbo (politician), Yaya Touré (soccer player)

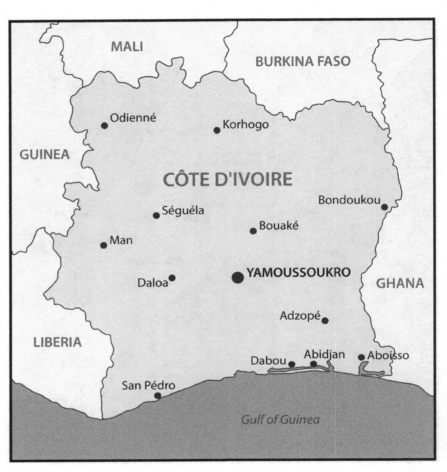

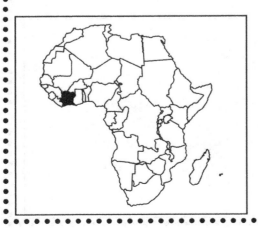

Find the Words

```
T S T P A U L S Q O T P
W Q O Y I E Q E S R R L
C B K D O R T Y U K E A
U A S L R I Z I H U I T
O B T M J O Q O N O C E
K O X H S V G A R S H A
B U T S E I J B C S V U
S A N P E D R O A U I A
A K O H I E R L W O L Z
N E A B X T E A I M L Z
J N A O Z O S U L A E G
R P R U S C F S L Y Y M
```

ABIDJAN
BOUAKE
CATHEDRAL
COTE DIVOIRE
DROGBA
PLATEAU
SAN PEDRO
ST PAULS
TREICHVILLE
YAMOUSSOUKRO

National Symbol

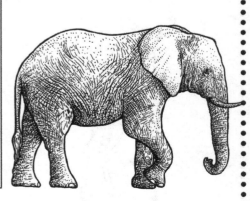

African Elephant

CROATIA

National Motto: God and Croats

Capital: Zagreb

Area: 21,851 square miles (56,594 square kilometers)

Major Cities: Dubrovnik, Zadar, Split

Population: 4,105,267

Bordering Countries: Hungary, Serbia, Bosnia and Herzegovina, Montenegro, Slovenia

Language: Croatian

Major Landmarks: Plitvice Lakes, Diocletian's Palace, Krka National Park

Famous Croatians: Nikola Tesla (inventor), Rudolf Steiner (philosopher)

National Symbol

Pine Marten

Find the Words

```
A J A C R O A T I A N B
S M G I Z H O L G R A P
S K P H Z L S D J N L K
W R A H W A B P R O I U
A K D D I K G A L N C P
Y A R H Z T D R V I A W
J P I Q F A H O E L T C
T A A F Z J R E U L K G
S R T C W B Z P A P O M
U K I I U W B Q U T D P
T G C D P O B T P L E S
T O M I S L A V X L Y R
```

ADRIATIC	PULA
AMPHITHEATER	SPLIT
CROATIAN	TOMISLAV
DUBROVNIK	ZADAR
KRKA PARK	ZAGRELO

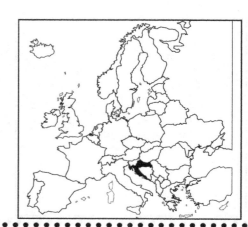

CUBA

National Motto: Fatherland or Death

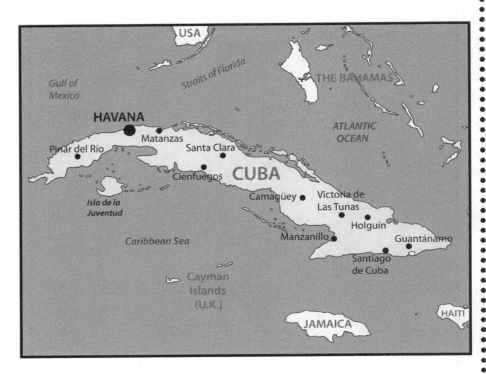

Capital: Havana

Area: 42,426 sq mi (109,884 sq km)

Major Cities: Havana, Santiago de Cuba, Camagüey, Holguín

Population: 11.326 million

Bordering Countries: Maritime borders with the Bahamas, Haiti, Honduras, Jamaica, Mexico, the United States

Language: Spanish

Major Landmarks: Old Havana, Varadero Beach, Morro Castle, Viñales Valley

Famous Cubans: Fidel Castro (former President), Celia Cruz (singer), Yoani Sánchez (blogger)

Find the Words

```
V R V G Y P E G C L O R
Y H D R P G R S L Y J J
R N A Y U A T A P H W C
F E G V G M B C N E U A
K C V U A E B T P M F S
J D S O S N C A H I S T
N C H A L G A W P N R R
F U B X G U W V E G B O
K L V I J I T H H W D G
T U H A V D C I X A A X
C I G A R S B B O Y O E
Q D A M O J I T O N C T
```

BASEBALL	HEMINGWAY
CASTRO	MOJITO
CHE	REVOLUTION
CIGARS	RUMBA
HAVANA	SUGAR

National Symbol

Cuban Trogon

CYPRUS

National Motto: No official motto

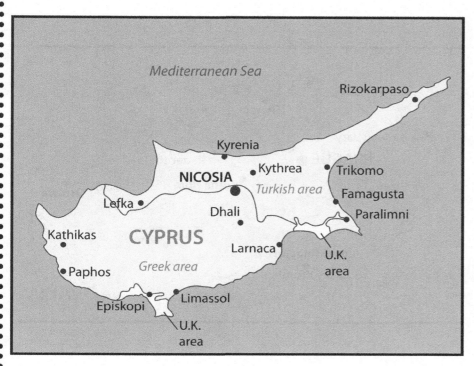

Mediterranean Sea

Rizokarpaso

Kyrenia

NICOSIA — Kythrea — Trikomo

Turkish area

Lefka — Dhali — Famagusta — Paralimni

Kathikas — CYPRUS — Larnaca — U.K. area

Greek area

Paphos

Episkopi — Limassol

U.K. area

Capital: Nicosia

Area: 3,572 square miles (9,251 square kilometers)

Major Cities: Larnaca, Limassol, Paphos

Population: 1,207,359

Neighboring Countries: Turkey, Syria, Lebanon, Israel, Egypt, Greece

Language: Greek, Turkish

Major Landmarks: Petra tou Romiou, Nissi Beach, Tombs of the Kings, Kykkos Monastery

Famous Cyprians: Marcos Baghdatis (tennis player), Simon Fuller (TV personality), Makarios III (president)

National Symbol

Cyprus Mouflon

Find the Words

```
L P C O M C T A P Z I D
A A P Y M A I U O N N D
N P Z X R S K I R A X K
A H U U O P G A L K E I
T O V C R R U S R E E W
O S I Q Y A I S R I H Y
L N J D P W P G Y I O Y
I N I S S I B E A C H S
A F I P I C H O K V L L
N X O I J U E A C S I N
Q N C P J A C J V Z H I
G J Q B L A R N A C A B
```

ANATOLIAN   MAKARIOS
CYRPUS   NICOSIA
GREEK   NISSI BEACH
ISLAND   PAPHOS
LARNACA   TURKEY

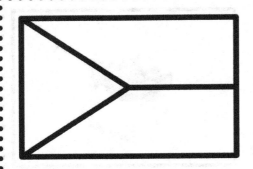

CZECH REPUBLIC

National Motto: Truth Prevails

Capital: Prague

Area: 30,452 square miles (78,867 square kilometers)

Major Cities: Prague, Brno, Ostrava

Population: 10,708,981

Bordering Countries: Poland, Germany, Austria, Slovakia

Language: Czech

Major Landmarks: Prague Castle, Charles Bridge, St. Vitus Cathedral

Famous Czechs: Martina Navratilova (tennis player), Rainer Maria Rilke (author), Gregor Mendel (scientist), Charles IV (emperor)

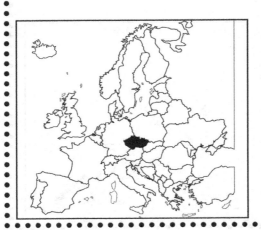

Find the Words

```
R J P X L M O R A V I A
X E I E W Q C L A X P Q
J J P N U U Z N C T D M
E B O U O U U Q A W P F
J D O M B R Y O T R R W
M U O H O L I B H T A Z
I L E K E L I Y E K G J
O W B K A M J C D O U U
S C R T A P I P R I E M
Y W N M O F O A A D T F
I S O S U Y K R L H D J
C A S T L E S A S L U L
```

BOHEMIA   KORUNA
BRNO   MORAVIA
CASTLES   OLOMOUC
CATHEDRALS   PRAGUE
KAFKA   REPUBLIC

National Symbol

Double-tailed Lion

DENMARK

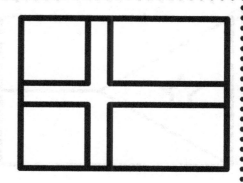

National Motto: God's help, the love of the people, Denmark's strength

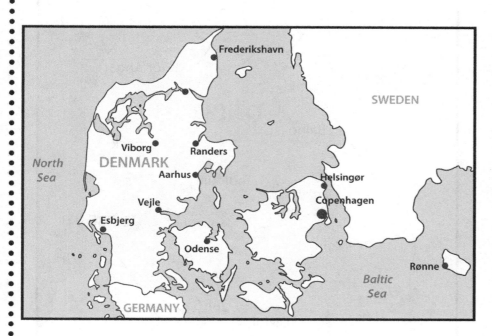

Capital: Copenhagen

Area: 16,577 square miles (42,943 square kilometers)

Major Cities: Aarhus, Odense, Aalborg

Population: 5,792,202

Neighboring Countries: Germany, Norway, Sweden

Language: Danish

Major Landmarks: Tivoli Gardens, The Little Mermaid, Kronberg

Famous Danes: Søren Kierkegaard (philosopher), Hans Christian Andersen (author), Jacob Riis (journalist)

National Symbol

Mute Swan

Find the Words

```
F O N H W A G E S A N B
J Z E J D H J U R E N G
Z T J A C A H P G Y Y Y
R R I I N R N A K M H A
T A R V A D H I T P A D
U L Z A O N E Q S S V E
U W T P E L I R C H N N
F K Y P T J I F S R K M
B E O F J R J K S E A A
H C I E Y Q E C E C N R
K O D E N S E O K D Z K
W G A A L B O R G G K P
```

AALBORG	DENMARK
AARHUS	NYHAVN
ANDERSEN	ODENSE
COPENHAGEN	TIVOLI
DANISH	ULRICH

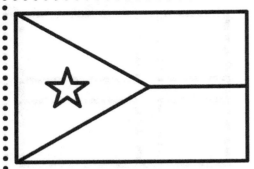

DJIBOUTI

National Motto: Unity, Equality, Peace

Capital: Djibouti

Area: 8,958 square miles (23,200 square kilometers)

Major Cities: Djibouti, Tadjoura, Obock, Dikhil

Population: 1.1 million

Bordering Countries: Eritrea, Ethiopia, Somalia

Languages: Arabic, French, Afar, Somali

Major Landmarks: Lake Assal, Day Forest, Hamoudi Mosque

Famous Djiboutians: Abdourahman Waberi (writer), Ayanleh Souleiman (runner)

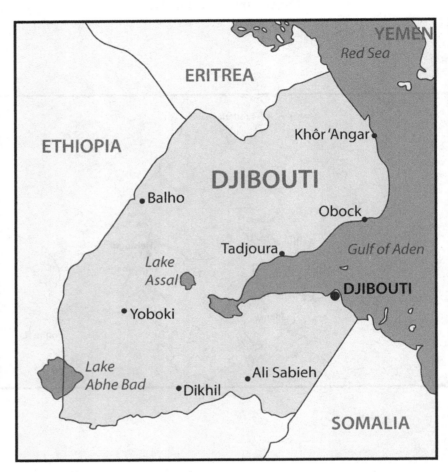

Find the Words

```
A A R U O J D A T L T T
L S Y H A N D O G A S A
I N D H J G T X J E H C
L A N J N A W V R C I R
A I O E I C O O C B Y D
K T D R I B F B A O P M
E U I L A Y O R O B V A
A O T H A M A U O C B F
S B P D J Y D U T A K D
S I A D I K H I L I M P
A J N V L Y N W E R C S
L D E R N B C P E B C B
```

APTIDON   DJIBOUTIANS
ARABIC   HANDOGA
DAY FOREST   LAKE ASSAL
DIKHIL   OBOCK
DJIBOUTI   TADJOURA

National Symbol

Somali Wild Ass

DOMINICA

National Motto: After God, the Earth

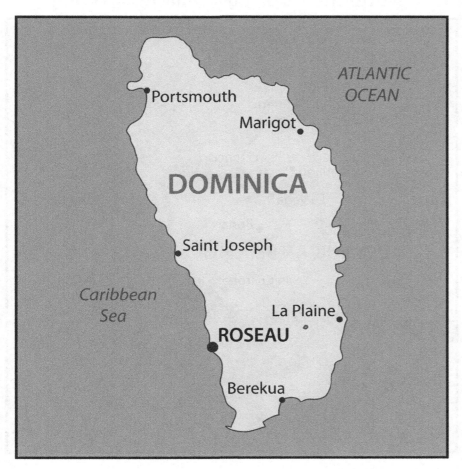

Portsmouth

Marigot

ATLANTIC OCEAN

DOMINICA

Saint Joseph

Caribbean Sea

La Plaine

ROSEAU

Berekua

Capital: Roseau

Area: 290 sq mi (751 sq km)

Major Cities: Roseau, Portsmouth, Marigot, Berekua

Population: 71,986

Bordering Countries: Maritime borders with Guadeloupe (France), Martinique (France)

Language: English

Major Landmarks: Morne Trois Pitons National Park, Boiling Lake, Trafalgar Falls

Famous Dominicans: Jean Rhys (author), Roosevelt Skerrit (current Prime Minister), Garth Joseph (basketball player)

National Symbol

Imperial Amazon Parrot

Find the Words

```
M L O O C A R N I V A L
T R A F A L G A R T E K
F X Z W L R D U U N X Q
S P C N I W O C Q T X M
B X A L J R N A R X T I
Q E J R E X S R W E C V
M L A S R U F I N S R O
S O S C A O C B Y U E L
N I R E H S T B H U O C
S U S N S E R E L F L A
A O X V E Y S A S S E N
R T X C X K K N K V G O
```

BEACHES   PARROT
CARIBBEAN   ROSEAU
CARNIVAL   SISSEROU
CREOLE   TRAFALGAR
MORNE   VOLCANO

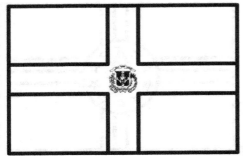

DOMINICAN REPUBLIC

National Motto: God, Fatherland, Liberty

Capital: Santo Domingo

Area: 18,792 sq mi (48,671 sq km)

Major Cities: Santo Domingo, Santiago, La Romana, San Cristóbal

Population: 10.84 million

Bordering Countries: Haiti; maritime borders with Colombia, Puerto Rico (US), Venezuela

Language: Spanish

Major Landmarks: Punta Cana Beaches, Basilica Cathedral of Santa María la Menor, Los Haitises National Park

Famous Dominicans: Juan Luis Guerra (singer), Sammy Sosa (baseball player), Junot Díaz (author)

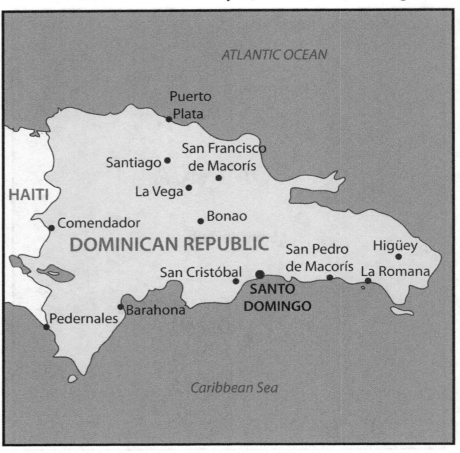

ATLANTIC OCEAN

Puerto Plata

San Francisco de Macorís

Santiago

La Vega

HAITI

Bonao

Comendador

DOMINICAN REPUBLIC

San Pedro de Macorís

Higüey

San Cristóbal

La Romana

SANTO DOMINGO

Pedernales

Barahona

Caribbean Sea

Find the Words

```
S T R E P U B L I C P O
N A B A S E B A L L I L
O F N C I G A R S A C H
D X X T Q M H H L L O X
B C L P O G D O C E D Z
A S P A O D I C U U U A
C G A S M N O G A P A C
H Q F M A B N M Z D R S
A K R P A E E G I Z T O
T Q S B R N F R H N E H
A I A E K H S F E T G P
H C M P W J G A Y P F O
```

AMBER
BACHATA
BASEBALL
CIGARS
HISPANIOLA

MERENGUE
PICO DUARTE
REPUBLIC
SAMANSA
SANTO DOMINGO

National Symbol

Palmchat

EAST TIMOR

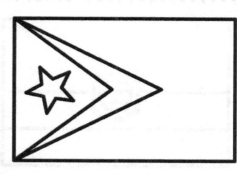

National Motto: Unity, Action, and Progress

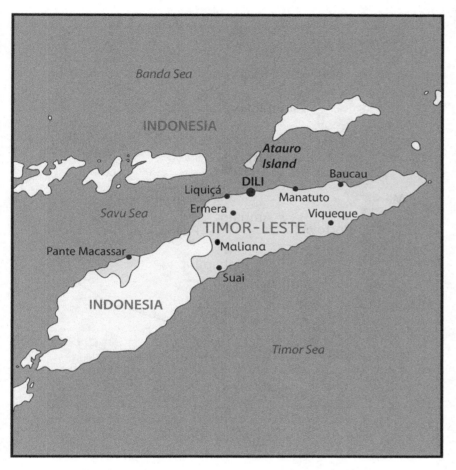

Capital: Dili

Area: 5,794 square miles (15,007 square kilometers)

Major Cities: Maliana, Suai

Population: 1,321 million

Bordering Countries: Indonesia, maritime border with Australia

Languages: Tetum, Portuguese

Major Landmarks: Cristo Rei of Dili, Jaco Island, Atauro Island, Tais Market, Lake Maubara

Famous Timorese: Xanana Gusmão (politician), José Ramos-Horta (politician)

National Symbol

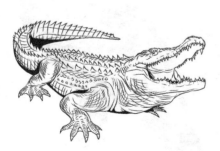

Crocodile

Find the Words

```
G P D A U D F J J G C A
A U B I K Q X V H K W U
E T S E L R O M I T M C
F K U M W I O D U R A U
L O S P A L O S I K L A
K L G J X O Z D X W I B
I M A I L E U Q O Z A Y
A T A U R O I S L A N D
E S E U G U T R O P A A
L D H W M U T E T J C C
```

AILEU	LOSPALOS
ATAURO ISLAND	MALIANA
BAUCUA	PORTUGUESE
DILI	TETUM
GUSMAO	TIMOR LESTE

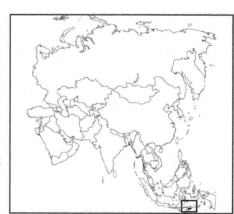

ECUADOR

National Motto: God, Homeland, and Freedom

Capital: Quito
Area: 109,484 sq mi (283,561 sq km)
Major Cities: Quito, Guayaquil, Cuenca, Santo Domingo
Population: 17.64 million
Bordering Countries: Colombia, Peru
Languages: Spanish, Kichwa, Shuar
Major Landmarks: Galápagos Islands, Cotopaxi, Quito's Historic Center
Famous Ecuadorians: Antonio Valencia (footballer), Rafael Correa (former President), Jefferson Pérez (race walker)

San Lorenzo
COLOMBIA
Esmeraldas
PACIFIC OCEAN
QUITO
Nueva Loja
ECUADOR
Manta
Ambato
Portoviejo
Puyo
Riobamba
Guayaquil
La Libertad
Cuenca
PERU
Machala
Loja

Find the Words

```
J T C J O G J O N P Q C
C O N D O R T Y U C G O
U R M R C A R A K E R M
U M S G C O N A X V E B
H B R N A A P H J I I D
V Q E Y N L C R M C N C
Y U U A C A A P G H C A
C Y B I O B N P C E A C
T R J R T E H H A U F A
A N D E S O A O I G V O
I K T M A F Z P K W O X
N H A M A Z O N E I Y S
```

AMAZON
ANDES
BANANA
CACAO
CEVICHE
CONDOR
CUENCA
GALAPAGOS
INCA
QUITO

National Symbol

Andean Condor

EGYPT

National Motto: No official motto

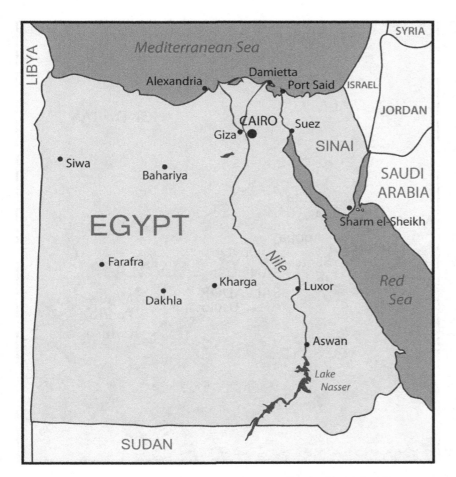

National Symbol

Golden Eagle

Capital: Cairo

Area: 386,662 square miles (1,001,449 square kilometers)

Major Cities: Cairo, Luxor, Alexandria, Giza, Aswan

Population: 109 million

Bordering Countries: Libya, Sudan, Israel

Language: Arabic

Major Landmarks: Pyramids of Giza, Great Sphinx, Abu Simbel, Luxor Temple, Valley of the Kings

Famous Egyptians: Cleopatra (queen), Mohamed Salah (soccer player), Omar Sharif (actor), Anwar Sadat (politician)

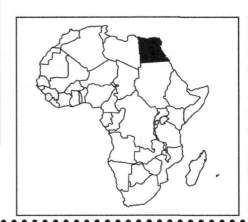

Find the Words

```
F W B A B U S I M B E L
D U S S G Q A C A I R O
H G D T R Z I E R H C I
R A I I E O R Z G U Q E
Q S M K A N D M R Y S V
O W A L T A N O G Q P V
N A R G S E A S L H O T
I N Y X P C X E E H R Y
B W P Z H C E S J O M D
I P T K I G L V X M W N
R H C A N E A U U M B T
O Z E M X H L M H C S I
```

ABU SIMBEL	GREAT SPHINX
ALEXANDRIA	LUXOR
ASWAN	MOSES
CAIRO	MUMMY
EGYPT	PYRAMIDS

EL SALVADOR

National Motto: God, Union, Liberty

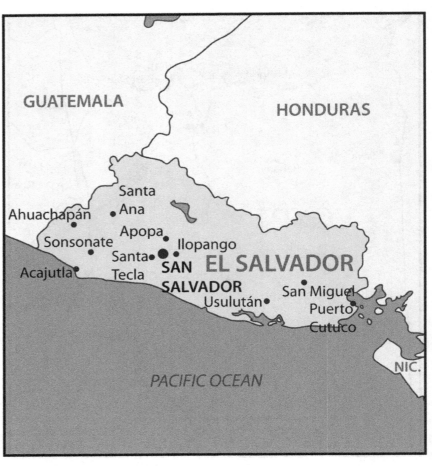

Capital: San Salvador

Area: 8,124 sq mi (21,041 sq km)

Major Cities: San Salvador, Santa Ana, San Miguel

Population: 6.486 million

Bordering Countries: Guatemala, Honduras

Language: Spanish

Major Landmarks: Joya de Cerén, Tazumal, Coatepeque Lake

Famous Salvadorans: Óscar Romero (Archbishop and martyr), Claudia Lars (poet), Mauricio Funes (former President)

Find the Words

T	F	C	L	Q	L	U	N	K	S	E	T
P	S	F	T	I	Y	L	E	M	P	A	Q
N	T	A	P	Q	S	M	X	Y	L	D	U
Z	H	I	N	Z	B	P	A	A	I	N	I
L	P	I	C	S	B	U	Z	Y	P	O	A
I	R	C	Z	G	A	T	T	D	A	R	D
B	P	Z	T	A	E	L	R	X	U	M	C
E	U	V	W	U	L	D	V	U	D	Q	E
R	P	F	Q	M	S	C	U	A	J	X	R
T	U	M	G	X	V	B	O	B	D	X	E
Y	S	P	A	C	I	F	I	C	E	O	N
O	A	N	P	W	M	E	C	N	U	A	R

CEREN   PACIFIC
IZALCO   PIPIL
LEMPA   PUPUSA
LIBERTY   QUETZAL
MAYA   SAN SALVADOR

National Symbol

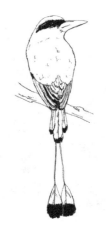

Turquoise-browed Motmot

EQUATORIAL GUINEA

National Motto: Unity, Peace, Justice

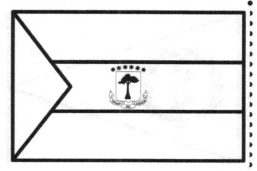

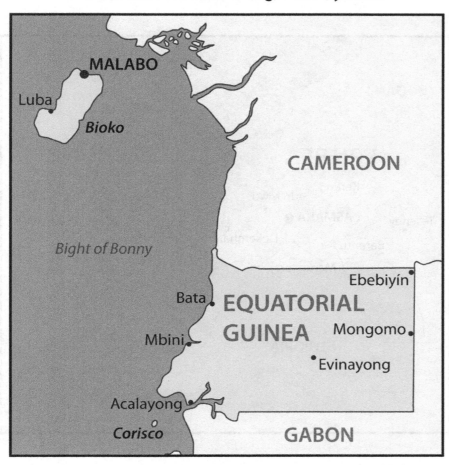

Capital: Malabo

Area: 10,831 square miles (28,051 square kilometers)

Major Cities: Bata, Malabo

Population: 1.63 million

Bordering Countries: Cameroon, Gabon

Language: Spanish, Portuguese, French

Major Landmarks: Malabo Cathedral, Monte Alen National Park, Pico Malabo volcano

Famous Equatoguineans: Teodoro Obiang Nguema Mbasogo (politician), Juan Tomás Ávila Laurel (writer)

National Symbol

Gorilla

Find the Words

D	E	U	R	E	C	A	M	P	Z	D	Y
L	O	M	O	G	N	O	M	M	G	C	L
U	E	L	I	D	U	D	S	N	Q	I	S
Q	J	Q	L	G	F	L	O	I	M	U	A
K	V	J	U	A	M	Y	K	Q	B	G	N
G	Q	G	D	A	A	O	E	K	M	N	A
A	D	I	K	N	T	A	C	Y	O	A	N
E	S	A	I	Y	T	O	L	A	E	V	T
N	Y	V	R	A	M	R	R	G	X	E	O
I	E	Q	B	G	A	C	R	I	X	Z	N
U	P	Q	O	B	A	L	A	M	A	K	I
G	M	S	E	O	J	Z	Y	N	B	L	O

BATA
DE URECA
EQUATORIAL
EVA NGUI
EVINAYONG

GUINEA
MALABO
MOCA
MONGOMO
SAN ANTONIO

ERITREA

National Motto: Victory to the Masses!

Capital: Asmara

Area: 45,406 square miles (117,600 square kilometers)

Major Cities: Asmara, Mitsiwa, Keren

Population: 3.62 million

Bordering Countries: Djibouti, Ethiopia, Sudan

Languages: Tigrinya, Arabic, and English

Major Landmarks: Asmara, Massawa, Qohaito

Famous Eritreans: Meb Keflezighi (runner), Nafkote Tamirat (writer), Dawit Isaak (artist)

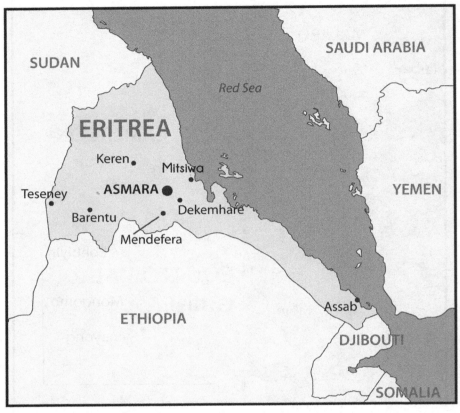

Find the Words

```
L E A T N E N Q V B L E
D C R V I Q Q Y W E K R
E A A J I G A Y I J E I
Q L M R Y W R S H W R T
Y A S C I K A I Y Q E R
R P A S J V U R N C N E
X X T I Y O U A A Y F A
O I D B E E G E N Y A N
M Y A D I U G R I T A S
Z E U D I U G O F W T U
A E R T I R E N X H N H
Y Q C Z V B T C N L Q V
```

ADI UGRI   KEREN
ARAYA   MITSIWA
ASMARA   PALACE
ERITREA   TIGRINYA
ERITREANS   ZEUDI

National Symbol

Arabian Camel

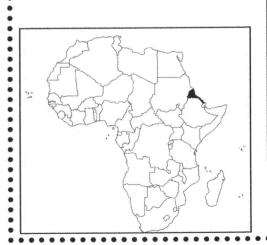

ESTONIA

National Motto: No official motto

FINLAND
Gulf of Finland
Baltic Sea
Paldiski • Muuga • Kunda
TALLINN • Kohtla-Järve • Narva
Hiiumaa • Haapsalu • Paide
ESTONIA Lake Peipus
Saaremaa • Pärnu • Viljandi • Tartu
• Valga
Gulf of Riga RUSSIA
LATVIA

Capital: Tallinn

Area: 17,505 square miles (45,227 square kilometers)

Major Cities: Tartu, Narva

Population: 1,326,535

Bordering Countries: Russia, Latvia

Language: Estonian

Major Landmarks: Alexander Nevsky Cathedral, Kumu, Lahemaa National Park

Famous Estonians: Louis Kahn (architect), Wolfgang Köhler (psychologist)

National Symbol

Barn Swallow

Find the Words

```
G O J C V C X W Y V W A
F I B E J T F M U F S M
Z F A S Z L J T N D K V
O O L T Z O N N N H N Q
S L T O T E L A A N D A
B Z I N J A L D I R W P
N U C I L S R L T U V O
Q Y A A I J L T M O Q A
N S O N P A A U U B W G
F Q V M T X K G J U P N
D L B L E N U S A D A M
F O R E S T S W G F N D
```

BALTIC   LENUSADAM
ESTONIAN   NARVA
FORESTS   OLD TOWN
ISLANDS   TALLINN
KUMU   TARTU

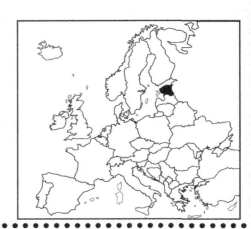

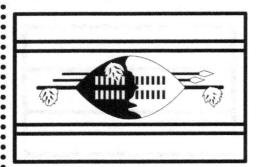

ESWATINI

National Motto: We Are the Fortress

Capital: Mbabane
Area: 6,704 square miles (17,364 square kilometers)
Major Cities: Manzini, Mbabane
Population: 1.192 million
Bordering Countries: South Africa, Mozambique
Languages: Swati, English
Major Landmarks: Mlilwane Wildlife Sanctuary, Hlane Royal National Park, Mantenga Cultural Village
Famous Emaswati: Mswati III (king), Bongani Khumalo (soccer player)

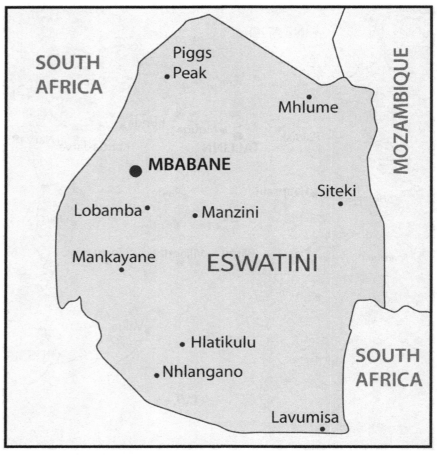

Find the Words

A	V	E	Q	W	J	Y	M	A	M
Z	K	X	S	K	O	A	I	L	B
U	F	R	Z	W	N	H	K	L	A
H	C	Q	F	Z	A	G	E	S	B
B	J	I	I	U	G	T	T	A	A
O	J	N	M	E	N	U	I	I	N
S	I	Y	I	A	A	K	S	N	E
Z	E	G	A	L	L	I	V	T	I
S	W	A	T	I	H	S	L	S	Z
G	W	W	P	C	N	Z	I	L	D

ALL SAINTS   NHLANGANO
ESWATINI   SITEKI
ISLAMIC   SOBHUZA
MANZINI   SWATI
MBABANE   VILLAGE

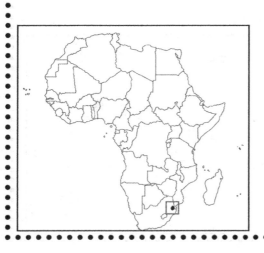

National Symbol

African Elephant

ETHIOPIA

National Motto: No official motto

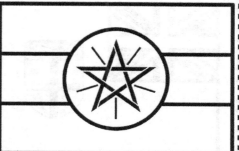

Capital: Addis Ababa

Area: 426,373 square miles (1,104,300 square kilometers)

Major Cities: Addis Ababa, Dire Dawa, Gondar

Population: 120.3 million

Bordering Countries: Eritrea, Somalia, Kenya, South Sudan, Sudan

Languages: Oromo, Amharic, Somali, Tigrinya, Sidama

Major Landmarks: Lalibela, Aksum, Harar, Blue Nile Falls

Famous Ethiopians: Haile Selassie (emperor), Liya Kebede (actress), Abebe Bikila (marathon runner)

National Symbol

Lion

Find the Words

A	D	R	K	A	K	S	U	M	L	V	L
L	V	J	I	I	K	Z	C	O	Q	E	A
A	E	H	X	F	T	T	G	V	A	H	L
K	O	B	E	U	T	U	J	W	K	X	I
E	W	R	H	A	J	V	A	Y	E	I	B
T	G	H	O	R	E	D	A	E	D	X	E
A	Z	I	A	M	E	V	F	L	E	F	L
N	P	R	I	R	I	F	U	T	L	M	A
A	A	G	I	Z	O	A	C	X	U	E	Y
H	L	D	V	C	L	W	H	G	I	I	Y
I	X	A	D	D	I	S	A	B	A	B	A
T	G	B	D	A	L	L	O	L	D	B	Q

ADDIS ABABA   HARAR JUGOL

AKSUM   LAKE TANA

COFFEE   LALIBELA

DALLOL   OROMIA

DIRE DAWA   RIFT VALLEY

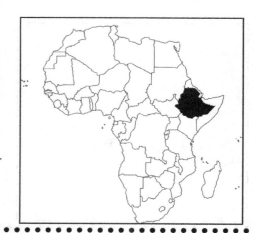

FIJI

National Motto: Fear God and Honor the King

Capital: Suva

Area: 7,054 square miles (18,270 square kilometers)

Major Cities: Suva, Lautoka, Nadi

Population: 924,610

Bordering Countries: No direct bordering countries

Languages: English, Fijian, and Fiji Hindi

Major Landmarks: Great Astrolabe Reef, Sri Siva Subramaniya Temple, Bouma National Heritage Park, Sigatoka Sand Dunes National Park

Famous Fijians: Waisale Serevi (rugby player), Roy Krishna (footballer), Satendra Nandan (author), Laisenia Qarase (politician)

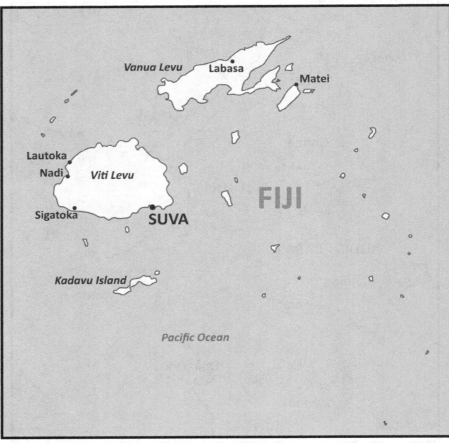

Find the Words

```
Q H P F Y O S P F D L X
B S G R I H E W F A C P
E T O X S J A I Y S K J
E L R L A N I C U T R O
I I U O P X I A N R R N
Q F E L P F O A N O E S
N F J O I I E R A L E X
A A Q C F C C H W A F A
D I A A O R P S Q B B J
I P P A Z P U M X E H S
I I S L A N D S W Y W I
S D R Y I N P S U V A Q
```

ASTROLABE	OCEAN
FIJIAN	PACIFIC
ISLANDS	REEF
LORY	SUVA
NADI	TROPICS

National Symbol

Collared Lory

FINLAND

National Motto: No official motto

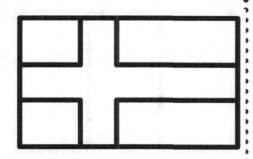

Capital: Helsinki

Area: 130,672 square miles (338,455 square kilometers)

Major Cities: Tampere, Turku, Oulu

Population: 5,540,720

Bordering Countries: Norway, Russia, Sweden

Language: Finnish, Swedish

Major Landmarks: Suomenlinna Fortress, Helsinki Cathedral, Turku Castle

Famous Finns: Jean Sibelius (composer), Linus Torvalds (computer programmer)

National Symbol

Brown Bear

Find the Words

```
M E V W N F G F N Y X Y
S A U N A S F Z D S G S
W Y H U B N B C Q A F C
S U O M E N L I N N A A
H H T C T O J H H V S N
B E I L Z U S L V T E D
T H L U A I R P R R A I
D S L S N P Y K E P R N
C U M N I Z L P U V C A
O D I D J N M A I Y T V
M F W H S A K M N K I I
V P I W T F Q I K D C A
```

ARCTIC   SAUNAS
FINNISH   SCANDINAVIA
HELSINKI   SUOMENLINNA
LAPLAND   TAMPERE
OULU   TURKU

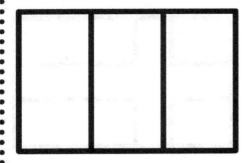

FRANCE

National Motto: Liberty, Equality, Fraternity

Capital: Paris
Area: 244,300 square miles (551,500 square kilometers)
Major Cities: Marseille, Lyon, Strasbourg
Population: 65,273,511
Bordering Countries: Belgium, Luxembourg, Germany, Switzerland, Italy, Spain, Andorra
Language: French
Major Landmarks: Eiffel Tower, Louvre Museum, Palace of Versailles, Notre-Dame Cathedral
Famous French: Napoleon Bonaparte (military commander), Louis XIV (king), Voltaire (author), René Descartes (philosopher)

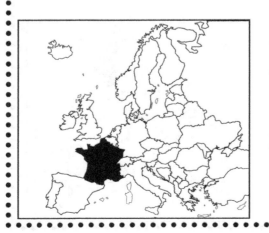

Find the Words

```
M A Z O E T E M S X P Z
A C K C M X I M T D W Q
R U P A N S F N R A T B
S B W O N E F Q A S L A
E R Y O A I E J S W O G
I L F G P T L V B A U U
L Q R H O A T W O R V E
L T E E L B O D U E R T
E M N O E E W C R P E T
O G C F O H E Y G G V E
X I H Y N S R P A R I S
V E R S A I L L E S W K
```

BAGUETTE   MARSEILLE
EIFFEL TOWER   NAPOLEON
FRENCH   PARIS
LOUVRE   STRASBOURG
LYON   VERSAILLES

National Symbol

Gallic Rooster

GABON

National Motto: Union, Work, Justice

CAMEROON

EQUATORIAL GUINEA

• Bitam

• Oyem

REPUBLIC OF THE CONGO

LIBREVILLE
Owendo
• Kango

Makokou •

Port-Gentil

• Booué

GABON

Lambaréné •

• Lastoursville

Koulamoutou •

Moanda •

• Franceville

Mouila •

Gamba •

ATLANTIC OCEAN

Tchibanga •

REPUBLIC OF THE CONGO

Capital: Libreville

Area: 103,347 square miles (267,668 square kilometers)

Major Cities: Libreville, Port-Gentil, Franceville, Oyem

Population: 2.341 million

Bordering Countries: Equatorial Guinea, Cameroon, Republic of the Congo

Language: French

Major Landmarks: Loango National Park, Pointe Denis, Lopé National Park

Famous Gabonese: Omar Bongo (politician), Pierre-Emerick Aubameyang (soccer player)

National Symbol

Black Panther

Find the Words

E	V	I	L	I	T	N	E	G	U	N	E
L	N	A	H	D	Z	O	N	B	C	L	U
L	G	L	T	C	X	V	M	P	L	Z	A
I	A	P	A	Y	A	N	T	I	H	P	J
V	B	U	E	M	O	G	V	K	D	O	B
E	O	H	O	B	B	E	X	T	O	R	H
C	N	S	A	K	R	A	H	V	A	T	C
N	E	G	K	B	K	P	R	A	E	G	N
A	S	C	I	Q	K	U	D	E	K	G	E
R	E	L	G	R	M	I	B	N	N	T	R
F	M	E	K	W	A	T	A	B	L	E	F
E	S	T	M	I	C	H	A	E	L	E	L

EKWATA
FRANCEVILLE
FRENCH
GABON
GABONESE

GENTIL
LAMBARENE
LIBREVILLE
PORT
ST MICHAEL

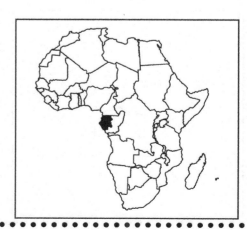

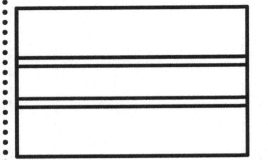

GAMBIA

National Motto: Progress, Peace, Prosperity

Capital: Banjul

Area: 4,008 square miles (10,380 square kilometers)

Major Cities: Serekunda, Brikama, Bakau

Population: 2.64 million

Bordering Countries: Senegal

Languages: English, Mandinka, Wolof

Major Landmarks: Wassu Stone Circles, Kunta Kinteh Island, Abuko Nature Reserve

Famous Gambians: Yahya Jammeh (politician), Fatou Bensouda (lawyer), Kebba Tolbert (musician)

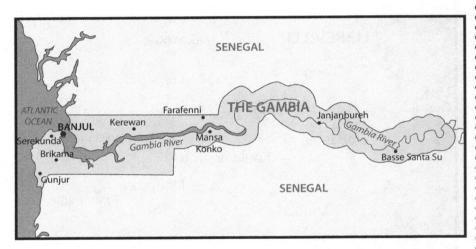

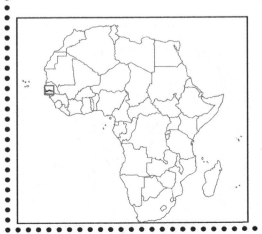

Find the Words

```
X G Y H S I L G N E N R
S X S T A T E H O U S E
E M F R O U D W I B A A
R I F O O Y I A Y T D L
R A P R R S R J D U F U
E M E B V T F A O K J O
K A F A A S B S M U T P
U K K N B R N U A F Q D
N I T J L E C K L J A K
D R M U B U A H D L Y J
A B K L K B T J T F E A
G A M B I A V B B X K N
```

ARCH
BAKAU
BANJUL
BENSOUDA
BRIKAMA

ENGLISH
FORT BULLEN
GAMBIA
SERREKUNDA
STATE HOUSE

National Symbol

Spotted Hyena

GEORGIA

National Motto: Strength Is in Unity!

Capital: Tbilisi

Area: 26,911 square miles (69,700 square kilometers)

Major Cities: Batumi, Kutaisi, Rustavi

Population: 3,989,167

Bordering Countries: Russia, Azerbaijan, Armenia, Turkey

Language: Georgian

Major Landmarks: Svetitskhoveli Cathedral, Uplistsikhe, Narikala Fortress, Gergeti Trinity Church, Vardzia

Famous Georgians: Sergei Parajanov (director), Katie Melua (musician)

National Symbol

Snow Leopard

Find the Words

```
J W P C B Y C R H I J S
I W K S E L B J M H U P
C I G O K N A U O S I I
T N E G X U T C A R T X
B E O J E A T C K E K S
I B R O B C U A H S D A
L P G J Z A V K I Q E L
I K I I C U A I E S B A
S Q A T L K Q I M E I T
I N N N A R I K A L A J
W V A R D Z I A T L U J
G W G E X N W J A P D Q
```

BATUMI   KUTAISI
BLACK SEA   NARIKALA
CAUCASUS   TBILISI
GEORGIAN   VARDZIA
KAKHETI   WINE

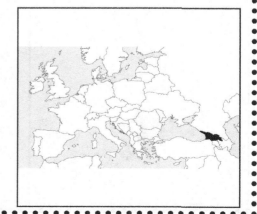

GERMANY

National Motto: Unity and Justice and Freedom

Capital: Berlin

Area: 137,988 square miles (357,022 square kilometers)

Major Cities: Munich, Frankfurt, Hamburg

Population: 83,783,942

Bordering Countries: Denmark, Netherlands, Belgium, Luxembourg, France, Switzerland, Austria, Czech Republic, Poland

Language: German

Major Landmarks: Neuschwanstein Castle, Brandenburg Gate, Berlin Wall, Cologne Cathedral

Famous Germans: Beethoven (composer), Albert Einstein (physicist), Karl Marx (philosopher), Igor Stravinsky (composer)

Find the Words

```
H B F K K I F M M S Z B
Z F R A N K F U R T E R
G E R M A N I Z U P N A
H G L E F T X L G E X N
A E Z S H D H I V B L D
M A I E A C P O B E E E
B R O N I U H F W R K N
U P E N S T S X K L N B
R V U Q E T G A I I S U
G M G E Y R E X G N N R
D I B I N H W I R E V G
A U T O B A H N N Z S Y
```

AUTOBAHN   FRANKFURT
BEETHOVEN   GERMAN
BERLIN   HAMBURG
BRANDENBURG   MUNICH
EINSTEIN   SAUSAGES

National Symbol

Eagle

GHANA

National Motto: Freedom and Justice

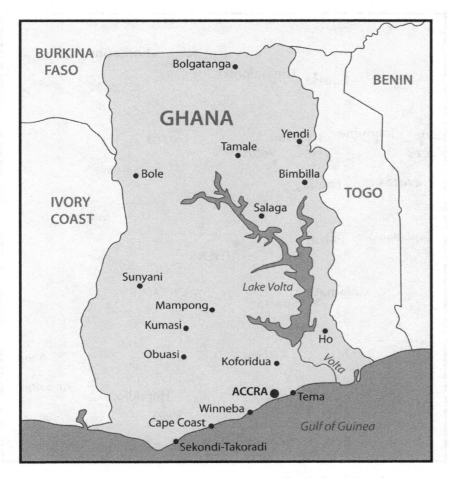

National Symbol

Lion

Find the Words

G	H	A	N	A	W	X	E	Q	G	Y	R
U	K	Q	Y	P	X	L	L	F	C	H	C
I	O	Y	T	R	W	W	T	T	X	H	P
D	C	A	H	I	D	I	S	A	M	U	K
A	O	A	S	N	A	I	A	N	A	H	G
R	H	O	P	S	I	A	C	C	R	A	D
O	Q	I	W	E	U	K	U	K	V	H	E
K	A	P	C	N	C	C	S	T	D	L	W
A	N	Q	W	S	S	O	O	F	T	G	A
T	N	L	Q	T	G	W	A	S	P	I	K
K	A	M	V	E	I	Q	A	S	V	C	S
S	N	M	E	N	Q	C	L	F	T	F	J

ACCRA	GHANAIANS
ANNAN	KUMASI
CAPE COAST	OSU CASTLE
CASTLE	PRINSENSTEN
GHANA	TAKORADI

Capital: Accra

Area: 92,098 square miles (238,534 square kilometers)

Major Cities: Accra , Kumasi, Tamale, Cape Coast, Sekondi-Takoradi

Population: 32.83 million

Bordering Countries: Côte d'Ivoire, Burkina Faso, Togo

Languages: English, Akan

Major Landmarks: Cape Coast Castle, Osu Castle, Kakum National Park, Lake Volta

Famous Ghanaians: Kofi Annan (diplomat), Kwame Nkrumah (politician), Abedi Pele (soccer player)

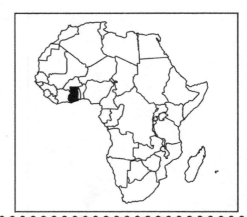

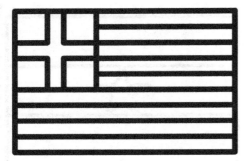

GREECE

National Motto: Freedom or Death

Capital: Athens

Area: 50,949 square miles (131,957 square kilometers)

Major Cities: Athens, Thessaloniki, Heraklion

Population: 10,423,054

Bordering Countries: Albania, Bulgaria, North Macedonia, Turkey

Language: Greek

Major Landmarks: The Parthenon, Acropolis, Academy of Athens, Colossus of Rhodes

Famous Greeks: Aristotle (philosopher), Alexander the Great (ruler), Homer (author), Hippocrates (physician)

Find the Words

```
A R I S T O T L E U I N
M P B P P T T D A N O R
Y L H E E M K E R N A S
K T M I A B S Y E F T D
O O I A L N U H S H H E
N H S S A O T U Z J E M
O E P E L R S V S R N O
S I G J A A F O E U S C
P E L P A C N M P O I R
A N V N U R O D C H P A
E N D F Y H X Z S L Y C
W A C R O P O L I S B Y
```

ACROPOLIS   HOMER
AEGEAN SEA   ISLANDS
ARISTOTLE   MYKONOS
ATHENS   PARTHENON
DEMOCRACY   PHILOSOPHY

National Symbol

Dolphin

GRENADA

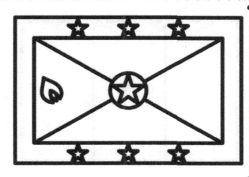

National Motto: Ever Conscious of God We Aspire, Build and Advance as One People

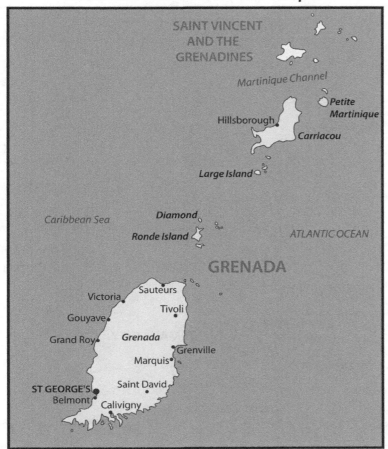

Capital: St. George's

Area: 132 sq mi (344 sq km)

Major Cities: St. George's, Gouyave, Victoria, Grenville

Population: 112,523

Bordering Countries: Maritime borders with Saint Vincent and the Grenadines, Trinidad and Tobago

Language: English

Major Landmarks: Grand Anse Beach, Belmont Estate, Underwater Sculpture Park

Famous Grenadians: Kirani James (Olympic sprinter), Maurice Bishop (former Prime Minister), Eric Gairy (first Prime Minister)

National Symbol

Grenada Dove

Find the Words

```
S T G E O R G E E Q C Y
G R E N A D A T P C U V
K C S R E X A U G A Z H
C F O C I L Q N C R Y W
O A I U O Q H D A R B I
N P L C C V T E T I X M
S U O Y R O H R L A A Q
K H T M P R U W A C V A
C G F M S S R A N O K X
J D T A E O O T T U Z C
S N U N Y G R E I E Q A
Q D A J Z R E R C X S N
```

ATLANTIC
CALYPSO
CARRIACOU
CHOCOLATE
COUCOU

GRENADA
NUTMEG
SPICE
ST GEORGE
UNDERWATER

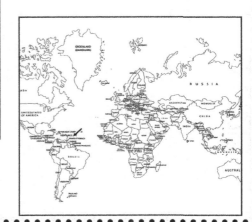

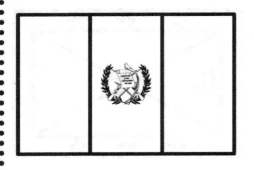

GUATEMALA

National Motto: Grow Free and Fertile

Capital: Guatemala City

Area: 42,042 sq mi 108,889 sq km)

Major Cities: Guatemala City, Mixco, Villa Nueva, Quetzaltenango

Population: 17.915 million

Bordering Countries: Belize, El Salvador, Honduras, Mexico

Languages: Spanish, various Mayan languages

Major Landmarks: Tikal National Park, Antigua Guatemala, Lake Atitlán

Famous Guatemalans: Rigoberta Menchú (indigenous rights activist and Nobel Peace Prize laureate), Carlos Ruiz (footballer), Miguel Ángel Asturias (author)

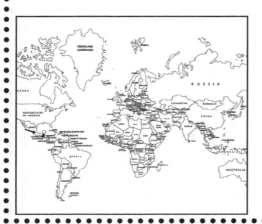

Find the Words

```
M A R I M B A Y P A Y J
Y C F Y M C A A U R I R
M A Y A N S N K T K N X
G E A X X U R N E H D E
F U O T F Y U I K A I P
E V A I I O N R T N G E
H W R T C T O N J T E T
Z A M U E A L E B I N E
G F W N K M N A G G O N
A X K R A C A J N U U Y
A L W O W L D L J A S H
N V T I K A L W A I A E
```

ANTIGUA   INDIGENOUS
ATITLAN   MARIMBA
COUNTRY   MAYANS
GARIFUNA   PETEN
GUATEMALA   TIKAL

National Symbol

Quetzal

GUINEA

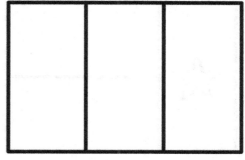

National Motto: Work, Justice, Solidarity

SENEGAL
MALI
THE GAMBIA
GUINEA-BISSAU
Siguiri
Labé
Boké
GUINEA
Fria
Port Kamsar
Kindia
Kankan
CONAKRY
Kissidougou
Guéckédougou
Macenta
SIERRA LEONE
Nzérékoré
ATLANTIC OCEAN
LIBERIA
IVORY COAST

Capital: Conakry

Area: 94,926 square miles (245,857 square kilometers)

Major Cities: Conakry, Kissidougou, Nzérékoré, Kankan

Population: 13.53 million

Bordering Countries: Guinea-Bissau, Senegal, Mali, Côte d'Ivoire, Liberia, Sierra Leone

Language: French

Major Landmarks: Fouta Djallon, Conakry Grand Mosque, Chutes de la Sala waterfalls

Famous Guineans: Sekou Toure (politician), Mory Kante (musician)

National Symbol

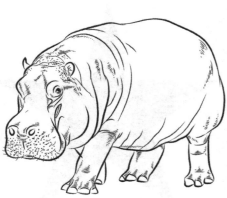

Hippopotamus

Find the Words

T	C	K	I	T	R	X	F	K	E	P	G
C	J	O	V	D	A	E	L	I	U	X	T
A	M	Y	N	T	N	N	Y	S	Q	B	Y
T	I	A	U	A	O	D	N	S	S	K	H
H	N	O	C	I	K	N	R	I	O	D	P
E	F	F	I	E	O	R	H	D	M	H	Q
D	C	V	X	L	N	K	Y	O	D	S	Y
R	L	C	L	L	N	T	W	U	N	N	K
A	U	A	R	D	S	W	A	G	A	H	M
L	J	N	Z	E	R	E	K	O	R	E	X
D	G	U	I	N	E	A	S	U	G	Q	L
E	I	R	A	M	E	T	N	A	S	R	M

CATHEDRAL   GUINEA
CONAKRY   KISSIDOUGOU
DJALLON   MACENTA
FOUTA   NZEREKORE
GRAND MOSQUE   SANTE MARIE

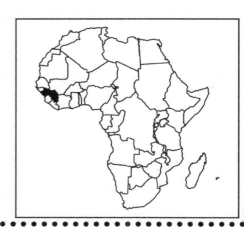

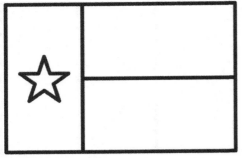

GUINEA-BISSAU

National Motto: Unity, Struggle, Progress

Capital: Bissau

Area: 13,948 square miles (36,125 square kilometers)

Major Cities: Bissau, Gabú, Bafatá

Population: 2.061 million

Bordering Countries: Senegal, Guinea

Languages: Portuguese, Guinea-Bissau Creole

Major Landmarks: Bissau Velho, Cacheu, Orango Islands National Park

Famous Bissau-Guineans: Amilcar Cabral (politician), Manecas Costa (musician)

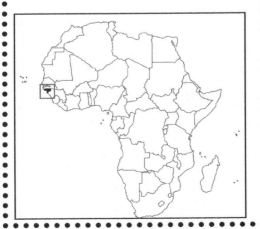

Find the Words

```
Y P U E Q K G U I N E A
K P Y O Q L P S M G C D
P C O R P F L K G A B U
E U F R E U Q A B U B X
C B X Y T A G P J T R Q
A V B G I U A M L K N C
L U L K D R G E J U V R
A A T T O B F U E P N U
P S K S T C R H E H M B
A S S F B V C U M S M A
V I Y V E A J L M N E N
B B C G C I R L D A O E
```

BISSAU
BISSORA
BRUMA
BUBAQUE
CACHEU

GABU
GUINEA
PALACE
PORTUGUESE
RUBANE

National Symbol

Black Star of Africa

GUYANA

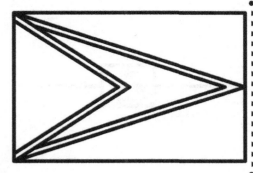

National Motto: One People, One Nation, One Destiny

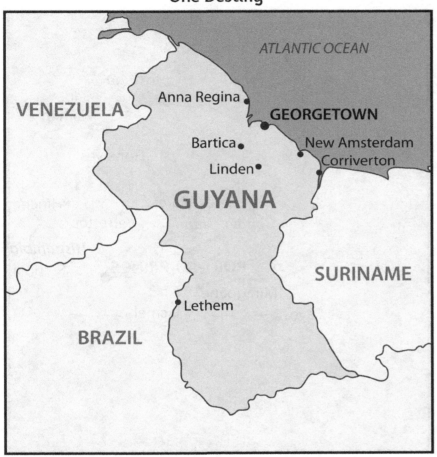

Capital: Georgetown
Area: 83,000 sq mi (214,969 sq km)
Major Cities: Georgetown, Linden, New Amsterdam, Bartica
Population: 786,552
Bordering Countries: Brazil, Suriname, Venezuela
Languages: English, Creole
Major Landmarks: Kaieteur Falls, St George's Cathedral, Iwokrama Forest
Famous Guyanese: Cheddi Jagan (former President), Eddy Grant (musician), Shivnarine Chanderpaul (cricketer)

National Symbol

Hoatzin

Find the Words

```
Y D K R U P U N U N I H
D R S T A B R O E K F H
E R G A K J C K X A Y E
M A C E Q A W Z M R O Q
E I A S O Y I A O B S E
R N N O R R R E I I L M
A F J K K K G U T O S K
R O E D O E Q E E E Q M
A R M W D E A R T L U I
K E I B S D C E X O W R
M S M S S L L T I P W A
W T E P W F M N K F Q N
```

CANJE   IWOKRAMA
CREOLE   KAIETEUR
DEMERARA   RAINFOREST
ESSEQUIBO   RUPUNUNI
GEORGETOWN   STABROEK

HAITI

National Motto: Liberty, Equality, Fraternity

Capital: Port-au-Prince

Area: 10,714 sq mi (27,750 sq km)

Major Cities: Port-au-Prince, Cap-Haïtien, Gonaïves, Les Cayes

Population: 11.402 million

Bordering Countries: Dominican Republic; maritime borders with Colombia, Cuba, the Bahamas, Jamaica, Turks and Caicos Islands

Languages: French, Haitian Creole

Major Landmarks: Citadelle Laferrière, Sans-Souci Palace, Labadee

Famous Haitians: Wyclef Jean (rapper), Toussaint Louverture (leader of the Haitian Revolution), Jean-Bertrand Aristide (former President)

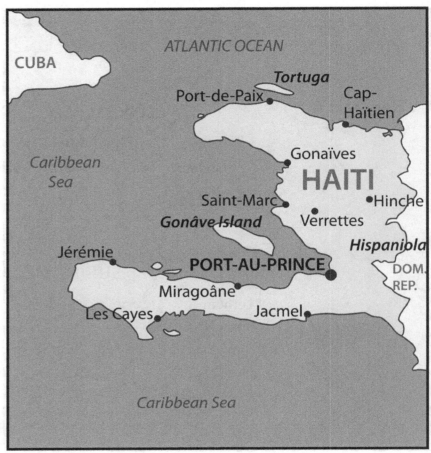

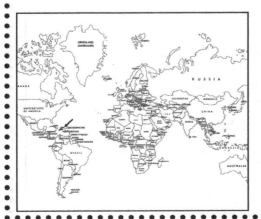

Find the Words

```
P V O O D O O O M S P E
M O I L M C A F E V L B
O N R U A F R N M L E T
R L H T I B I E E S S O
I R X Q A L A D O W L U
N S M D A U A D I L J S
G C Y S L T P S E Y E S
A J S O I L T R R E C A
F E B C D T R E I B Z I
D F S M T G Y X H N L N
A R T I B O N I T E C T
J O V H Y F P Z E K H E
```

ARTIBONITE
CITADELLE
CREOLE
DESSALINES
LABADEE
MORINGA
PORT AU PRINCE
RHUM
TOUSSAINT
VOODOO

National Symbol

Hispaniolan Trogon

HONDURAS

National Motto: Free, Sovereign, and Independent

Capital: Tegucigalpa
Area: 43,278 sq mi (112,090 sq km)
Major Cities: Tegucigalpa, San Pedro Sula, Choloma, La Ceiba
Population: 9.904 million
Bordering Countries: El Salvador, Guatemala, Nicaragua
Language: Spanish
Major Landmarks: Copán Ruins, Roatán Island, Rio Platano Biosphere Reserve
Famous Hondurans: Carlos Roberto Flores (former President), David Suazo (footballer)

National Symbol

Scarlet Macaw

Find the Words

```
T D M U M B F O Q A N O
L E F F I O G P N L C M
E M G O A Z R U L U I O
M S V U T E F A S Y I S
P X X D C I C U Z E Y Q
I G F O R I C O Y A B U
R B C A T H G G P L N I
A Y G N E W W A T A N T
H O N D U R A S L R N O
V F L E N C A Q V P M T
C H C R O A T A N D A Y
S E Z O U B M D P K F T
```

COPAN
CUSUCO
GARIFUNA
HONDURAS
LEMPIRA
LENCA
MORAZAN
MOSQUITO
ROATAN
TEGUCIGALPA

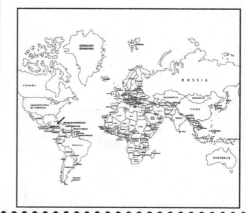

HUNGARY

National Motto: With the help of God for Homeland and Freedom

Capital: Budapest

Area: 35,919 square miles (93,022 square kilometers)

Major Cities: Szeged, Debrecen, Miskolc

Population: 9,660,351

Bordering Countries: Austria, Serbia, Croatia, Slovenia, Romania, Ukraine, Slovakia

Language: Hungarian

Major Landmarks: Buda Castle, Danube River, Széchenyi Medicinal Bath

Famous Hungarians: Harry Houdini (magician), George Soros (investor), John von Neumann (mathmetician)

Find the Words

```
Y W M U S K O L C P S L
B T D Z I J G F P A H A
B U U E D V C H P V U N
V F D Y B A D S O T N D
S K S A W R L E S V G L
Z Y R I C A E E Q W A O
E Z W U R A P C X B R C
G U E E E A S G E O I K
E W N Q D Q K T X N A E
D I K U O N B R L J N D
M H B J B R O D Y E R O
U D A N U B E R I V E R
```

BRODY   HUNGARIAN
BUDA CASTLE   LANDLOCKED
BUDAPEST   MINERAL SPAS
DANUBE RIVER   MUSKOLC
DEBRECEN   SZEGED

National Symbol

Turul

ICELAND

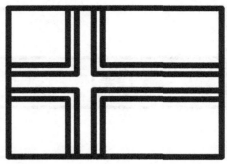

National Motto: No official motto

Capital: Reykjavik

Area: 39,769 square miles (103,125 square kilometers)

Major Cities: Vik, Akureyri, Hafnarfjrdur

Population: 341,243

Bordering Countries: None

Language: Icelandic

Major Landmarks: Blue Lagoon, Jokulsarlon Glacier Lagoon, Gullfoss

Famous Icelanders: Leif Ericson (explorer), Bjork (singer)

National Symbol

Icelandic Horse

Find the Words

T	C	I	C	E	L	A	N	D	I	C	W
A	X	B	X	G	V	S	D	N	U	T	K
S	T	U	L	O	W	H	J	G	M	I	Q
A	H	I	T	U	G	C	X	T	V	I	M
V	G	E	E	J	E	E	C	A	J	S	R
I	U	X	E	A	S	L	J	I	E	L	J
K	L	Z	L	P	T	K	A	K	W	A	K
E	L	F	J	A	Y	Y	R	G	H	N	Y
N	F	Q	Y	E	V	O	F	Q	O	D	M
V	O	Q	R	G	J	A	O	X	V	O	G
K	S	I	K	B	V	G	Y	U	Z	H	N
E	S	G	L	A	C	I	E	R	S	A	Q

BJORK   ISLAND
BLUE LAGOON   LAVA
GLACIERS   REYKJAVIK
GULLFOSS   SHEEP
ICELANDIC   VIK

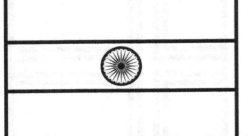

INDIA

National Motto: Truth Alone Triumphs

Capital: New Delhi

Area: 1,269,219 square miles (3,287,263 square kilometers)

Major Cities: Mumbai, Bangalore, Kolkata, Chennai

Population: 1.408 billion

Bordering Countries: Nepal, Pakistan, Bhutan, China, Bangladesh, Myanmar, Afghanistan, Sri Lanka, Maldives

Language: Hindi, Urdu, Bengalis, English, Punjabi, Marathi, Gujarati

Major Landmarks: Taj Mahal, Jaipur's Pink City and Amber Fort, Varanasi (Ganges River, Ghats), Golden Temple

Famous Indians: Mahatma Gandhi (politician), Sachin Tendulkar (cricketer), Amitabh Bachchan (actor), Kalpana Chawla (astronaut)

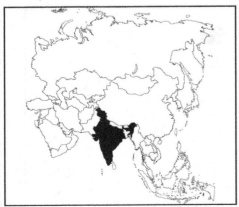

Find the Words

```
M L T W V N G A N G E S
T L X E A E G A N D H I
V P J T R W N M C N O E
Q L D Q A D G J D Y R E
T L K I N E P D Q O I P
R A I Z A L N R L D I M
M Z J A S H Z A N A X Q
K U G M I I G I N J N C
Z B M J A N H N O O Y Q
U X D B A H E U R D U K
L H V B A H A F T N D X
X U R F C I C L D N K P
```

BANGALORE   MUMBAI
CHENNAI   NEW DELHI
GANDHI   TAJ MAHAL
GANGES   URDU
HINDI   VARANASI

National Symbol

Bengal Tiger

INDONESIA

National Motto: Unity in Diversity

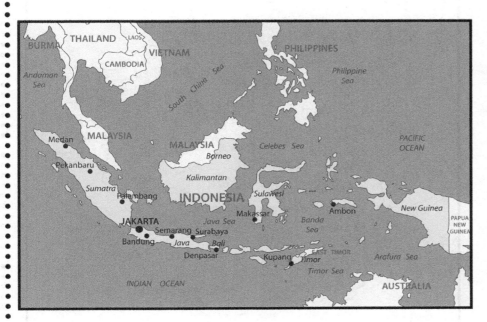

Capital: Jakarta
Area: 579,937 square miles (1,502,029 square kilometers)
Major Cities: Bandung, Surabaya, Makassar
Population: 273.8 million
Bordering Countries: Timor-Leste, Papua New Guinea, Malaysia
Languages: Indonesian, Javanese, Sundanese
Major Landmarks: Borobudur Temple, Tanah Lot Temple, Ubud Monkey Forest, Komodo National Park, Mount Bromo, Prambanan Temple
Famous Indonesians: Sukarno (politician), Pramoedya Ananta Toer (writer), R.A. Kartini (feminist activist), Susi Pudjiastuti (politician)

National Symbol

Komodo Dragon

Find the Words

D	E	X	M	K	G	N	K	U	P
O	S	A	S	A	H	A	B	L	T
H	L	U	B	H	O	N	Q	U	B
T	A	T	R	A	K	A	J	N	A
E	Q	O	L	A	I	B	W	D	N
M	L	W	R	I	B	M	V	A	D
R	A	S	S	A	K	A	M	N	U
X	S	W	G	G	H	R	Y	U	N
K	O	M	O	D	O	P	C	A	G
I	N	D	O	N	E	S	I	A	K

BAHASA   MAKASSAR
BANDUNG   METHOD
INDONESIA   PRAMBANAN
JAKARTA   SURABAYA
KOMODO   ULUN DANU

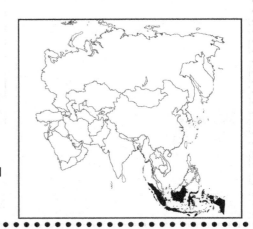

IRAN

National Motto: God Is the Greatest

Capital: Tehran

Area: 636,372 square miles (1,648,195 square kilometers)

Major Cities: Isfahan, Mashhad, Shiraz, Tabriz

Population: 87.92 million

Bordering Countries: Azerbaijan, Armenia, Turkmenistan Pakistan, Afghanistan, Turkey, Iraq

Languages: Persian, Azeri, Kurdish

Major Landmarks: Persepolis, Nasir al-Mulk Mosque (Pink Mosque), Imam Mosque, Golestan Palace, Yazd's Historic City

Famous Iranians: Rumi (poet), Ayatollah Khomeini (religious leader), Shohreh Aghdashloo (actress), Shirin Ebadi (activist)

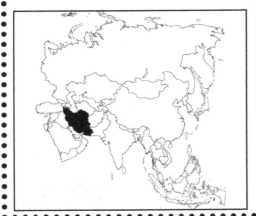

Find the Words

```
Q T C C P U L N I R Q L
A N Z I R B A T E R L H
L A K S R K V W I V A W
I H P H I P O Z Y Y P N
T A B I A T B R I D G E
J F U R D M T E H R A N
W S I A G L E P G O V Z
T I L Z L F L N V N E P
G I M N A I S R E P G V
M O J U E H U E T I Q Z
```

ALI	PERSIAN
IRAN	SHIRAZ
ISFAHAN	TABIAT BRIDGE
KHAMENEI	TABRIZ
MILAD TOWER	TEHRAN

National Symbol

Persian Nightingale

IRAQ

National Motto: God Is the Greatest

Capital: Baghdad
Area: 169,235 square miles (438,317 square kilometers)
Major Cities: Mosul, Basrah, Kirkuk
Population: 43.53 million
Bordering Countries: Iran, Jordan, Kuwait, Saudi Arabia, Syria, Turkey
Languages: Arabic, Kurdish
Major Landmarks:
Ziggurat of Ur, Al-Mustansiriya School, Erbil Citadel, Hatra Archaeological Site, Marshes of Southern Iraq
Famous Iraqis: Saddam Hussein (politician), Umm Kulthum (singer), Nadia Murad (activist), Ibrahim al-Jaafari (politician)

National Symbol

Mesopotamian Fallow Deer

Find the Words

```
O X R H C H N P P A C G
U Z U P A O U R S P D A
L F Q R L C E S Z R N Z
E Z S Y I T U M S H Z U
N A B B U I P H O E K S
B A A I N G H N E S I P
B R Z B I R R H J F U N
A M J T C I A T B E A L
M P D K N S T U J R C Z
N F L P Z T E P Q B Q A
T I K R I T S N Q I N V
Q V B A G H D A D L K O
```

ARABIC
BABYLON
BAGHDAD
BASRA
ERBIL

EUPHRATES
HUSSEIN
MOSUL
TIGRIS
TIKRIT

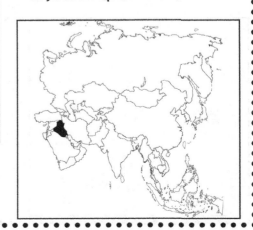

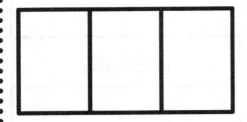

IRELAND

National Motto: Ireland forever

Capital: Dublin

Area: 32,595 square miles (70,273 square kilometers)

Major Cities: Belfast, Cork, Derry

Population: 4,937,786

Bordering Countries: United Kingdom

Language: English and Irish

Major Landmarks: Cliffs of Moher, Belfast Castle, Bangor Cathedral

Famous Irish : C. S. Lewis (author), Bono (musician), William Butler Yeats (author), Kenneth Branagh (actor)

Find the Words

```
R D K G U I N N E S S E
H S E X U K E L L S L Z
O S B R K G W N S S M Y
G O E T R Z B F I O K F
V I L K G Y F D S R Y L
W H F B Z I L O O X S N
C I A W L A D C T K S I
Y B S C R M F U I D J R
A N T E M K O V B F L I
Y G M M B D P H F L C S
N E M F P C G O E B I H
M H J U Y Z D A G R D N
```

BELFAST   EMERALD ISLE
CLIFFS   GUINNESS
CORK   IRISH
DERRY   KELLS
DUBLIN   MOHER

National Symbol

Red Deer

ISRAEL

National Motto: No official motto (Unofficial: If you will it, it is no dream)

Capital: Jerusalem
Area: 8,522 square miles (22,072 square kilometers)
Major Cities: Tel Aviv, Haifa, Ashdod
Population: 9.364 million
Bordering Countries: Egypt, Jordan, Lebanon, Syria, Palestine
Languages: Hebrew, Arabic, English, Russian
Major Landmarks: Western Wall (Wailing Wall), Dome of the Rock, Masada, Old City of Jerusalem, Yad Vashem Holocaust Memorial
Famous Israelis: David Ben-Gurion (politician), Golda Meir (politician), Amos Oz (writer), Natalie Portman (actress)

National Symbol

Hoopoe

Find the Words

I	Q	I	J	X	T	Y	A	F	O
D	O	M	E	O	F	R	O	C	K
W	M	H	R	L	L	A	W	H	G
W	A	U	U	U	L	J	K	A	W
P	I	R	S	E	D	B	D	I	E
V	I	V	A	L	E	T	O	F	R
A	E	R	L	B	B	F	L	A	B
O	S	T	E	D	I	L	A	C	E
I	Y	N	M	D	Z	C	T	P	H

ARABIC   JERUSALEM
DOME OF ROCK   LOD
HAIFA   TEL AVIV
HEBREW   WALL
ISRAEL   YAFO

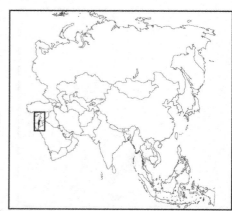

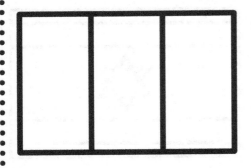

ITALY

National Motto: Union, Strength and Liberty!

Capital: Rome
Area: 116,348 square miles (301,340 square kilometers)
Major Cities: Venice, Florence, Milan
Population: 60,461,826
Bordering Countries: Austria, France, Holy See, San Marino, Slovenia, Switzerland
Language: Italian
Major Landmarks: Colosseum, Pantheon, Trevi Fountain, Mount Vesuvius, Leaning Tower of Pisa, Lake Como
Famous Italians: Leonardo da Vinci (Renaissance man), Julius Caesar (statesman), Christopher Colombus (explorer)

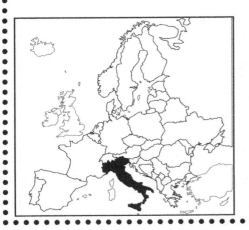

Find the Words

```
W G F L O R E N C E X W
G Z O C K T A I X F O P
F T L D M Y C P B P E O
G Q R N L I O K U A L N
C O L O S S E U M N C T
P V E L G N D N Q T O X
D A F V A E A P K H L Q
M X S Z E I L E V E O D
E K Z T L N M A G O M D
E I U A A O I Q T N B O
P Z T P R L K C H O U R
F I V A D K X F E G S E
```

COLOMBUS PANTHEON
COLOSSEUM PASTA
FLORENCE PIZZA
GELATO ROME
ITALIAN VENICE

National Symbol

Italian Wolf

JAMAICA

National Motto: Out of Many, One People

Caribbean Sea

Montego Bay
Falmouth
Discovery Bay
Negril
Ocho Rios
Bluefields
JAMAICA
Port Antonio
Spanish Town
Mandeville
KINGSTON

Capital: Kingston

Area: 4,244 sq mi (10,991 sq km)

Major Cities: Kingston, Montego Bay, Spanish Town, Portmore

Population: 2.961 million

Bordering Countries: Maritime borders with Colombia, Cuba, Haiti

Languages: English, Jamaican Patois

Major Landmarks: Dunn's River Falls, Bob Marley Museum, Blue and John Crow Mountains National Park

Famous Jamaicans: Usain Bolt (sprinter), Bob Marley (singer), Marcus Garvey (political leader)

National Symbol

Red-billed Streamertail

Find the Words

```
B A E B O B S L E D B N
J L Y N N L H B W R E W
A Z U L T A J A E K V U
M R P E T W S O C A M J
A U E C M I N I N C A P
I U E G O O H P K K R C
C V C T G C U F J E K O
A N A Z K A F N X E L V
S P N R B M E S T C E A
D C E K M R C W M A Y V
B J P B K R A S T A I W
E K I N G S T O N X M N
```

ACKEE
BLUE MOUNTAIN
BOB SLED
JAMAICA
JERK CHICKEN
KINGSTON
MARKLEY
PATOIS
RASTA
REGGAE

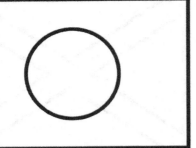

JAPAN

National Motto: Let the Rising Sun Bloom

Capital: Tokyo
Area: 145,920 square miles (377,930 square kilometers)
Major Cities: Osaka, Yokohama, Nagoya
Population: 125.7 million
Bordering Countries: Maritime borders with China, Northern Mariana Islands, Philippines, Russia, South Korea, China, North Korea
Language: Japanese
Major Landmarks: Mount Fuji, Kyoto's Temples and Shrines, Shibuya Crossing, Imperial Palace, Hiroshima Peace Memorial Park, Itsukushima Shrine
Famous Japanese: Emperor Hirohito (emperor), Hayao Miyazaki (filmmaker), Ichiro Suzuki (baseball player), Haruki Murakami (writer)

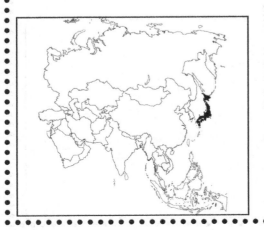

Find the Words

M	D	O	T	O	N	B	O	R	I
U	C	K	Y	O	T	O	B	A	E
R	O	R	R	P	N	S	M	T	A
A	O	B	O	F	T	I	V	N	Y
K	Y	O	H	S	H	H	A	I	U
A	K	R	H	S	S	P	C	V	B
M	O	Q	O	U	A	I	T	J	I
I	T	R	T	J	S	M	N	T	H
E	I	A	K	A	S	O	O	G	S
H	N	E	S	E	N	A	P	A	J

CROSSING	KYOTO
DOTONBORI	MURAKAMI
HIROSHIMA	OSAKA
JAPAN	SHIBUYA
JAPANESE	TOKYO

National Symbol

Japanese Macaque

JORDAN

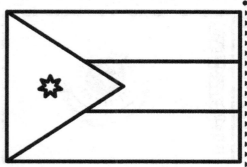

National Motto: God, HomeLand, King

Capital: Amman
Area: 34,495 square miles
(89,342 square kilometers)
Major Cities: Zarqa, Irbid
Population: 11.15 million
Bordering Countries:
 Syria, Iraq, Saudi Arabia,
Israel, Palestine
Language: Arabic
Major Landmarks: Dead
Sea, Ajloun Castle, Jerash,
Petra, Wadi Rum, Ammam
Citadel
Famous Jordanians: King
Abdullah II (king), Queen
Rania (queen consort),
Abdulhadi al-Khawaja
(activist)

National Symbol

Arabian Oryx

Find the Words

```
A M M A N O J Y O O U D
T D W B D Z R A X Y I G
E E U A O I R L L B H R
G P Y M D T L E R L I Z
K W C R E I D I Z O D E
M J B P A A R U W X E O
Z Z Q C T J V U G M A E
A U H I C U L J M M D V
R S C S Q E I O H E S X
Q K C A S T L E U D E X
A M P G Y W N B F N A E
Y J E R A S H G E T Q S
```

AJLOUN	IRBID
AMMAN	JERASH
CASTLE	PETRA
CITADEL	WADI RUM
DEAD SEA	ZARQA

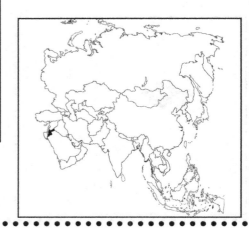

KAZAKHSTAN

National Motto: Freedom, Unity, Progress!

Capital: Astana

Area: 982,600 square miles (2,544,900 square kilometers)

Major Cities: Almaty, Shymkent , Aktobe

Population: 19 million

Bordering Countries: Russia, China, Kyrgyzstan, Uzbekistan, Turkmenistan

Languages: Kazakh, Russian

Major Landmarks: Charyn Canyon, Lake Kaindy, Astana Bayterek Tower, Big Almaty Lake, Mausoleum of Khoja Ahmed Yasawi

Famous Kazakhs: Nursultan Nazarbayev (politician), Dimash Kudaibergen (singer), Mukhtar Auezov (author)

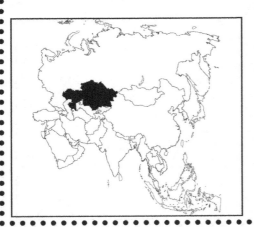

Find the Words

C	B	K	T	B	A	L	K	H	A	S	H
U	H	X	A	P	R	V	N	E	J	M	U
S	X	A	X	Z	O	S	V	G	U	E	W
H	I	A	R	V	A	U	O	E	N	A	T
Y	S	K	J	Y	H	K	L	M	N	J	N
M	U	T	B	X	N	O	H	A	R	S	A
K	L	O	F	S	S	C	T	G	Y	A	Z
E	T	B	B	U	A	S	A	U	N	N	K
N	A	E	A	J	A	J	P	N	V	D	X
T	N	M	P	Y	A	Q	W	Z	Y	G	U
L	A	K	E	K	A	I	N	D	Y	O	I
A	A	L	M	A	T	Y	A	V	X	O	N

AKTOBE	KAZAKH
ALMATY	LAKE KAINDY
ASTANA	MAUSOLEUM
BALKHASH	SHYMKENT
CHARYN CANYON	SULTAN

National Symbol

Snow Leopard

KENYA

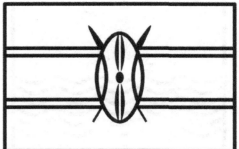

National Motto: All Pull Together

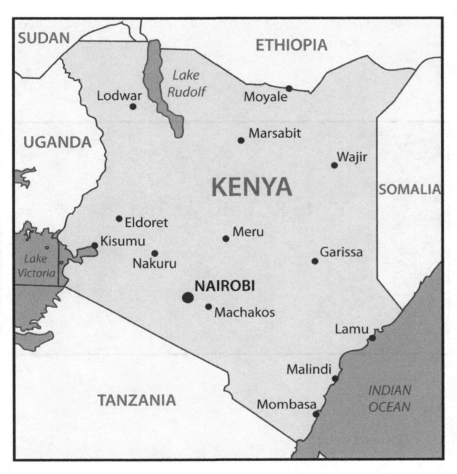

Capital: Nairobi

Area: 224,081 square miles (580,367 square kilometers)

Major Cities: Nairobi, Mombasa, Kisumu, Nakuru

Population: 53 million

Bordering Countries: South Sudan, Ethiopia, Somalia, Tanzania, Uganda

Languages: Swahili, English

Major Landmarks: Masai Mara National Reserve, Mount Kenya, Lamu Island

Famous Kenyans: Jomo Kenyatta (politician), Wangari Maathai (activist), David Rudisha (athlete)

National Symbol

African Lion

Find the Words

E	K	U	M	U	S	I	K	B	Q	J	F
E	Y	E	A	M	N	A	I	R	O	B	I
S	L	T	N	H	R	B	O	M	A	S	X
E	W	D	C	Y	P	U	A	S	X	O	T
C	S	D	R	X	A	S	A	U	A	A	P
M	J	W	N	J	A	H	S	S	N	A	I
A	E	T	A	B	V	H	P	E	A	Y	J
A	S	H	M	H	B	D	A	J	Y	T	U
T	I	O	O	T	I	N	R	T	N	R	A
H	M	C	I	L	P	L	Q	R	E	F	U
A	A	R	U	K	A	N	I	O	K	O	I
L	X	L	H	A	F	C	B	F	M	O	K

BOMAS   MAATHAI
FORT JESUS   MOMBASA
KENYA   NAIROBI
KENYAN   NAKURA
KISUMU   SWAHILI

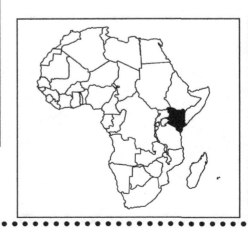

KIRIBATI

National Motto: Health, Peace and Prosperity

Capital: Tarawa

Area: 313.1 square miles (811 square kilometers)

Major Cities: Tarawa, Betio Village, Bikenibeu

Population: 128,874

Bordering Countries: Cook Islands, Tokelau, French Polynesia

Language: English

Major Landmarks: Phoenix Islands Protected Area, Tarawa Atoll, Christmas Island, Equator and International Date Line Monuments

Famous Kiribatians: Anote Tong (politician), David Katoatau (weightlifter)

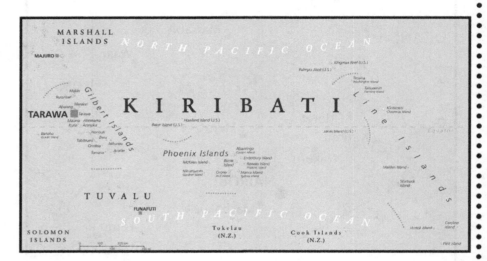

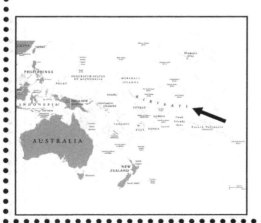

Find the Words

K	Z	B	I	K	E	N	I	B	E	U	A
G	I	H	B	Q	E	C	F	B	D	K	C
H	D	R	E	E	A	H	Z	O	N	I	W
J	A	H	I	W	T	R	G	K	O	S	D
L	G	T	A	B	C	I	A	I	C	L	N
S	J	R	O	Q	A	S	O	K	Q	A	V
T	A	J	V	L	K	T	T	O	U	N	C
T	B	R	K	J	L	M	I	K	Z	D	R
S	O	U	T	H	P	A	C	I	F	I	C
Z	E	U	E	Z	M	S	X	K	U	W	A
P	H	O	E	N	I	X	H	O	K	E	O
C	H	W	E	V	F	Y	F	I	Z	Y	H

ATOLL   ISLAND
BETIO   KIRIBATI
BIKENIBEU   PHOENIX
BOKIKOKIKO   SOUTH PACIFIC
CHRISTMAS   TARAWA

National Symbol

Bokikokiko

KOREA, NORTH

National Motto: Powerful and Prosperous Nation

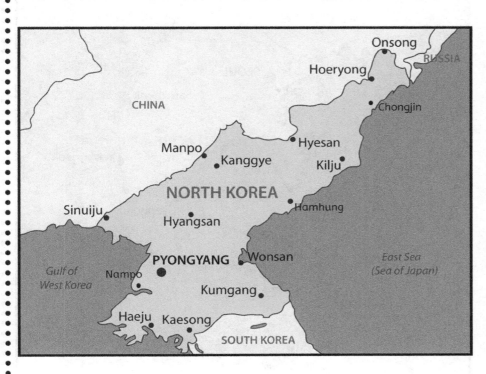

Capital: Pyongyang
Area: 46,540 square miles
(120,538 square kilometers)
Major Cities: Nampo,
Chongjin, Hamhung
Population: 25.97 million
Bordering Countries:
China, Russia, South Korea
Language: Korean
Major Landmarks: Kumsu-
san Palace of the Sun, Juche
Tower, Demilitarized Zone
(DMZ), Mansu Hill Grand
Monument, Koryo Museum
Famous North Koreans:
Kim Il-sung (politician), Kim
Jong-il (politician), Kim Jong-
un (politician), Ri Chun-hee
(news presenter)

National Symbol

Chollima

Find the Words

M	J	U	C	H	E	T	O	W	E	R	O
R	F	W	Z	N	Z	N	G	R	H	A	M
P	X	F	I	C	N	N	F	D	V	U	G
Y	W	F	B	B	O	A	B	C	E	K	H
O	N	D	C	S	K	N	M	S	I	O	A
N	E	Z	E	H	Y	I	U	P	P	R	M
G	P	A	O	B	O	M	M	S	O	E	H
Y	K	N	Q	F	O	N	S	J	U	A	U
A	S	M	T	Y	T	Q	G	J	O	N	N
N	E	Y	R	R	L	W	R	J	O	N	G
G	T	O	W	O	N	S	A	N	I	Q	G
X	K	I	Y	J	N	D	Y	O	Y	N	U

CHONGJIN	KOREAN
HAMHUNG	KORYO MUSEUM
JUCHE TOWER	NAMPO
KAESONG	PYONGYANG
KIM JONG	WONSAN

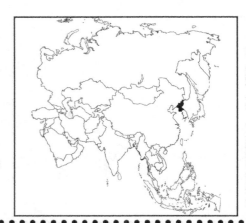

KOREA, SOUTH

National Motto: No official motto

Capital: Seoul
Area: 38,690 square miles
(100,210 square kilometers)
Major Cities: Busan,
Incheon, Daegu
Population: 51.74 million
Bordering Countries:
North Korea
Language: Korean
Major Landmarks:
Gyeongbokgung Palace,
Changdeokgung Palace
and Huwon (Secret Garden), Jeju Island, Bukchon
Hanok Village, DMZ (Demilitarized Zone) and Joint
Security Area (JSA)
Famous South Koreans:
Park Geun-hye (politician),
Kim Yuna (athlete), Bong
Joon-ho (filmmaker)

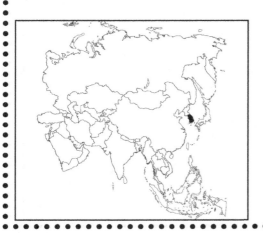

Find the Words

```
S U F Q U Q N H K D P J
D E E H K M T T N I Y N
A S C F N U G A Q N X B
E B X R O P L F L C R U
G X O S E S B U I H D S
U S F R I T O W H E J C
V F Z U D E G O N O O A
B R J N S E F A E N W N
L E L I U B R J R A E E
J E L K O R E A N D G R
Q Y E L L O W S E A E U
V W P D U Q C A R R A N
```

BORDER   KOREAN
BUSCAN   SECRET GARDEN
DAEGU   SEOUL
INCHEON   SOUTH
JEJU ISLAND   YELLOW SEA

National Symbol

Korean Tiger

KOSOVO

National Motto: Honour, Duty, Homeland

Capital: Pristina

Area: 4,203 square miles (10,887 square kilometers)

Major Cities: Prizren, Peja, Mitrovica

Population: 4,935,259

Bordering Countries: Serbia, North Macedonia, Albania, Montenegro

Language: Albanian, Serbian

Major Landmarks: Mother Teresa Cathedral, Gracanica Monastery, Prizren's Fortress

Famous Kosovans: Era Istrefi (singer)

National Symbol

Roe Deer

Find the Words

```
I E A P R I Z R E N M F
I N L L Q V Q G A C I X
S N D N B A T N J J T Y
L K M E I A I A D Y R B
A E B B P T N B S S O A
M A R C S E X I D F V L
G E W I G P N R A C I K
S C R B T N E D C N C A
K P O G J Q W J E X A N
I D Q T R A Z N A N S S
G F O T T O M A N S C F
R L K R Z I W V T J U E
```

ALBANIAN	OTTOMANS
BALKANS	PEJA
INDEPENDENCE	PRISTINA
ISLAM	PRIZREN
MITROVICA	SERBIA

KUWAIT

National Motto: No official motto

Capital: Kuwait City

Area: 6,880 square miles (17,818 square kilometers)

Major Cities: Al Ahmadi, Al Fahahil

Population: 4.25 million

Bordering Countries: Iraq, Saudi Arabia

Languages: Arabic, English

Major Landmarks: Grand Mosque, Kuwait Towers, The Avenues Mall, Sadu House, Failaka Island

Famous Kuwaitis: Sheikh Jaber Al-Ahmad Al-Sabah (politician), Tareq Al-Suwaidan (scholar), Mubarak Al-Hajri (athlete)

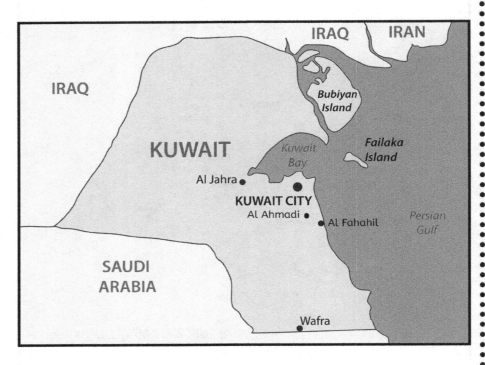

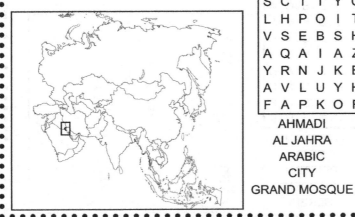

Find the Words

```
K U W A I T T O W E R S
I D A M H A U D E X T Z
O E U Q S O M D N A R G
S C I T Y C D A H S R R
L H P O I T R D A F T X
V S E B S H K C W T I R
A Q A I A Z C P A A A E
Y R N J K B Z F L J W B
A V L U Y H N C L K U A
F A P K O F Z F Y W K J
```

AHMADI   HAWALLY
AL JAHRA   JABER
ARABIC   KUWAIT
CITY   KUWAIT TOWERS
GRAND MOSQUE   SHEIKH

National Symbol

Falcon

KYRGYZSTAN

National Motto: No official motto

Capital: Bishkek

Area: 77,202 square miles (199,951 square kilometers)

Major Cities: Osh, Karakol, Jalal-Abad

Population: 6.692 million

Bordering Countries: Kazakhstan, China, Tajikistan, Uzbekistan

Languages: Kyrgyz, Russian

Major Landmarks: Issyk-Kul Lake, Ala Archa National Park, Burana Tower, Song Kol Lake, Osh Bazaar

Famous Kyrgyzstani: Chingiz Aitmatov (author), Kurmanbek Bakiyev (politician), Roza Otunbayeva (politician)

National Symbol

Snow Leopard

Find the Words

```
M M Z M O U N T A I N S
A B V Q K L P A M I R V
N K U B I S H T E K T P
A Y Y R I P H F T D L D
S R A F A Q O A Z L U Y
P G Q L Z N B N O Y X P
E Y J L A A A K G Y R P
A Z Y L R A A T Q F E S
K P K H F R R G O Y W X
O M S U A W H C E W B D
V A I K H S L N H Z E A
T J M J O O J I J A I R
```

ALA ARCHA
BISHTEK
BURANA TOWER
KARAKOL
KYRGYZ

MANAS PEAK
MOUNTAINS
OSH
PAMIR
TASH RABAT

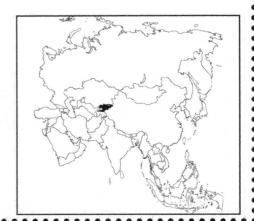

LAOS

Capital: Vientiane

Area: 91,400 square miles (236,800 square kilometers)

Major Cities: Luang Prabang, Savannakhet, Pakse

Population: 7.425 million

Bordering Countries: China, Vietnam, Cambodia, Thailand, Myanmar

Language: Lao

Major Landmarks: Luang Prabang's Temples, Kuang Si Waterfalls, Plain of Jars, Wat Phu, Pha That Luang, Buddha Park

Famous Laotians: Khamtai Siphandon (politician), Souphanouvong (politician), Anou Savanh (singer)

National Motto: Peace, Independence, Democracy, Unity and Prosperity

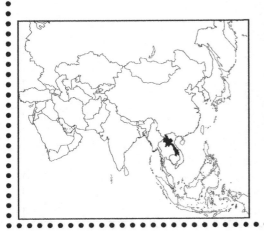

Find the Words

```
M L E Z Z C A W H U B T
B U D D H A P A R K E V
F P P Q W B Q N V H C I
Q X P C L A Z H K S B E
A X Q G H I T A R K X N
A Z L P E A N P E T G T
T G A I A N M H H O M I
T Y O L A K K P X U Y A
A G K V X A S A A V I N
P M A M H C V E X S L E
E S D T P Q T I F Y A A
U U A M U A N G X A Y K
```

ATTAPEU
BUDDHA PARK
CHAMPASAK
LAO
MUANG XAY

PAKSE
SAVANNAKHET
THAKHEK
VIENTIANE
WAT PHU

National Symbol

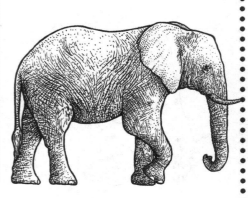

Elephant

LATVIA

National Motto: For Fatherland and Freedom

Capital: Riga

Area: 24,938 square miles (62,157 square kilometers)

Major Cities: Daugavpils, Ventspils, Jelgava

Population: 1,886,198

Bordering Countries: Estonia, Russia, Belarus, Lithuania

Language: Lettish

Major Landmarks: Rundāle Palace, Gauja National Park, Turaida Castle

Famous Latvians: Mikhail Baryshnikov (dancer), Isaiah Berlin (philosopher), Catherine I (monarch)

National Symbol

White Wagtail

Find the Words

T	P	G	W	I	O	A	T	Q	O	Y	N
B	Z	M	I	K	J	W	G	A	U	J	A
Y	D	Z	H	A	B	A	L	H	D	Z	I
Y	N	T	P	W	E	T	E	C	J	B	Q
B	O	E	T	M	A	E	T	W	N	D	F
R	I	W	H	E	C	R	T	P	V	A	O
L	X	R	X	W	H	F	I	W	Z	V	R
Z	T	P	I	R	E	A	S	Q	E	N	E
W	W	S	D	G	S	L	H	P	S	H	S
A	Y	Q	K	W	A	L	Q	S	W	B	T
C	J	U	R	M	A	L	A	A	K	J	S
M	E	I	S	E	N	S	T	E	I	N	K

BEACHES   LETTISH
EISENSTEIN   LIEPAJA
FORESTS   RIGA
GAUJA   ROTHKO
JURMALA   WATERFALL

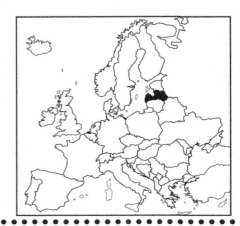

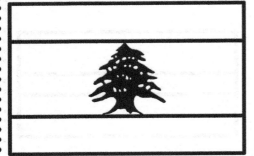

LEBANON

National Motto: We Are All for the Country, the Sublime and the Flag

Capital: Beirut

Area: 4,036 square miles (10,452 square kilometers)

Major Cities: Tripoli, Sidon, Tyre

Population: 5.593 million

Bordering Countries: Syria, Israel

Language: Arabic

Major Landmarks: Baalbek Roman Ruins, Byblos, Jeita Grotto, National Museum of Beirut, Pigeon Rocks (Raouche Rocks)

Famous Lebanese: Fairuz (singer), Gibran Khalil Gibran (poet, writer) Rafic Hariri (politician), Amal Clooney (human rights lawyer)

El Mina
Tripoli
Chekka
Hermel
Batroun
Mediterranean Sea
Byblos
Baalbek
Jounieh
BEIRUT
Zahlé
LEBANON
SYRIA
Sidon
Jezzine
Tyre
Naqoura
ISRAEL

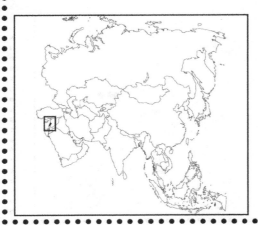

Find the Words

```
E S A S D A N T Y R E M
J P I G E O N R O C K S
R E A S I D O N F R M J
B U I G J J Y H A B M M
R U I T O Y G C I S F O
T S K N A X R N R R U W
R Z I B S G A K U S S Y
I X D K E R R V Z O N G
P S A O B I P O L O L E
O J L I P C R B T L A X
L C G E W H Y U Q T K K
I T E Q T B Y W T L O E
```

BEIRUT
BYBLOS
FAIRUZ
GIBRAN
JEITA GROTTO
PIGEON ROCKS
RUINS
SIDON
TRIPOLI
TYRE

National Symbol

Lebanese Nightingale

LESOTHO

National Motto: Peace, Rain, Prosperity

SOUTH AFRICA

- Leribe
- Teyateyaneng
- **MASERU**
- Mokhotlong
- Thaba-Tseka

LESOTHO

- Mafeteng
- Mohale's Hoek
- Qacha's Nek
- Quthing

Capital: Maseru
Area: 11,720 square miles (30,355 square kilometers)
Major Cities: Maseru, Teyateyaneng, Mafeteng
Population: 2.281 million
Bordering Countries: South Africa
Languages: Sotho, English
Major Landmarks: Maletsunyane Falls, Sani Pass, Thaba-Bosiu
Famous Basothos: Moshoeshoe I (king), Le-hlohonolo Majoro (soccer player)

National Symbol

Black Rhinoceros

Find the Words

L	E	G	N	E	T	E	F	A	M	A	C
E	C	K	G	B	M	A	S	E	R	U	L
R	V	C	P	O	S	L	P	U	D	I	R
I	I	Y	L	Y	X	Q	D	E	I	E	C
B	I	A	P	E	Z	A	O	C	O	B	F
E	I	X	S	S	S	X	N	S	N	A	H
L	E	O	H	M	S	O	T	H	O	S	S
Q	I	R	X	P	E	U	T	H	J	O	X
E	S	S	C	J	P	Q	O	H	T	T	C
O	T	Q	I	A	I	T	Y	N	O	H	B
Q	E	M	M	U	O	E	G	R	C	O	I
B	L	D	N	A	B	A	H	T	Y	S	M

BASOTHOS   MAFETENG
LERIBE   MAPUTSOE
LESOTHO   MASERU
LETSIE III   SOTHO
LISIU   THABA

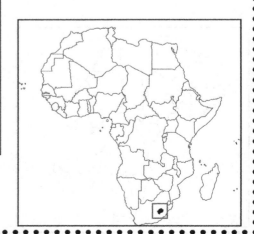

LIBERIA

National Motto: The Love of Liberty Brought Us Here

Capital: Monrovia

Area: 43,000 square miles (111,369 square kilometers)

Major Cities: Monrovia, Gbarnga, Buchanan

Population: 5.193 million

Bordering Countries: Sierra Leone, Guinea, Côte d'Ivoire

Language: English

Major Landmarks: Sapo National Park, Robertsport

Famous Liberians: Ellen Johnson Sirleaf (politician), Leymah Gbowee (activist), George Weah (soccer player)

Map

SIERRA LEONE

Voinjama

GUINEA

Yekepa

Tubmanburg

Robertsport

Gbarnga

CÔTE D'IVOIRE

LIBERIA

MONROVIA

Harbel

Buchanan

Zwedru

ATLANTIC OCEAN

Greenville

Harper

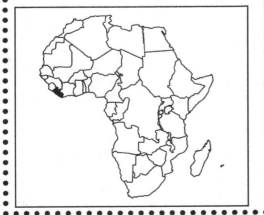

Find the Words

D	L	G	V	C	W	E	N	F	D	B	Y
L	I	M	B	V	G	N	D	I	E	S	C
A	B	M	O	A	S	P	V	N	L	R	L
I	E	G	Z	N	R	X	A	E	H	D	I
N	R	H	E	S	R	N	T	H	Y	B	B
N	I	L	O	V	A	O	G	W	Q	B	E
E	A	X	M	H	H	M	V	A	F	Y	R
T	N	W	C	R	I	P	L	I	Q	B	I
N	S	U	O	X	X	Y	F	R	A	R	A
E	B	C	P	A	V	I	L	I	O	N	I
C	U	P	I	Q	A	T	A	K	A	K	N
D	S	M	R	A	F	I	K	L	U	W	E

BUCHANAN
CENTENNIAL
DUCOR HOTEL
GBARNGA
KAKATA

LIBERIA
LIBERIANS
MONROVIA
PAVILION
WULKI FARMS

National Symbol

Asiatic Lion

LIBYA

National Motto: No official motto

Capital: Tripoli

Area: 679,362 square miles (1,759,540 square kilometers)

Major Cities: Tripoli, Benghazi, Misrata

Population: 6.735 million

Bordering Countries: Egypt, Sudan, Niger, Chad, Tunisia, Algeria

Language: Arabic

Major Landmarks: Leptis Magna, Cyrene, Sabratha

Famous Libyans: Muammar Gaddafi (politician), Omar Mukhtar (resistance leader), Queen Fatima

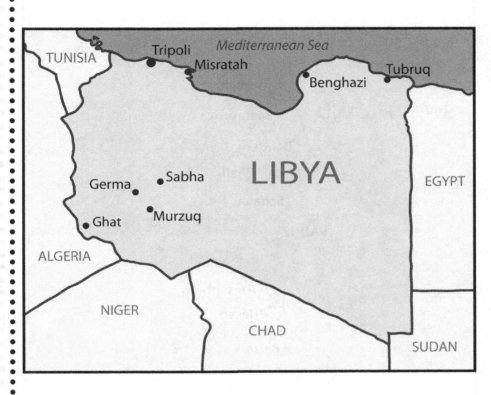

National Symbol

Barbary Lion

Find the Words

E	L	T	S	A	C	D	E	R	Z	C	R
S	N	A	Y	B	I	L	M	K	I	E	K
I	C	T	R	I	G	M	Z	B	J	F	P
A	O	O	M	I	S	R	A	T	A	S	I
X	U	Q	N	K	P	R	L	T	N	D	Z
Q	L	R	D	Z	A	L	G	R	T	H	A
Q	U	E	E	N	F	A	T	I	M	A	H
G	E	B	L	L	Y	C	D	P	Q	R	G
P	T	Q	I	B	I	J	L	O	W	C	N
O	R	J	B	H	N	U	T	L	L	U	E
R	I	E	Y	A	F	W	S	I	V	R	B
G	S	O	A	Z	Q	M	J	D	S	P	K

ARABIC
AURELIUS
BENGHAZI
LIBYA
LIBYANS

MISRATA
QUEEN FATIMA
RED CASTLE
SIRTE
TRIPOLI

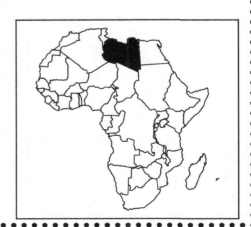

LIECHTENSTEIN

National Motto: For God, Prince and Fatherland

Capital: Vaduz

Area: 61.78 square miles (160 square kilometers)

Major Cities: Triesenberg, Schaan, Triesen

Population: 38,128

Bordering Countries: Switzerland, Austria

Language: German

Major Landmarks: Vaduz Castle, Alte Rheinbrucke, The Main Square

Famous Liechtensteiners: Josef Rheinberger (composer)

Find the Words

```
S C H E L L E N B E R G
L Y H N G J M R H I N E
A Y S Q R H O V A D U Z
L U C A A Q N K T C O M
P G H I U Z A J L A Z M
I V A B S O R Y R S J A
N J A N P L C E D T P L
E H N F I C H E D L U R
A T X R T O Y G J E M C
F R I I Z R W I O S P C
P R I N C I P A L I T Y
T R I E S E N B E R G C
```

ALPINE   RHINE
CASTLES   SCHAAN
GRAUSPITZ   SCHELLENBERG
MONARCHY   TRIESENBERG
PRINCIPALITY   VADUZ

National Symbol

Kestrel

LITHUANIA

National Motto: Let Unity Flourish

Baltic Sea

LATVIA

Mažeikiai

Būtingė
Palanga
Klaipėda

Šiauliai

Panevėžys

LITHUANIA

Utena

Kuršių

Kėdainiai

Jonava

Kaunas

VILNIUS

RUSSIA

Marijampolė Lake Galvė

Alytus

POLAND

BELARUS

Capital: Vilnius

Area: 25,212 square miles (65,300 square kilometers)

Major Cities: Kaunas, Klaipeda, Siauliai

Population: 2,673,113

Bordering Countries: Latvia, Belarus, Poland, Russia

Language: Lithuanian

Major Landmarks: Trakai Island Castle, Hill of Crosses, Gates of Dawn

Famous Lithuanians: Emma Goldman (author), Jascha Heifetz (violinist)

National Symbol

White Stork

Find the Words

B	E	H	U	K	A	U	N	A	S	V	K
N	E	M	A	N	R	I	V	E	R	A	R
L	O	T	Y	K	G	W	S	C	O	W	B
N	I	T	K	J	K	U	M	E	A	B	H
I	E	T	E	H	I	Z	Z	B	B	A	J
N	E	M	H	N	G	U	W	I	W	L	W
T	C	G	L	U	M	O	A	E	O	T	J
H	I	I	V	L	A	K	L	N	K	I	Q
F	V	H	E	Y	A	N	T	D	U	C	Y
O	E	T	F	R	Q	L	I	B	M	S	W
R	S	T	T	C	J	P	A	A	Y	A	X
T	V	P	A	L	A	N	G	A	N	M	N

BALTICS   NINTH FORT
GOLDMAN   PALANGA
KAUNAS   STELMUZE OAK
LITHUANIAN   TRAKAI
NEMAN RIVER   VILNIUS

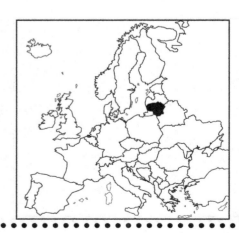

LUXEMBOURG

National Motto: We Wish to Remain What We Are

Capital: Luxembourg

Area: 998 square miles (2,586 square kilometers)

Major Cities: Dudelange, Differdange, Echternach

Population: 625,978

Bordering Countries: Belgium, France, Germany

Language: Luxembourgish, French, German

Major Landmarks: Mudam, Grand Ducal Palace, Neumünster Abbey

Famous Luxembourgers: Andy Schleck (cyclist), Hugo Gernsback (author)

BELGIUM
Troisvierges
GERMANY
Diekirch
LUXEMBOURG
Mertert
Grevenmacher
LUXEMBOURG
Differdange
Esch
Dudelange
FRANCE

Find the Words

```
C A S E M A T E S G H R
L L B L Y Y J W B R V E
X U K K J H Y E E A V C
S Y X L D H J G U N D H
J M L E T M N H N D I T
Q L A L M A G S E D F E
W H A L L B L E S U O R
O E J E L E O C C C O N
W N D M N E E U O H S A
F U V N F J S Q R Y S C
D T U E D U L T C G L H
L T E T T E L B R U C K
```

CASEMATES   LUXEMBOURG
DUDELANGE   SMALLEST
ECHTERNACH   TUNNELS
ETTELBRUCK   UNESCO
GRAND DUCHY   WEALTHY

National Symbol

Lion

MADAGASCAR

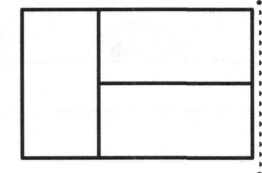

National Motto: Love, Ancestral-land, Progress

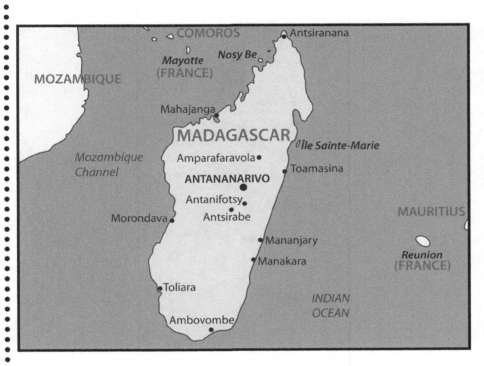

Capital: Antananarivo
Area: 226,658 square miles (578,041 square kilometers)
Major Cities: Toamasina, Antsirabe, Mahajanga
Population: 27,691,018
Bordering Countries: Maritime borders with Comoros, France, Mauritius, Mozambique, Seychelles
Languages: Malagasy, French
Major Landmarks: Avenue of the Baobabs, Tsingy de Bemaraha Strict Nature Reserve, Isalo National Park
Famous Madagascans: Marc Ravalomanana (politician), Erick Manana (musician)

National Symbol

Ring-tailed Lemur

Find the Words

```
L A G N A J A H A M L S
G P Q K M P Q I S G L Q
H T O A M A S I N A E M
O V I R A N A N A T N A
M M A D A G A S C A R Y
A D I O V G G U S B W S
L P F A F C G S A A A A
A B R E R N F J G B T T
G U Y S O N A C A L E I
A X O O D X S L D S R C
S H A N T S I R A B E A
Y J Y W L O G Q M X K L
```

ANTANANARIVO
ANTSIRABE
LAC ANOSY
LAC ITASY
MADAGASCANS

MADAGASCAR
MAHAJANGA
MALAGASY
TOAMASINA
WATER

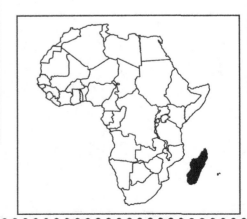

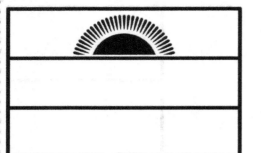

MALAWI

National Motto: Unity and Freedom

Capital: Lilongwe

Area: 45,747 square miles (118,484 square kilometers)

Major Cities: Lilongwe, Blantyre, Zomba, Mzuzu

Population: 19.89 million

Bordering Countries: Zambia, Tanzania, Mozambique

Languages: English, Chichewa

Major Landmarks: Lake Malawi, Liwonde National Park, Mount Mulanje

Famous Malawians: Hastings Kamuzu Banda (founding father), Joyce Banda (politician), William Kamkwamba (inventor)

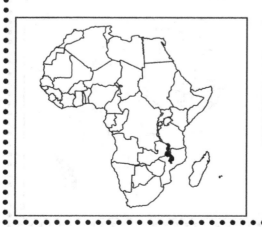

Find the Words

```
E  D  I  B  B  A  T  F  X  W  X  U
I  B  Q  L  H  W  I  X  V  S  W  G
L  C  L  Y  V  T  Y  M  V  L  W  I
A  L  I  L  O  N  G  W  E  E  I  B
B  C  N  Z  S  O  U  A  Q  G  M  L
M  J  H  E  A  Z  Y  F  Q  N  E  A
U  X  M  U  U  M  P  Z  I  A  M  N
K  L  Q  Z  R  E  B  T  K  L  O  T
J  L  M  J  I  C  W  A  B  L  R  Y
I  W  A  L  A  M  H  V  X  A  I  R
F  S  N  A  I  W  A  L  A  M  A  E
E  K  M  Q  M  B  J  R  Z  V  L  E
```

ALL ANGELS   MALAWI
BLANTYRE   MALAWIANS
CHURCH   MZUZU
KUMBALI   WWI MEMORIAL
LILONGWE   ZAMBA

National Symbol

African Fish Eagle

MALAYSIA

National Motto: Unity Is Strength

Capital: Kuala Lumpur
Area: 127,724 square miles (330,803 square kilometers)
Major Cities: George Town, Ipoh, Johor Bahru
Population: 33.57 million
Bordering Countries: Brunei, Indonesia, Thailand, martime borders with Phillippines, Singapore, Vietnam
Language: Malay
Major Landmarks: Petronas Twin Towers, Batu Caves, Georgetown Historic City, Langkawi Archipelago, Mount Kinabalu
Famous Malaysians: Mahathir Mohamad (politician), Michelle Yeoh (actress), Nicol David (athlete), Yasmin Ahmad (filmmaker)

National Symbol

Malayan Tiger

Find the Words

```
G E O R G E T O W N
K I H E R U P M U L
Q U G I A A V P M A
B G C L C K Y E I I
E A A H T J U T V S
G U H Z I Y L R B Y
K V M A A N F O A A
T X Z L S A G N H L
S H E N T A W A R A
W M R O H O J S U M
```

BAHASA   KUCHING
BAHRU   LUMPUR
GEORGE TOWN   MALAYSIA
JOHOR   MELAYU
KUALA   PETRONAS

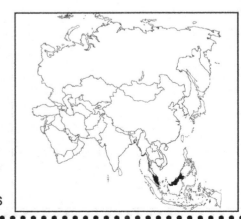

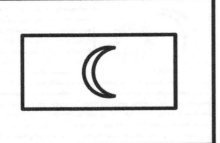

MALDIVES

National Motto: State of the Mahal Dibiyat

Capital: Malé

Area: 120 square miles (300 square kilometers)

Major Cities: Malé

Population: 521,457

Bordering Countries: Maritime borders with India and Sri Lanka

Language: Dhivehi

Major Landmarks: Malé's Old Friday Mosque, Bioluminescent Beaches, Baa Atoll Biosphere Reserve, Hanifaru Bay

Famous Maldivians: Mohamed Nasheed (politician), Ali Hafez (athlete), Ahmed Naseem (politician), Mariyam Zakir (surfer)

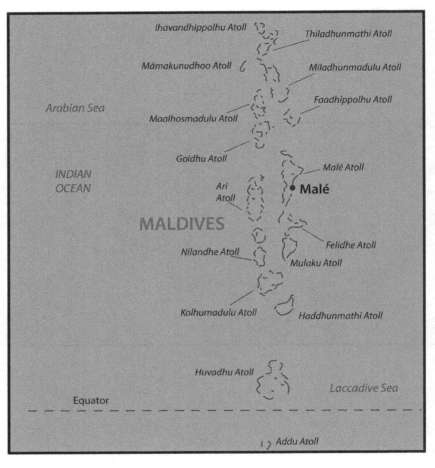

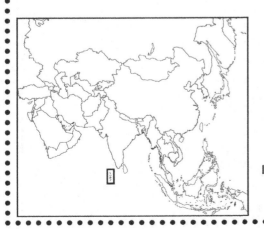

Find the Words

M	M	I	N	I	C	O	Y	M	U	J
M	A	P	I	F	F	U	P	S	N	P
M	P	L	G	S	R	W	E	E	N	D
O	E	Q	D	U	L	V	M	L	A	H
S	T	P	K	I	I	A	A	A	F	I
Q	Z	U	W	D	V	F	N	M	A	V
U	H	I	L	C	N	I	L	D	A	E
E	A	A	C	I	K	T	A	Z	M	H
R	M	K	P	Q	R	D	J	N	C	I
F	E	E	H	T	A	L	D	A	M	I

DHIVEHI   MALDIVES
HUKURU   MALDIVIAN
IMAD LATHEEF   MALE
ISLAND   MINICOY
MAAFANNU   MOSQUE

National Symbol

White-breasted Waterhen

MALI

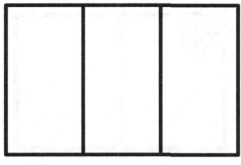

National Motto: One People, One Goal, One Faith

Capital: Bamako
Area: 478,841 square miles (1,240,192 square kilometers)
Major Cities: Bamako, Sikasso, Ségou
Population: 21.9 million
Bordering Countries: Algeria, Niger, Burkina Faso, Côte d'Ivoire, Guinea, Senegal, Mauritania
Languages: French, Bambara, Tamajaq, Tamasheq
Major Landmarks: Timbuktu, Djenne, Bandiagara Escarpment
Famous Malians: Salif Keita (musician), Alpha Oumar Konaré (politician)

National Symbol

West African Lion

Find the Words

```
N F T B O A X H Y R T U
H I K I V V Z X E F I P
M G G J T N B V O T M B
O A O E S S I O O K B K
P O D L R R A O F K U W
T H G O I R K H S W K U
I S Z J G A I C E H T F
B Z N W M O O V Q L U E
Z A R A L W N C E J F R
B K B K S I F H K R U F
A Z I D S E G O U A K S
Q A N S O N G O B B U M
```

ANSONGO
BAMAKO
BANJI RIVER
DOGON
GAO

MOPTI
NIGER RIVER
SAHEL
SEGOU
TIMBUKTU

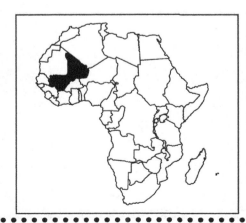

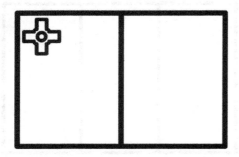

MALTA

National Motto: Strength and Consistency

Capital: Valletta

Area: 122 square miles (316 square kilometers)

Major Cities: Mdina, Rabat, Qormi

Population: 441,543

Bordering Countries: None

Language: Maltese, English

Major Landmarks:

Hypogeum of Paola, Mnajdra, Skorba Temples, Qawra Tower

Famous Maltese: Edward de Bono (psychologist), Joseph Calleja (singer)

Find the Words

```
A M Q N S H P J A V C W
R M J C Z A G M A A H P
C M A M O B V M G L I X
H M W L R M S T D L S W
I W D Y T I I N S E T W
P E I H R E A N P T O X
E K T U J L S K O T R F
L N O H S P A E D A I M
A T C I V O P O R O C V
G G E O R G E C R O S S
O S B L U E G R O T T O
J R A M L A B E A C H Z
```

ARCHIPELAGO   ISLAND
BLUE GROTTO   MALTESE
COMINO   RAMLA BEACH
GEORGE CROSS   TOURISM
HISTORIC   VALLETTA

National Symbol

Blue Rock Thrush

MARSHALL ISLANDS

National Motto: Accomplishment/Achievement through Joint Effort

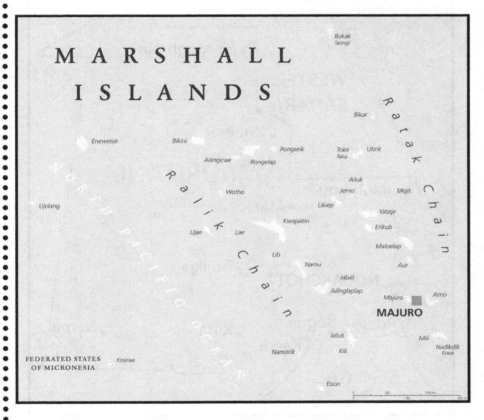

Capital: Majuro, Delap-Uliga-Djarrit

Area: 69.88 square miles (181 square kilometers)

Major Cities: Majuro, Ebaye, Arno

Population: 42,050

Bordering Countries: Maritime borders with the Federated States of Micronesia, Kiribati and Nauru

Languages: Marshallese, English

Major Landmarks: Bikini Atoll, Majuro Atoll, Arno Atoll

Famous Marshallese: Amata Kabua (president), Tony de Brum (politician), Kathy Jetnil-Kijiner (poet)

National Symbol

Black-footed Cat

Find the Words

O	M	T	S	O	I	V	X	M	G	O	E
V	F	A	O	C	E	A	N	Y	R	Y	S
G	R	T	R	J	Y	O	A	U	A	D	A
X	W	A	Y	S	T	L	J	B	N	P	K
B	J	M	L	I	H	A	E	A	C	T	N
J	F	S	P	I	M	A	L	N	G	U	R
A	C	O	A	V	K	S	L	D	A	F	A
R	H	U	C	X	I	B	N	L	E	N	T
N	H	R	I	C	S	B	T	S	E	Y	A
O	D	G	F	J	D	V	P	W	Y	S	K
B	I	K	I	N	I	A	T	O	L	L	E
C	C	B	C	V	C	S	M	U	J	R	U

ARNO
BIKINI ATOLL
EBAYE
ISLANDS
MAJURO

MARSHALLESE
OCEAN
PACIFIC
RALIK
RATAK

MAURITANIA

National Motto: Honor, Fraternity, Justice

Capital: Nouakchott

Area: 397,955 square miles (1,030,700 square kilometers)

Major Cities: Nouakchott, Nouadhibou, Kiffa

Population: 4.615 million

Bordering Countries: Algeria, Mali, Senegal, Western Sahara

Languages: Arabic, Wolof, French

Major Landmarks: Banc d'Arguin National Park, Richat Structure, Ancient Ksour of Ouadane, Chinguetti, Tichitt, and Oualata

Famous Mauritanians: Moktar Ould Daddah (politician), Noura Mint Seymali (singer)

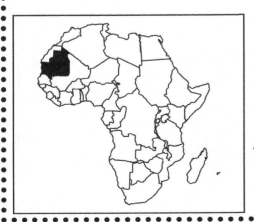

Find the Words

```
A I N O U A D H I B O U
S A H A R A D E S E R T
S E N E G A L R I V E R
T X L T E E I W E E U A
I D T T D T K I F F A Z
C H B N R A T A R T I O
H N O U A K C H O T T U
I W Q D C T Y W L R Q G
T Q F Y L C A G Z W R U
T C U C Q W O L O F M I
A D R A R P L A T E A U
S J Y F B A Q E P J Q G
```

ADRAR PLATEAU
ATAR
AZOUGUI
KIFFA
NOUADHIBOU

NOUAKCHOTT
SAHARA DESERT
SENEGAL RIVER
TICHITT
WOLOF

National Symbol

Dama Gazelle

MAURITIUS

National Motto: Star and Key of the Indian Ocean

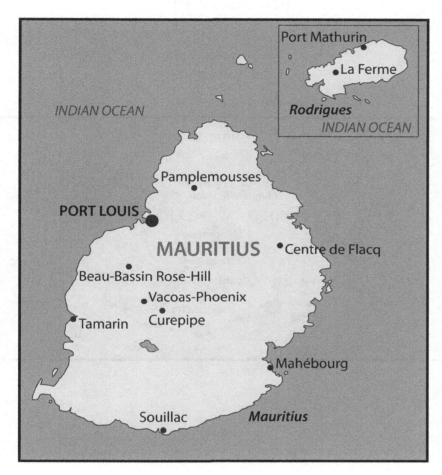

Capital: Port Louis
Area: 788 square miles
(2,040 square kilometers)
Major Cities: Port Louis, Vacoas, Beau Bassin-Rose Hill
Population: 1.266 million
Bordering Countries:
Maritime borders with France and Seychelles
Languages: English, French, Creole
Major Landmarks: Le Morne Brabant, Black River Gorges National Park, Pamplemousses Botanical Garden
Famous Mauritians:
Seewoosagur Ramgoolam (politician), Kaya (musician)

National Symbol

Dodo

Find the Words

```
M A H E B O U R G Q D D
B E G G P D E M J G H S
L L R R A T D U A Z N H
E P A O A K H G A A N L
M O U C Q N M T I P E Y
O R C N K X D T H R P V
R T Q R X R I B A W W A
N L Q Z E R I M A W H C
E O Q G U O A V T I G O
U U J A F H L Y E R E A
E I M R C J X E U R N S
E S F L I C E N F L A C
```

BLACK RIVER   LE MORNE
CHAMAREL   MAHEBOURG
CREOLE   MAURITIANS
FLIC EN FLAC   PORT LOUIS
GRAND BAIE   VACOAS

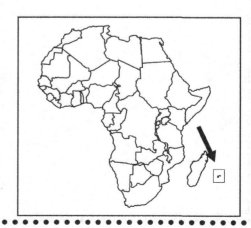

MEXICO

National Motto: No official motto, (Unofficial: The Homeland Is First)

Capital: Mexico City

Area: 761,610 sq mi (1,964,375 sq km)

Major Cities: Mexico City, Guadalajara, Monterrey, Puebla

Population: 128.932 million

Bordering Countries: Belize, Guatemala, the United States

Language: Spanish

Major Landmarks: Chichen Itza, Teotihuacan, Cancun Beaches, Copper Canyon

Famous Mexicans: Frida Kahlo (painter), Guillermo del Toro (film director), Carlos Slim (business magnate)

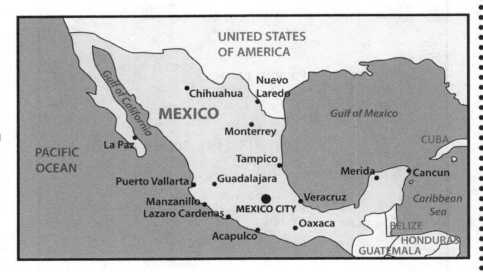

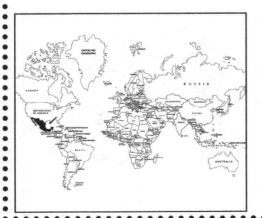

Find the Words

```
Z O C A L O G A M T G B
C A N C U N U S Z A R H
Q M M G U B A O G T Y P
S T A I D V D M N U E A
N Q R R W K A B C N S C
V M I R M F L R S T V T
X D A R A P A E I K K E
Y E C A R Y J R V X E Q
R Z H J Q W A O Z D N U
X D I B Z Q R G U O A I
B O R D E R A P V Q L L
S J T O R T I L L A F A
```

AZTEC
BORDER
CANCUN
GUADALAJARA
MARIACHI

MAYA
SOMBRERO
TEQUILA
TORTILLA
ZOCALO

National Symbol

Golden Eagle

MICRONESIA

National Motto: Peace, Unity, Liberty

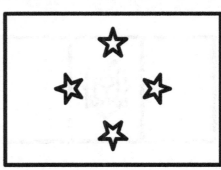

FEDERATED STATES OF
M I C R O N E S I A

Capital: Palikir
Area: 271 square miles (702 square kilometers)
Major Cities: Algiers, Oran, Constantine, Annaba
Population: 113,131
Bordering Countries: Maritime borders with the Marshall Islands, Palau, Papua New Guinea, and Guam (United States)
Languages: Chuuk, Kosraean, Ponapean, Yapese, English
Major Landmarks: Nan Madol, Truk (Chuuk) Lagoon, Sokehs Rock
Famous Micronesians: Bailey Olter (president), John Haglelgam (politician), Alik L. Alik (politician)

National Symbol

Chuuk Flying Fox

Find the Words

```
K M L B O A L O K K P L
R M S N U X R N C J A Q
Q J I O O N S O V N L Y
L C G C O S R C A I I A
R P H O R S H R A P K N
C T G U H O O T D R I N
V A T E U R N O R H R A
L B K O H K J E V U O B
C O T D S L S K S D K A
S A L G I E R S Y I B R
W G E F U L M C K P A T
Y L A N A N M A D O L Q
```

ALGIERS	NAN MADOL
ANNABA	ORAN
CHUUK	PALIKIR
LAGOON	SOKEHS ROCK
MICRONESIA	TRUK

MOLDOVA

National Motto: No official motto

Capital: Chişinău (Kishinev)

Area: 13,068 square miles (33,800 square kilometers)

Major Cities: Tiraspol, Balti, Orhei

Population: 4,033,963

Bordering Countries: Ukraine, Romania

Language: Romanian

Major Landmarks: Victory Memorial and Eternal Flame, Triumphal Arch, St. Teodora de la Sihla Church

Famous Moldavians: Vladimir Voronin (politician), Cleopatra Stratan (singer)

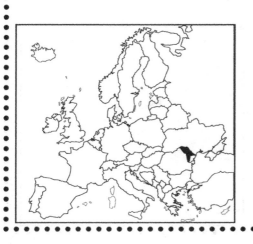

Find the Words

```
F P V T E I E O R H E I
L O K I A M T R T C P X
N R M R M O E X F H F B
T R S A G N R W N I B E
Z I H S M A N M E S I S
K D P P W S A L X I R S
A G W O Q T L E D N L A
E E U L H E F S V A I R
B A L T I R L W J U B A
C Y K J A I A R I R A B
M H H G V E M S E N Q I
F M T M C S E R R W E A
```

BALTI MONASTERIES
BESSARABIA ORHEI
BIRLIBA PORRIDGE
CHISINAU TIRASPOL
ETERNAL FLAME WINE

National Symbol

Eurasian Skylark

MONACO

National Motto: With God's Help

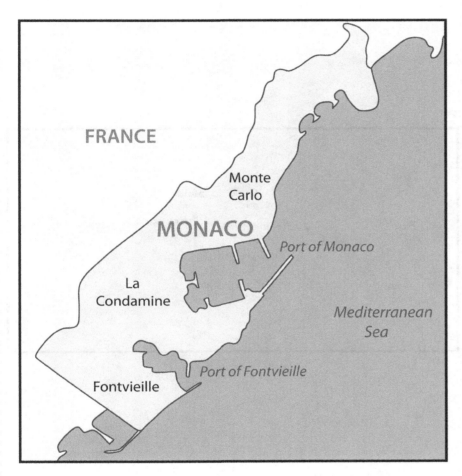

FRANCE

Monte
Carlo

MONACO

Port of Monaco

La
Condamine

Mediterranean
Sea

Fontvieille

Port of Fontvieille

Capital: Monaco
Area: 499 acres
Major Cities: La Condamine
Population: 39,244
Bordering Countries: France
Language: French
Major Landmarks: Prince's Palace, Monaco Courthouse, Saint Nicholas Cathedral, Monte Carlo Casino
Famous Monégasques: Léo Ferré (artist), Albert II (prince)

National Symbol

Hedgehog

Find the Words

```
W D Q P O M I N Q F P F
C Y P W C A S I N O A R
C A T H E D R A L S L E
G R A N D P R I X W A N
M O N T E C A R L O C C
K U N L Y W P C R R E H
P R I N C I P A L I T Y
W Y Z F R X K T K C L I
D Q A L P Z D Y S Y T T
F Q C I T Y S T A T E O
A Y Z R I V I E R A K S
Z L A C O N D A M I N E
```

CASINO	LA CONDAMINE
CATHEDRAL	MONTE CARLO
CITY STATE	PALACE
FRENCH	PRINCIPALITY
GRAND PRIX	RIVIERA

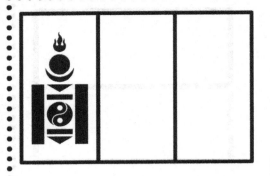

MONGOLIA

National Motto: No official motto

Capital: Ulaanbaatar (Ulan Bator)

Area: 603,910 square miles (1,564,110 square kilometers)

Major Cities: Erdenet, Darkhan

Population: 3.348 million

Bordering Countries: Russia, China

Language: Khalkha Mongol

Major Landmarks: Genghis Khan Statue Complex, Erdene Zuu Monastery, Gobi Desert, Terelj National Park, Orkhon Valley

Famous Mongolians: Genghis Khan (founder of the Mongol Empire), Damdin Sükhbaatar (military leader), Anu Namshir (artist)

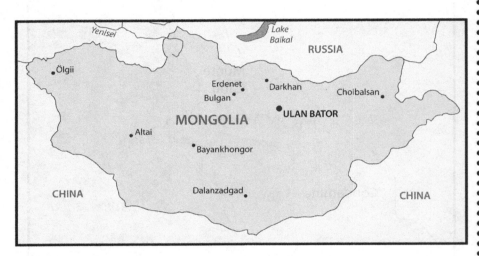

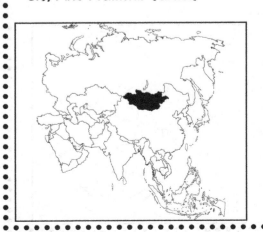

Find the Words

```
G G E N G H I S K H A N
O R V T U U D I P M J H
B K H R L D A L H O Y M
I W M P A S R E I N E V
D B O F A P K M V G R W
E X N J N E H O E O D D
S G A G B M A N R L E Y
E I S Q A P N G D I N I
R B T I A I O O E A E D
T B E H T R G L N N Z J
Y A R N A E A K E S U A
H A Y S R S H X T Z U Z
```

DARKHAN	GOBI DESERT
EMPIRE	MONASTERY
ERDENE ZUU	MONGOL
ERDENET	MONGOLIANS
GENGHIS KHAN	ULAANBAATAR

National Symbol

Snow Leopard

MONTENEGRO

National Motto: May Montenegro Be Eternal!

BOSNIA AND HERZEGOVINA

SERBIA

Pljevlja

Bijelo Polje

MONTENEGRO

Berane

•Nikšić

Herceg Novi

CROATIA

PODGORICA

Tivat •Cetinje

Lake Skadar

Budva

Adriatic Sea

•Bar

ALBANIA

Ulcinj

Capital: Podgorica

Area: 5,333 square miles (13,812 square kilometers)

Major Cities: Nikšić, Pljevlja, Herceg Novi

Population: 621,718

Bordering Countries: Croatia, Bosnia and Herzegovina, Serbia, Albania, Kosovo

Language: Montenegrin

Major Landmarks: Tare River Canyon, Kotor Old City, The Old Town, Biogradska Gora

Famous Montenegrins: Petar I (monarch)

National Symbol

Golden Eagle

Find the Words

T	A	R	A	R	I	V	E	R	R	H	P
B	B	H	T	S	W	R	H	O	D	E	O
A	W	O	E	O	Q	X	T	I	O	R	D
U	D	S	B	M	U	O	B	R	X	C	G
L	Y	R	O	O	K	R	G	F	N	E	O
C	M	B	I	F	T	E	I	D	G	G	R
I	L	B	O	A	N	O	K	S	T	N	I
N	A	Y	X	E	T	B	V	K	M	O	C
J	A	E	T	G	X	I	I	K	D	V	A
B	I	N	B	S	K	N	C	E	U	I	W
E	O	G	F	V	B	L	H	I	W	K	F
M	L	A	K	E	S	K	A	D	A	R	W

ADRIATIC	MONTENEGRO
BAY OF KOTOR	PODGORICA
BOBOTOV KUK	TARA RIVER
HERCEG NOVI	TOURISM
LAKE SKADAR	ULCINJ

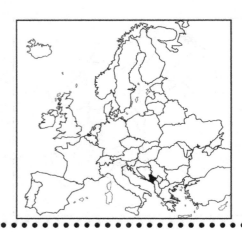

MOROCCO

National Motto: God, the Country, the King

Capital: Rabat

Area: 275,117 square miles (712,550 square kilometers)

Major Cities: Rabat, Casablanca, Marrakesh, Fes, Tangier

Population: 37.08 million

Bordering Countries: Algeria, Western Sahara

Languages: Arabic, Berber, French

Major Landmarks: Djemaa El Fna, Erg Chebbi, Hassan II Mosque, Bahia Palace

Famous Moroccans: Mohammed VI (king), French Montana (rapper)

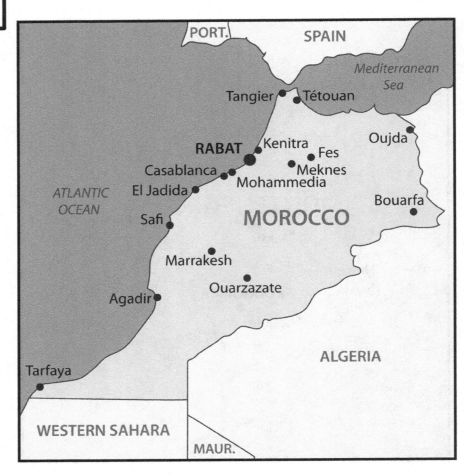

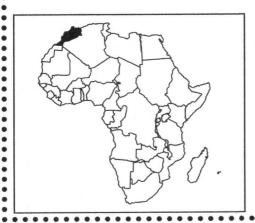

Find the Words

```
M O R O C C A N D T Q R
O M W T I T A B A R P J
C H A I A A H I F X A L
B Q W R V C I M N Z I S
E Z D R R N A I S I H R
R T N U A A R Y O X A M
B D H S A L K U A W B O
E D A S C B K E C P J R
R H C E Q A E P S U O O
U S A B K S K Q F H Z C
F E S E C A L A P S B C
K N I F U C A I U G B O
```

BAHIA   MARRAKESH
BERBER   MOROCCAN
CASABLANCA   MOROCCO
FES   PALACE
HASAN II   RABAT

National Symbol

Barbary Lion

MOZAMBIQUE

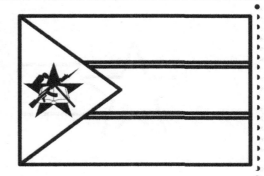

National Motto: No official motto

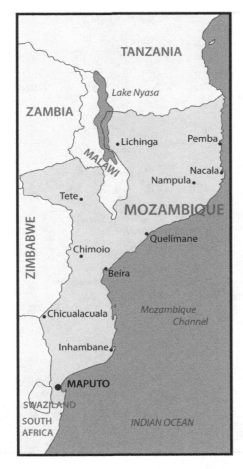

Capital: Maputo
Area: 309,496 square miles
(801,590 square kilometers)
Major Cities: Maputo,
Napula, Beira, Quelimane,
Nacala
Population: 32.08 million
Bordering Countries:
Tanzania, Malawi, Zambia,
Zimbabwe, South Africa,
Eswatini
Languages: Portuguese,
Makhuwa, Changana, Nyan-
ja, Ndau, Sena, Chwabo,
and Tswa
Major Landmarks:
Gorongosa National Park,
Ilha de Moçambique,   Tofo
Beach
Famous Mozambicans:
Samora Machel (president),
Eusébio (soccer player),
Mia Couto (writer)

National Symbol

African Elephant

Find the Words

Z	A	M	B	E	Z	I	R	I	V	E	R
B	E	I	R	A	B	A	T	E	R	S	C
I	T	Q	R	D	L	C	V	R	N	Q	A
N	D	U	U	A	N	W	J	A	S	I	B
H	X	V	C	E	K	I	C	L	F	T	O
A	T	A	X	G	L	I	A	R	R	E	D
M	N	C	K	U	B	I	O	S	W	T	E
B	N	S	L	M	O	T	M	R	S	O	L
A	S	G	A	I	U	P	C	A	X	A	G
N	H	Z	T	P	C	Q	E	Z	N	E	A
E	O	I	A	P	C	D	X	T	T	E	D
M	M	M	M	A	T	O	L	A	V	U	O

BEIRA	MOZAMBICANS
CABO DELGADO	NACALA
INHAMBANE	NIASSA
MAPUTO	QUELIMANE
MATOLA	ZAMBEZI RIVER

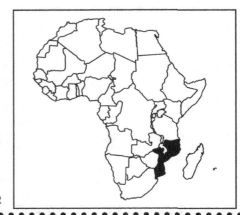

MYANMAR

National Motto: Happiness through Harmony

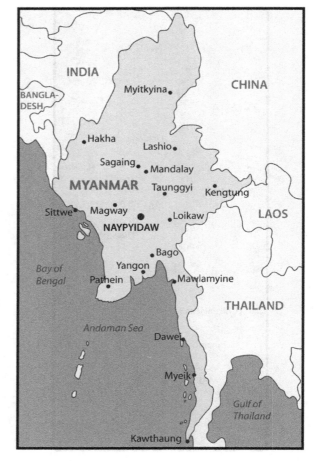

Capital: Naypyidaw
Area: 261,228 square miles
(676,578 square kilometers)
Major Cities: Yangon, Mandalay, Mawlamyine, Bago
Population: 53.8 million
Bordering Countries: China, Laos, Thailand, Bangladesh, India
Language: Burmese
Major Landmarks: Bagan's Temples and Pagodas, Shwedagon Pagoda (Yangon), Inle Lake, Mandalay Palace, Golden Rock (Kyaiktiyo Pagoda)
Famous Burmese: Aung San Suu Kyi (politician), U Thant (diplomat), Bogyoke Aung San (independence leader)

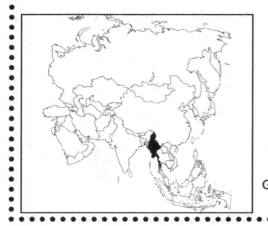

Find the Words

M	Y	A	N	M	A	R	V	A	E
N	N	A	S	G	N	U	A	P	S
M	A	N	D	A	L	A	Y	O	E
P	B	Y	N	Y	S	V	I	P	M
X	E	A	P	A	A	J	I	T	R
D	E	U	G	Y	B	N	G	N	U
J	Y	I	H	O	I	R	G	U	B
K	C	O	R	N	E	D	L	O	G
D	Y	Y	K	A	G	A	A	M	N
E	K	A	L	E	L	N	I	W	X

AUNG SAN   MANDALAY
BAGO   MOUNT POPA
BURMESE   MYANMAR
GOLDEN ROCK   NAYPYIDAW
INLE LAKE   YANGON

National Symbol

Grey Peacock Pheasant

NAMIBIA

National Motto: Unity, Liberty, Justice

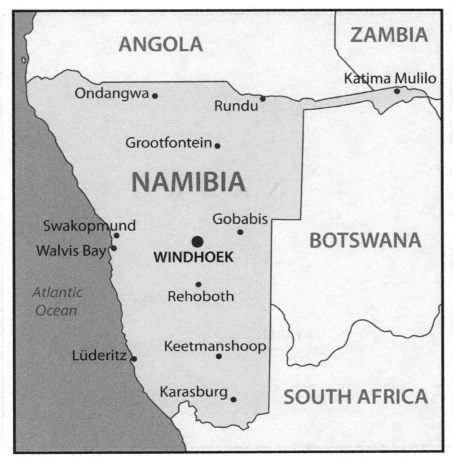

Capital: Windhoek

Area: 318,696 square miles (825,418 square kilometers)

Major Cities: Windhoek, Rundu, Walvis Bay

Population: 2.53 million

Bordering Countries: Angola, Zambia, Botswana, South Africa

Languages: English, Oshiwambo, Afrikaans

Major Landmarks: Etosha National Park, Sossusvlei, Fish River Canyon

Famous Namibians: Hage Geingob (politician), Frankie Fredericks (sprinter), Behati Prinsloo (model)

National Symbol

Oryx

Find the Words

```
S P S E T O S H A Y Y D
P O S O H Y K H A H N W
I S S G S T X B R U V I
T D I H G S S I M S E N
Z P M F I I U P J H Y D
K R K O V W O S J S I H
O F U L W K A N V Y K O
P L A N A O Q M W L X E
P W L W D X K P B F E K
E A S L Q U G C Z O V I
H H I M B A P E O P L E
D A M A R A L A N D D S
```

DAMARALAND
ETOSHA
HIMBA PEOPLE
OSHIWAMBO
RUNDU

SOSSUSVLEI
SPITZKOPPE
SWAKOPMUND
WALVIS BAY
WINDHOEK

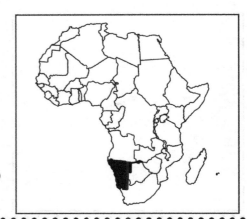

NAURU

National Motto: God's Will First

Capital: Yaren

Area: 8.1 square miles (21 square kilometers)

Major Cities: Yaren

Population: 12, 511

Bordering Countries: No direct bordering countries

Language: Nauruan

Major Landmarks: Command Ridge, Anibare Bay, Buada Lagoon

Famous Nauruans: Hammer DeRoburt (president), Bernard Dowiyogo (president), Marcus Stephen (weightlifter)

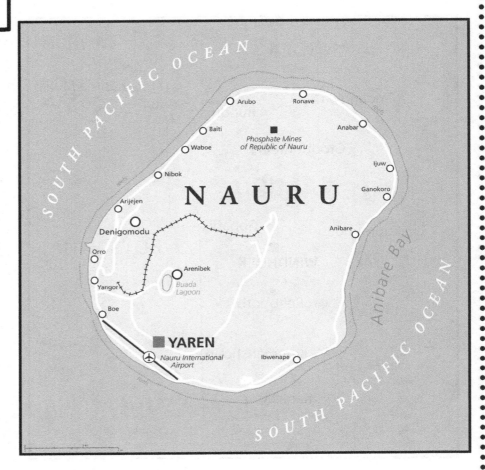

Find the Words

H	R	U	V	I	H	G	N	F	L	G	E
T	F	H	K	Z	W	O	P	A	O	G	J
Q	I	R	G	P	O	R	J	I	D	Z	F
A	O	B	I	G	U	B	X	I	Y	W	P
N	N	C	A	G	H	R	R	W	V	P	A
C	D	L	E	U	A	D	W	O	X	Y	C
Y	K	M	R	A	N	T	I	G	U	A	I
Q	U	U	H	A	N	A	E	K	N	R	F
Z	A	W	M	V	O	W	G	B	S	E	I
N	X	M	R	B	U	A	D	A	I	N	C
F	O	T	V	I	S	L	A	N	D	R	T
C	A	N	I	B	A	R	E	B	A	Y	D

ANIBARE BAY
BUADA
COMMAND RIDGE
FRIGATEBIRD
ISLAND

LAGOON
NAURU
OCEAN
PACIFIC
YAREN

National Symbol

Great Frigatebird

NEPAL

National Motto: Mother and Motherland Are Greater than Heaven

Capital: Kathmandu
Area: 56,827 square miles (147,181 square kilometers)
Major Cities: Pokhara, Lalitpur, Bharatpur
Population: 30.03 million
Bordering Countries: India, China
Language: Nepali
Major Landmarks: Mount Everest, Kathmandu's Durbar Square and Temples, Pokhara and Phewa Lake, Chitwan National Park, Annapurna Circuit Trek
Famous Nepali's: Prithvi Narayan Shah (king), Tenzing Norgay Sherpa (mountaineer), Laxmi Prasad Devkota (poet)

National Symbol

Himalayan Monal

Find the Words

```
K K P L A R A H K O P I N M
G R A A V U L P J R U H E Q
S A O T A V P M U F L A P W
E A U X H L G P A A A R A S
V J X T Q M K Q H V L A L W
B T A S A A A E M P I B I J
K O P A N M O N A S T E R Y
M E S A V U A E D I P J T T
A M J N E P A L Q U U D R E
L E M A H T J V I J R A W K
```

BARAHI	LALITPUR
GAUTAMA	NEPAL
JANAKPUR	NEPALI
KATHMANDU	POKHARA
KOPAN MONASTERY	THAMEL

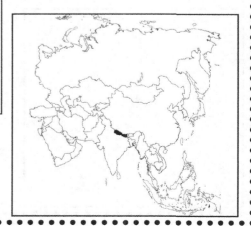

NETHERLANDS

National Motto: I Will Maintain

Capital: Amsterdam

Area: 15,907 square miles (41,198 square kilometers)

Major Cities: Rotterdam, The Hague, Utrecht

Population: 17,134,872

Bordering Countries: Germany, Belgium

Language: Dutch

Major Landmarks: Binnenhof, Castle De Haar, Circuit Zandvoort, Keukenhof

Famous Dutch: Vincent Van Gogh (artist), Rembrandt (artist), Baruch Spinoza (philosopher), M. C. Escher (artist)

Find the Words

```
A W V V C U T R E C H T
M C L A V A U T H R S K
S J U V N Y N Z O Q C S
T Q H F H G D A A B L Q
E H V G H D O F L L Z S
R A D M B L R G I S P H
D G M M A H T M H I D O
A U E Y C O D H L E B L
M E B T Q N J U P F H L
D R U D I V T C R V G A
G D Y W Z T B N U F W N
R O T T E R D A M V X D
```

AMSTERDAM   ROTTERDAM
CANALS   TULIPS
DUTCH   UTRECHT
HAGUE   VAN GOGH
HOLLAND   WINDMILLS

National Symbol

Lion

NEW ZEALAND

National Motto: No official motto, formerly Onward

Capital: Wellington
Area: 103,750 square miles (268,710 square kilometers)
Major Cities: Auckland, Wellington, Christchurch, Hamilton
Population: 5.123 million
Bordering Countries: Maritime borders with American Samoa, Australia, Fiji, French Polynesia, Kiribati, Samoa, and Tonga
Language: English
Major Landmarks: Milford Sound, Waitomo Glowworm Caves. Sky Tower
Famous New Zealanders: Edmund Hillary (explorer), Peter Jackson (filmmaker), Lorde (singer)

National Symbol

Kiwi

Find the Words

```
C W E L L I N G T O N D
P H K M L T E D M D N K
T Z R I W B D O J U J H
A A S I W M Q V O K R A
S J U S S I D S Q E X M
M M M C T T D U W L C I
A R F I K R C O W P S L
N I W N O L T H E V Y T
S S M F C Y A E U B M O
E U L W K L H N W R S N
A I U S F S F G D M C W
M E O N W A R D R I H H
```

AUCKLAND
CHRISTCHURCH
HAMILTON
KIWI
MILFORD SOUND

ONWARD
SHEEP
SKY TOWER
TASMAN SEA
WELLINGTON

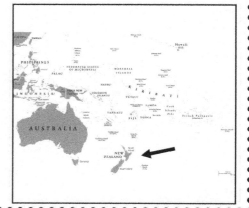

NICARAGUA

National Motto: In God We Trust

Capital: Managua

Area: 50,338 sq mi (130,373 sq km)

Major Cities: Managua, León, Masaya, Matagalpa

Population: 6.624 million

Bordering Countries: Costa Rica, Honduras

Language: Spanish

Major Landmarks: Ometepe Island, Masaya Volcano, Granada's Colonial Architecture

Famous Nicaraguans: Daniel Ortega (President), Rubén Darío (poet), Bianca Jagger (human rights advocate)

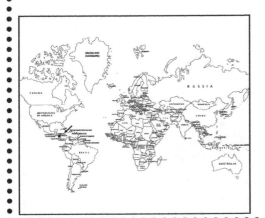

Find the Words

National Symbol

```
Q N M E N N Y I N D I O
S I G K B B H C G A Q T
O C Q A G F J H T P U Y
J A M A L V E S D A E W
G R G A Q L I J U O T L
A A E N R N O G Q C Z U
B G O P I I A P Y Q A X
Q U C D S N M F I O L Z
C A N A A L E B F N T R
T A V M Q A I Y A U T L
S I V G M A S A Y A T O
R C O R N I S L A N D I
```

CORN ISLAND   MASAYA
GALLO PINTO   NICARAGUA
INDIO   QUETZAL
MANAGUA   RIVAS
MARIMBA   SANDINISTA

Turquoise-browed Motmot

NIGER

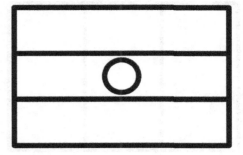

National Motto: Fraternity, Work, Progress

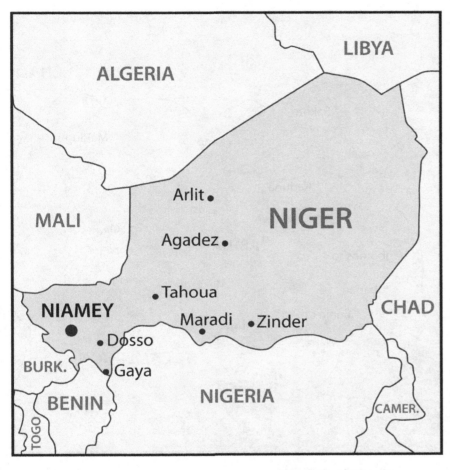

Capital: Niamey
Area: 489,191 square miles (1,267,000 square kilometers)
Major Cities: Niamey, Zinder, Maradi, Agadez
Population: 25.25 million
Bordering Countries: Algeria, Libya, Chad, Nigeria, Benin, Burkina Faso, Mali
Languages: French, Hausa
Major Landmarks: Agadez, Air and Ténéré Natural Reserves, W National Park
Famous Nigeriens: Mamadou Tandja (politician), Moustapha Alassane (film maker)

National Symbol

Dama Gazelle

Find the Words

T	E	R	M	I	T	M	A	S	S	I	F
W	H	B	J	U	G	Z	Z	B	D	H	C
G	N	N	I	G	E	R	R	I	V	E	R
A	G	A	D	E	Z	L	X	O	Q	V	R
F	I	W	U	W	V	V	M	Y	W	L	R
A	H	A	U	S	A	P	E	O	P	L	E
D	J	A	D	O	P	L	A	T	E	A	U
D	G	S	D	L	D	D	D	K	V	N	A
O	Y	D	L	K	F	N	I	A	M	E	Y
S	L	C	Z	I	N	D	E	R	K	B	N
S	B	I	R	N	I	N	K	O	N	N	I
O	S	A	H	A	R	A	Z	C	T	Q	B

AGADEZ
BIRNIN KONNI
DJADO PLATEAU
DOSSO
HAUSA PEOPLE

NIAMEY
NIGER RIVER
SAHARA
TERMIT MASSIF
ZINDER

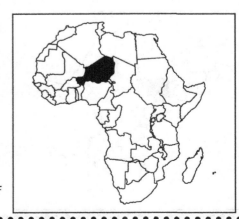

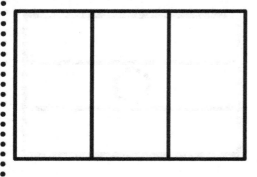

NIGERIA

National Motto: Unity and Faith, Peace and Progress

Capital: Abuja

Area: 356,669 square miles (923,768 square kilometers)

Major Cities: Abuja, Lagos, Ibadan, Kano

Population: 213.4 million

Bordering Countries: Niger, Chad, Cameroon, Benin

Languages: English, Hausa, Yoruba, Igbo, Fulfulde, Ibibio, Kanuri, and Tiv

Major Landmarks: Zuma Rock, Olumo Rock, Agodi Gardens

Famous Nigerians: Chinua Achebe (writer), Wole Soyinka (writer), Chimamanda Ngozi Adichie (writer)

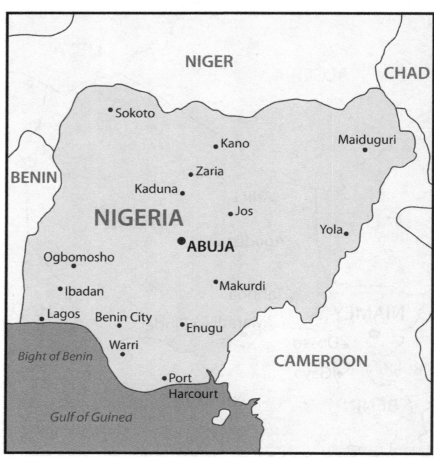

NIGER
CHAD
BENIN
•Sokoto
•Kano
Maiduguri
•Zaria
Kaduna•
NIGERIA
•Jos
Yola•
ABUJA
Ogbomosho
•Makurdi
•Ibadan
•Lagos Benin City
•Enugu
Warri
CAMEROON
Bight of Benin
•Port Harcourt
Gulf of Guinea

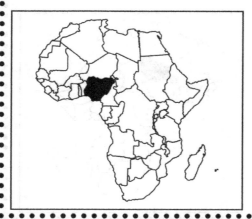

Find the Words

```
J N E T R L B B F O Y S
B A W Y B V H F B Q N Z
V B D T F O N G F E K U
S U O L J P I H D V A M
T J F D A A Y R F Q N A
P A O S S G A O I G O R
J L F U E G O L R I J O
Q O A Z I T I S F U R C
U H L D I B A D A N B K
F D O F X I B Y O R P A
E G Q E J W P V X V Y R
A D N O L L Y W O O D Y
```

ABUJA
AGODI GARDENS
HAUSA
IBADAN
IGBO
KANO
LAGOS
NOLLYWOOD
YORUBA
ZUMA ROCK

National Symbol

Eagle

NORTH MACEDONIA

National Motto: No official motto

SERBIA

BULGARIA

Kumanovo

SKOPJE

Tetovo

Gostivar

Veles Štip

NORTH MACEDONIA

Kičevo

Strumica

Prilep

Lake Ohrid

Doiran Lake

Lake Prespa

Bitola

GREECE

ALBANIA

Capital: Skopje

Area: 9,928 square miles (25,713 square kilometers)

Major Cities: Bitola, Kumanova, Prilep

Population: 2,083,374

Bordering Countries: Bulgaria, Greece, Serbia, Kosovo, Albania

Language: Macedonian

Major Landmarks: Matka Canyon, Vrelo Cave, Stobi

Famous Macedonians: Ptoly I Soter (monarch)

National Symbol

Eurasian Lynx

Find the Words

```
U M A C E D O N I A N N
Q V W M M H Y Z S H O K
B R C S O E F U G Y O P
I E X T Q U V B N D E Z
T L E A Z Y N A U L U S
O O A C G S C T I C U T
L C C Z E A K R A F K O
A A P M K S P O J I R B
K V P T E C S N P F N I
P E A K F V U M U J S S
X M A D W E D E W T E M
I L T E T O V A H T Q H
```

BITOLA   PRILEP
LAKES   SKOPJE
MACEDONIAN   STOBI
MATKA CANYON   TETOVA
MOUNTAINS   VRELO CAVE

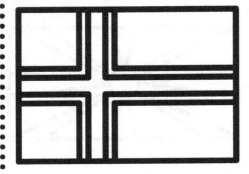

NORWAY

National Motto: No official motto

Capital: Oslo

Area: 148,718 square miles (385,178 square kilometers)

Major Cities: Bergen, Trondheim, Stavanger

Population: 5,421,241

Bordering Countries: Sweden, Finland, Russia

Language: Norwegian

Major Landmarks: North Cape, Preikestolen, Troll-tunga, Geirangerfjord, Akershus Fortress

Famous Norwegians: Henrik Ibsen (playwright), Edvard Munch (artist), Fridt-jof Nansen (scientist)

Find the Words

```
G L T R O L L T U N G A
W T I U G R F X V N S A
S R H L O Y D J E I I R
N O P D L Z X G O V Z B
O N Y U V E R X A R R L
R D P O T E H N A V D E
T H W R B E I A X I M S
H E V D N D T E M L W K
C I K O N N D F O M F R
A M R A D Q Q A I S E D
P K C N K G A R T C L R
E S N O R W E G I A N O
```

BERGEN
FJORDS
KRONE
LILLEHAMMER
NORTH CAPE

NORWEGIAN
OSLO
SCANDINAVIA
TROLLTUNGA
TRONDHEIM

National Symbol

Lion

OMAN

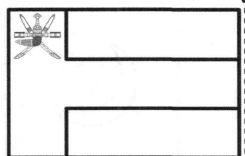

National Motto: No official motto

Capital: Muscat
Area: 119,500 square miles (309,500 square kilometers)
Major Cities: Nizwa, Salalah, Sohar
Population: 5,106,626
Bordering Countries: Yemen, United Arab Emirates, Saudi Arabia
Language: Arabic
Major Landmarks: Sultan Qaboos Grand Mosque, Wahiba Sands Mutrah Corniche, Nizwa Fort, Wadi Shab
Famous Omanis: Sultan Qaboos bin Said Al Said (politician), Haitham bin Tariq Al Said (politician)

National Symbol

Arabian Oryx

Find the Words

S	H	P	J	N	X	I	S	N	I	C
U	A	J	S	A	B	S	A	B	A	I
L	L	E	U	K	Y	M	U	W	S	B
T	A	N	H	H	O	Z	Z	R	K	A
A	L	I	N	A	B	I	D	A	W	R
N	A	E	J	L	N	Y	C	M	W	A
Z	S	J	D	F	M	U	S	C	A	T
Q	A	B	O	O	S	G	R	A	N	D
K	Q	M	G	R	D	Q	S	A	D	Q
Q	M	P	Y	T	S	C	B	Q	K	W

ARABIC QABOOS GRAND
MUSCAT SALALAH
NAKHAL FORT SULTAN
NIZWA SUR
OMAN WADI BANI

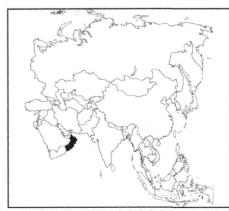

PAKISTAN

National Motto: Faith, Unity, Discipline

Capital: Islamabad

Area: 340,509 square miles (881,913 square kilometers)

Major Cities: Lahore, Karachi, Faisalabad

Population: 231.4 million

Bordering Countries: Iran, Afghanistan, China, India

Languages: Urdu, English

Major Landmarks: Badshahi Mosque, Lahore Fort, Mohenjo-daro Archaeological Site, K2, Shalimar Gardens

Famous Pakistanis: Muhammad Ali Jinnah (politician), Malala Yousafzai (activist), Imran Khan (politician)

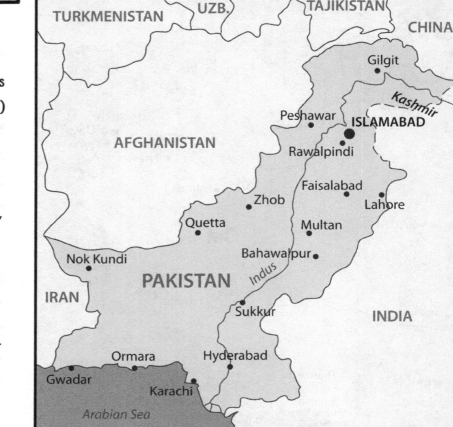

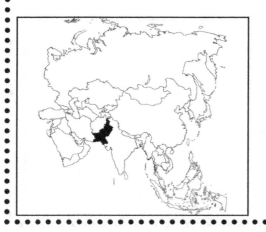

Find the Words

E	R	O	H	A	L	F	F	T	B
I	S	N	E	D	R	A	G	N	G
A	S	S	H	A	L	I	M	A	R
K	L	L	M	E	Q	S	J	T	H
A	J	J	A	J	T	A	E	S	S
R	O	D	I	M	Y	L	O	I	I
A	F	F	S	N	A	A	T	K	L
C	U	R	D	U	N	B	R	A	G
H	O	D	V	G	W	A	A	P	N
I	M	N	X	L	K	D	H	D	E

AL JINNAH	KARACHI
ENGLISH	LAHORE
FAISALABAD	PAKISTAN
GARDENS	SHALIMAR
ISLAMABAD	URDU

National Symbol

Markhor

PALAU

National Motto: No official motto

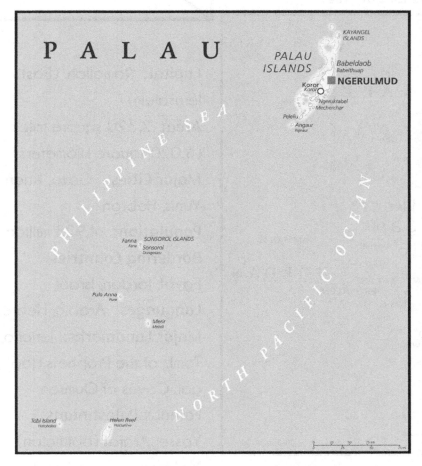

Capital: Ngerulmud
Area: 177.2 square miles (459 square kilometers)
Major Cities: Koror
Population: 44.6 million
Bordering Countries: Maritime borders with Micronesia, Indonesia, Philippines
Languages: Palauan, English
Major Landmarks: Rock Islands, Jellyfish Lake, Ngardmau Waterfall, Badrulchau Stone Monoliths
Famous Palauans: Tommy Remengesau (politician), Lazarus Salii (politician), Ymesei O. Ezekiel (poet), Ngeribongel Uriam (athlete)

National Symbol

Palau Fruit Dove

Find the Words

J	E	L	L	Y	F	I	S	H	N	I	P
M	D	C	Q	M	K	O	R	O	R	C	L
C	O	J	U	E	B	C	O	D	E	K	J
D	H	N	W	I	G	Y	U	P	W	L	X
O	L	H	O	H	X	M	P	A	A	G	U
V	C	G	W	L	L	C	H	L	T	I	I
E	A	I	D	U	I	O	K	A	E	F	U
F	G	Y	R	F	G	T	C	U	R	H	D
T	P	E	I	R	W	R	H	E	F	D	R
Y	G	C	A	I	C	Y	L	C	A	W	B
N	A	I	S	L	A	N	D	S	L	N	U
P	S	R	I	C	T	W	N	D	L	F	T

DOVE	NGERULMUD
ISLANDS	OCEAN
JELLYFISH	PACIFIC
KOROR	PALAU
MONOLITH	WATERFALL

PALESTINE

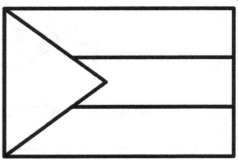

National Motto: No official motto (unofficial: From River To the Sea, Palestine will be free)

Capital: Ramallah, (East Jerusalem)

Area: 2,320 square miles (6,020 square kilometers)

Major Cities: Gaza, Khan Yunis, Hebron

Population: 4.923 million

Bordering Countries: Egypt, Jordan, Israel,

Languages: Arabic, Hebrew

Major Landmarks: Jericho, Tomb of the Prophets Haggai, Caves of Qumran

Famous Palestinians: Yasser Arafat (politician), Mahmoud Abbas (politician), Leila Khaled (activist), Edward Said (writer)

National Symbol

Gazelle

Find the Words

C	A	V	E	S	D	O	M	P	G	N	U	N
B	H	H	S	F	H	Y	C	A	A	U	U	A
O	E	U	I	C	G	I	H	L	Z	K	D	R
E	U	I	I	N	B	K	N	E	A	Z	X	M
D	P	R	T	A	D	V	T	S	B	T	Q	U
U	E	G	R	U	F	Q	J	T	S	R	E	Q
J	P	A	W	Y	N	W	G	I	F	Y	E	H
C	Z	X	L	O	X	I	R	N	E	X	K	W
J	A	B	A	L	I	A	A	E	I	H	S	U
M	E	L	A	S	U	R	E	J	T	S	A	E

ARABIC	HEBREW
BEITUNIA	JABALIA
CAVES	JERICHO
EAST JERUSALEM	PALESTINE
GAZA	QUMRAN

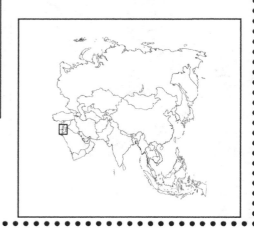

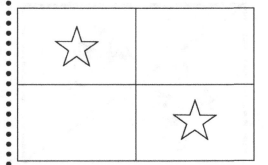

PANAMA

National Motto: For the Benefit of the World

Capital: Panama City

Area: 29,119 sq mi (75,417 sq km)

Major Cities: Panama City, San Miguelito, David, Colón

Population: 4.314 million

Bordering Countries: Colombia, Costa Rica

Language: Spanish

Major Landmarks: Panama Canal, Casco Viejo, Bocas del Toro

Famous Panamanians: Mariano Rivera (baseball player), Rubén Blades (singer, actor, politician), Mireya Moscoso (former President)

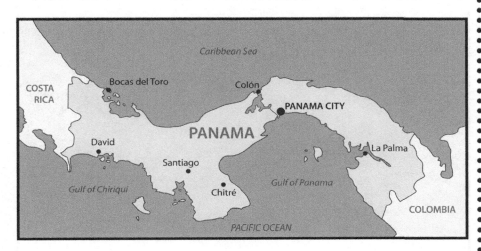

Find the Words

```
U J Q J H A T S V T Q L
R R B Z O U A P K K J C
P A D B H L X L G Z M P
K A L A B S C A N A L D
N A N N R P O L L E R A
B R A A U I I D E G A P
N S R E M I E Y L N T A
W M B M Q A N N U N Z C
W E C B N U C K K T P I
U X M E H H C I G Z T F
W W T R M R A A T S X I
N T S A U B U T C Y U C
```

BALBOA
CANAL
DARIEN
EMBERA
HAT

KUNA
PACIFIC
PANAMA CITY
POLLERA
SAN BLAS

National Symbol

Harpy Eagle

PAPUA NEW GUINEA

National Motto: Unity in Diversity

Capital: Port Moresby
Area: 178,704 square miles (462,840 square kilometers)
Major Cities: Port Moresby, Lae, Arawa
Population: 10.34 million
Bordering Countries: Maritime borders with Australia, Micronesia, Solomon Islands, New Caledonia
Languages: Tok Pisin, English, Hiri Motu
Major Landmarks: Kokoda Track, Mount Wilhelm, Sepik River, Port Moresby Nature Park
Famous Papua New Guineans: Michael Somare (prime minister), Dame Carol Kidu (politician), Dika Toua (weightlifter)

National Symbol

Bird-of-paradise

Find the Words

```
K P M T C O R A L S E A
K F O J O R O S O A U L
B W U R A K E E U X A W
H U N Q T E P P C D J K
K U T T L M A I O R I M
B I W R W P O K S K Q O
Y Z I R S W O R Z I V V
D H L A L K D I E X N D
G U H R P A E V Q S V T
Q K E A W K E E T O B I
S U L W P H V R X T N Y
E J M A P A R A D I S E
```

ARAWA
CORAL SEA
KOKODA
LAE
MOUNT WILHELM

PAPUA
PARADISE
PORT MORESBY
SEPIK RIVER
TOK PISIN

PARAGUAY

National Motto: Peace and Justice

Capital: Asunción

Area: 157,048 sq mi (406,752 sq km)

Major Cities: Asunción, Ciudad del Este, San Lorenzo, Luque

Population: 7.132 million

Bordering Countries: Argentina, Bolivia, Brazil

Languages: Spanish, Guarani

Major Landmarks: Jesuit Missions of La Santísima Trinidad, Itaipu Dam, Asunción's Historic Centre

Famous Paraguayans: Augusto Roa Bastos (author), Larissa Riquelme (model), José Luis Chilavert (footballer)

BOLIVIA

BRAZIL

Fuerte Olimpo

Mariscal Estigarribia

Filadelfia

Pedro Juan Caballero

Pozo Colorado   Concepción

Salto del Guairá

PARAGUAY

ASUNCIÓN   Caaguazú

Villarrica   Ciudad del Este

ARGENTINA

Pilar

Encarnación

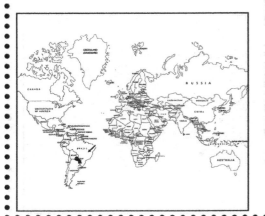

Find the Words

```
J Y M L B Q T W R G T E
U G E U W I Y Y P U I Q
N T V R U X A J A A T D
C O E S B U W K S R A A
G H E R G A G X A A I E
U J A A E J M C D N P K
M H R C M R K A O I U G
D A P Q O W E D T V U M
P U Y W G A I D V E R U
Z G O R A S U N C I O N
T F R V F Y J G H T I G
M I E S Z P A R A N A V
```

ASADO   JESUIT
ASUNCION   PARAGUAY
CHACO   PARANA
GUARANI   TERERE
ITAIPU   YERBA MATE

National Symbol

Pampas Fox

PERU

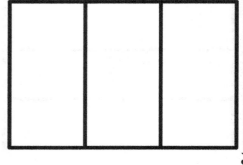

National Motto: Steady and Happy for the Union

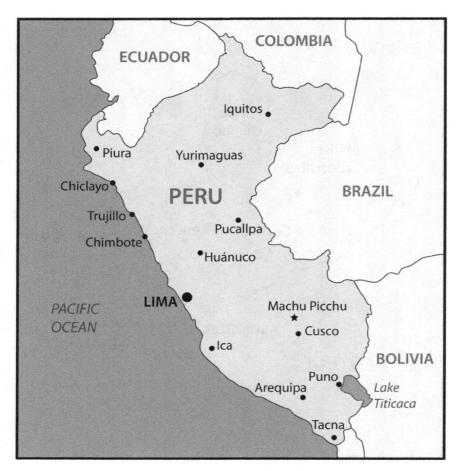

Capital: Lima
Area: 496,225 sq mi (1,285,216 sq km)
Major Cities: Lima, Arequipa, Trujillo, Chiclayo
Population: 32.971 million
Bordering Countries: Bolivia, Brazil, Chile, Colombia, Ecuador
Languages: Spanish, Quechua, Aymara
Major Landmarks: Machu Picchu, Nazca Lines, Amazon Rainforest, Lake Titicaca
Famous Peruvians: Mario Vargas Llosa (author), Paolo Guerrero (footballer), Alberto Fujimori (former President)

National Symbol

Vicuña

Find the Words

```
O A M A Z O N M C F B L
H M A C H U P I C C H U
T F Z A N D E S A V W T
W S M H T R D O D W M A
P R Z A R I N Q S D X H
E C N O H I T A F A F A
N E I U U L J I P P M O
A V H Q I U T L C I S Q
Z I T J S N A A L A S J
X C I W Z I C P Y O C E
A H D Y A U D A L G Z A
Z E G O G U K P S Q A F
```

ALPAXA
AMAZON
ANDES
CEVICHE
INCAS
LIMA
MACHU PICCHU
NAZXA
QUINOA
TITICACA

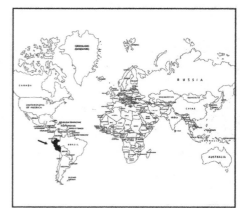

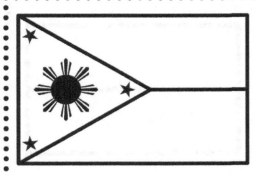

PHILIPPINES

National Motto: For God, for the People, for Nature and for the Country

Capital: Manila

Area: 120,000 square miles (300,000 square kilometers)

Major Cities: Quezon City, Davao City

Population: 113.9 million

Bordering Countries: Maritime borders with Taiwan, Japan, Indonesia, Malaysia, Brunei, Vietnam

Language: Filipino, English

Major Landmarks: Banaue Rice Terraces, Palawan's Underground River, Chocolate Hills, Mayon Volcano, Intramuros

Famous Filipinos: Jose Rizal (national hero), Manny Pacquiao (boxer), Imelda Marcos (politician), Lea Salonga (actress)

Find the Words

```
I N T R A M U R O S W O
Q M C L M A N I L A N M
U A A V T H M T U A J O
E R Q R G A J J C E A B
Z C B A F Z R L U I K V
O O Q B K I O S U R J N
N S B T U V L Q I G N O
C Q P Q N T C I C E B Y
I A A O X A I U P O R E
T A Y Z P I O R D I P S
Y A P R H B R A I V N M
M S Y B O R A C A Y B O
```

ADOBO   MARCOS
BORACAY   MAYON VOLCANO
FILIPINO   PACQUIAO
INTRAMUROS QUEZON CITY
MANILA   TARSIERS

National Symbol

Philippine Eagle

POLAND

National Motto: For Our Freedom and Yours

Capital: Warsaw
Area: 120,728 square miles (312,685 square kilometers)
Major Cities: Kraków, Łódź, Wrocław
Population: 37,846,611
Bordering Countries: Germany, Czech Republic, Slovakia, Ukraine, Belarus, Lithuania
Language: Polish
Major Landmarks: Poznań Fara, Wawel Castle, Malbork Castle, Wieliczka Salt Mine
Famous Polish: Marie Curie (scientist), John Paul II (pope), Nicolaus Copernicus (mathematician), Arthur Schopenhauer (philosopher)

National Symbol

White-tailed Eagle

Find the Words

```
W O A U M Y P E N C G C
S A H U C P I O I M A O
Y D W N Q R D L P Y P P
K Z Q E U P O E O E W E
R H M C L H O L K A R R
A L B W T C W L S L Z N
K J M A Z Y A R I V E I
O B C N J G A S W S Q C
W P K D O W C H T U H U
A L M A L B O R K L R S
D J S K L Z J R R Z E X
D I D G D A N S K W K W
```

CATHOLIC
COPERNICUS
CURIE
GDANSK
KRAKOW
MALBORK
POLISH
POPE
WARSAW
WAWEL CASTLE

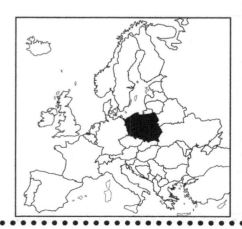

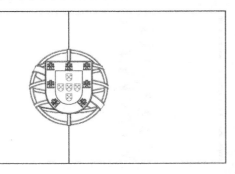

PORTUGAL

National Motto: No official motto

Atlantic Ocean

Chaves
Braga
Vila do Conde
Porto
Vila Real
Aveiro
Viseu
Guarda
Figueira da Foz
Coimbra
Castelo Branco
PORTUGAL
SPAIN
Santarém
Portalegre
LISBON
Almada
Setúbal
Évora
Beja
Portimão
Olhão
Faro

Capital: Lisbon

Area: 34,183 square miles (88,146 square kilometers)

Major Cities: Porto, Coimbra, Braga

Population: 10,196,709

Bordering Countries: Spain

Language: Portuguese

Major Landmarks: Dom Luis Bridge, Benagil Sea Cave, Pena Palace

Famous Portuguese: Ferdinand Magellan (explorer), Cristiano Ronaldo (soccer player)

Find the Words

```
E X P L O R E R S W J G
B N J P B I S P O Z T U
R D R O E Q B G O E I N
A P G R N A Q E U R O M
G H B T A D L I R B T E
A G X U G Z E G S I R O
M U I G I Q P I A I A Z
E C V U L R L Z P R B N
X R R E S Q L M I M V P
V C Y S E A E B F K A E
J R O E A O H D I Q R V
P E N A P A L A C E O L
```

ALGARVE   IBERIAN
BENAGIL SEA   LISBON
BRAGA   PENA PALACE
EMPIRE   PORTO
EXPLORERS   PORTUGUESE

National Symbol

Barcelos Rooster

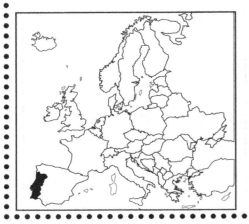

QATAR

National Motto: No official motto

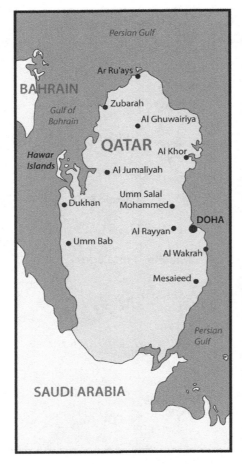

Capital: Doha
Area: 4,473 square miles
(11,586 square kilometers)
Major Cities: Al Rayyan,
Umm Salal Muhammad
Population: 2.688 million
Bordering Countries:
Saudi Arabia
Language: Arabic
Major Landmarks: The
Pearl-Qatar, Museum of
Islamic Art, Souq Waqif,
Katara Cultural Village,
Zubarah Fort and Archaeo-
logical Site
Famous Qataris: Sheikh
Hamad bin Khalifa Al Thani
(politician), Sheikha Moza
bint Nasser (philanthropist),
Nasser Al-Khelaifi (business
executive)

National Symbol

Arabian Oryx

Find the Words

A	S	P	I	R	E	P	A	R	K	X	S
R	I	Z	A	Q	X	Q	U	Q	Z	Y	P
S	T	S	R	L	K	S	P	K	A	F	J
O	K	X	L	R	J	T	B	W	E	N	D
U	A	B	F	A	X	A	R	X	A	H	G
Q	T	V	D	B	M	I	Z	Y	R	F	L
W	A	D	D	A	A	I	Y	E	N	G	Q
A	R	Z	H	R	N	A	C	C	E	K	F
Q	A	O	A	L	R	B	H	A	H	R	J
I	D	T	R	L	A	X	G	R	R	D	A
F	A	C	A	A	L	K	H	O	R	T	V
Q	A	M	Y	G	Z	U	B	A	R	A	H

AL JAZEERA   ISLAMIC ART
AL KHOR   KATARA
AL RAYYAN   QATAR AIRWAYS
ASPIRE PARK   SOUQ WAQIF
DOHA   ZUBARAH

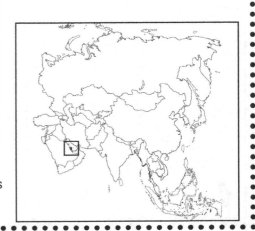

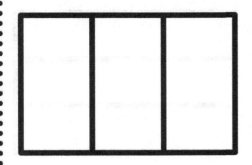

ROMANIA

National Motto: No official motto

Capital: Bucharest

Area: 92,046 square miles (238,397 square kilometers)

Major Cities: Iași, Timișoara, Cluj-Napoca

Population: 19,237,691

Bordering Countries: Ukraine, Moldova, Bulgaria, Serbia, Hungary

Language: Romanian

Major Landmarks: The Endless Column, Salina Turda, Bran Castle

Famous Romanians: Elie Wiesel (author), Nadia Comăneci (gymnast)

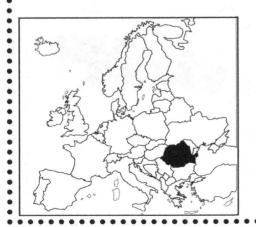

Find the Words

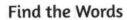

```
F S T W Y S G B Z B X C
H D R V V A C L L R R A
Y R A Z R L Q A S A O R
B A N H V I M C T N M P
R C S O F N Y K U C A A
A U Y Y D A U C N A N T
S L L H A T P H Q S I H
O A V R N U A U Q T A I
V N A T U R V R W L N A
K B N B B D A C E E F N
M Z I N E A M H L X U S
T W A B U C H A R E S T
```

BLACK CHURCH   DANUBE
BRAN CASTLE   DRACULA
BRASOV   ROMANIAN
BUCHAREST   SALINA TURDA
CARPATHIANS   TRANSYLVANIA

National Symbol

Lynx

RUSSIA

National Motto: No official motto (unofficial: Forward, Russia!)

Capital: Moscow

Area: 1,532,500 square miles (3,969,100 square kilometers)

Major Cities: Saint Petersburg, Yekaterinburg, Novosibirsk

Population: 145,934,462

Bordering Countries: North Korea, China, Mongolia, Kazakhstan, Azerbaijan, Georgia, Ukraine, Belarus, Latvia, Estonia, Finland, Norway

Language: Russian

Major Landmarks: St. Basil Cathedral, Winter Palace, Red Square, Hermitage Museum

Famous Russians: Sergei Rachmaninoff (composer), Anton Chekhov (playwright), Peter the Great (monarch), Vladimir Lenin (politician)

National Symbol

Bear

Find the Words

```
Q G F A J V B A F Q U J
V Z N I R V F X R W N I
R S O V I E T U N I O N
Y Q Q Y R L A R G E S T
S T P E T E R S B U R G
N T C O L D W A R A R S
V S T X G R M A V T U I
V O L G A R I V E R S B
W I J Z L E N I N K S E
C R A P B J K F B S I R
D J M O S C O W R W A I
Y W S T A L I N B H N A
```

COLD WAR   SIBERIA
LARGEST   SOVIET UNION
LENIN   ST PETERSBURG
MOSCOW   STALIN
RUSSIAN   VOLGA RIVER

RWANDA

National Motto: Unity, Work, Patriotism

Capital: Kigali

Area: 10,347 square miles (26,798 square kilometers)

Major Cities: Gisenyi, Butare, Gitarama

Population: 13.46 million

Bordering Countries: Uganda, Tanzania, Burundi, Democratic Republic of the Congo

Languages: Kinyarwanda, English, French

Major Landmarks: Volcanoes National Park, Kigali Genocide Memorial, Nyungwe National Park, Akagera National Park

Famous Rwandans: Paul Kagame (politician), Immaculée Ilibagiza (author), Sonia Rolland (actress)

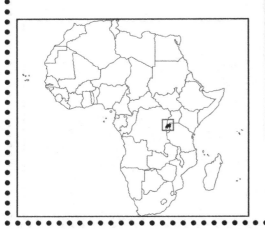

Find the Words

```
Q O R W A N D A N S Q A
M K B U T A R E I K D G
D I K U L X J L F N Z O
I B V V O A A U A D B R
H U N Y Q G K W L R U I
I N Y Y I E R E I K T L
U G E K A A B Y K U C L
A O W L Y M N Q U I I A
C S V N U E A X X Y V S
M H I D S V J T Q X J U
U K P I O G W V A N S M
X K G O G I T A R A M A
```

BUTARE
GISENYI
GITARAMA
GORILLAS
KIBUNGO

KIGALI
KINYARWANDA
LAKE KIVU
NYAMATA
RWANDANS

National Symbol

Leopard

SAINT KITTS AND NEVIS

National Motto: Country Above Self

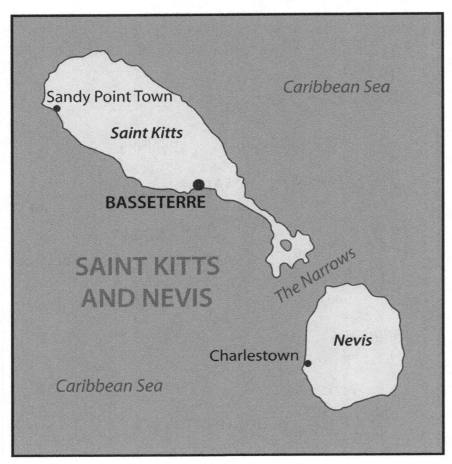

Capital: Basseterre

Area: 101 sq mi (261 sq km)

Major Cities: Basseterre, Charlestown, Sandy Point Town

Population: 53,199

Bordering Countries: Maritime borders with Antigua and Barbuda, Saint Eustatius (Netherlands), Saint Barthélemy (France), Saint Martin (France and the Netherlands)

Language: English

Major Landmarks: Brimstone Hill Fortress, Basseterre's Independence Square, Pinney's Beach

Famous Kittians or Nevisians: Alexander Hamilton (founding father of the United States), Robert L. Bradshaw (first Premier)

National Symbol

Brown Pelican

Find the Words

B	C	Y	K	I	T	T	I	T	I	A	N
R	U	A	W	L	M	W	Q	H	C	Q	N
I	B	V	R	Y	I	S	G	I	D	W	T
M	P	A	I	N	I	Z	T	V	O	E	S
S	G	Q	S	V	I	N	E	T	F	U	C
T	O	U	E	S	A	V	S	U	Y	N	R
O	Y	N	C	L	E	E	A	E	A	D	I
N	O	P	T	C	L	T	A	L	G	L	C
E	W	A	R	R	H	Q	E	O	O	K	K
C	D	P	A	I	F	H	Y	R	L	B	E
T	I	H	P	S	U	G	A	R	R	O	T
R	C	F	O	R	T	R	E	S	S	E	Y

ATLANTIC
BASSETERRE
BRIMSTONE
CARNIVAL
CHARLESTOWN
CRICKET
FORTRESS
KITTITIAN
NEVIS
SUGAR

SAINT LUCIA

National Motto: The Land, the People, the Light

Capital: Castries

Area: 238 sq mi (616 sq km)

Major Cities: Castries, Gros Islet, Vieux Fort, Soufrière

Population: 183,627

Bordering Countries: Maritime borders with Barbados, Martinique (France), Saint Vincent and the Grenadines

Languages: English, Creole

Major Landmarks: The Pitons, Pigeon Island National Park, Sulphur Springs

Famous Saint Lucians: Derek Walcott (poet), Darren Sammy (cricketer), Kenny Anthony (former Prime Minister)

Find the Words

```
C B M A T B O S F L Q E
A W J A C M N Q S C R M
S F Q B R O A W L E W P
T O J V T I X P I L F E
R I Q I O E G R W U Q O
I P P H E L F O M C C R
E Z H V P U C I T I F O
S T N V O P R A Y A E C
O U M S H X Z N N Z I E
G R O S P I T O N O B A
P H I I S L A N D W Z N
H E L E N E Q N P T Q Z
```

CASTRIES   MARIGOT
GROS PITON   OCEAN
HELEN   PITONS
ISLAND   SOUFRIERE
LUCIA   VOLCANO

National Symbol

Saint Lucia Parrot

SAINT VINCENT AND THE GRENADINES

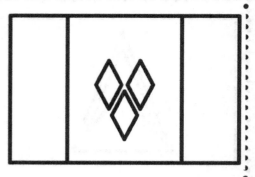

National Motto: Peace and Justice

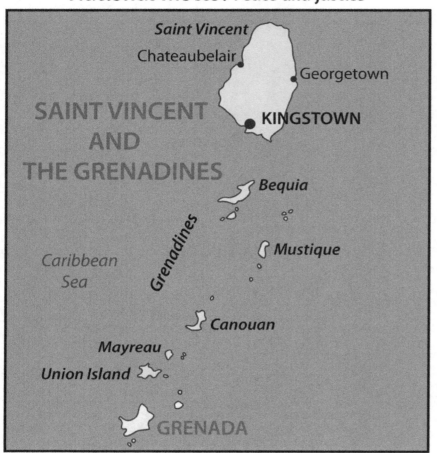

Saint Vincent
Chateaubelair
Georgetown
SAINT VINCENT
AND
THE GRENADINES
KINGSTOWN
Bequia
Grenadines
Caribbean
Sea
Mustique
Canouan
Mayreau
Union Island
GRENADA

Capital: Kingstown

Area: 150 sq mi (389 sq km)

Major Cities: Kingstown, Layou, Barrouallie, Chateaubelair

Population: 110,940

Bordering Countries: Maritime borders with Barbados, Grenada, Saint Lucia

Languages: English, Creole

Major Landmarks: La Soufriere Volcano, Kingstown's Botanical Gardens, Tobago Cays

Famous Vicentians: Ralph Gonsalves (Prime Minister), Kevin Lyttle (singer), Sir Louis Straker (politician)

National Symbol

Saint Vincent Parrot

Find the Words

X	Z	B	N	M	O	U	N	T	A	I	N
T	M	A	Y	R	E	A	Y	D	S	K	P
B	K	G	R	E	N	A	D	I	N	E	S
M	P	Q	R	K	P	C	I	C	G	N	M
S	T	I	E	I	G	A	T	F	B	V	U
O	H	B	J	N	A	N	F	Q	E	W	S
M	M	V	T	G	R	O	T	W	Q	U	T
U	M	S	Z	S	I	U	L	W	U	U	I
A	M	S	A	T	F	A	F	N	I	V	Q
H	O	Q	R	O	U	N	S	X	A	J	U
Y	J	J	Y	B	W	N	V	I	N	C	Y	E
B	X	E	N	N	A	F	O	R	E	S	T

BEQUIA   KINGSTOWN
CANOUAN   MAYREAY
FOREST   MOUNTAIN
GARIFUNA   MUSTIQUE
GRENADINES   VINCY

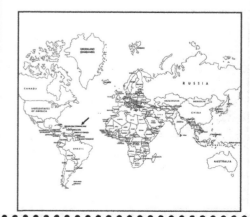

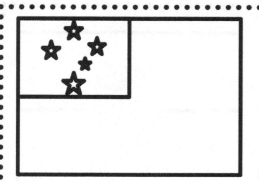

SAMOA

National Motto: God be the Foundation of Samoa

Capital: Apia

Area: 1,097 square miles (2,842 square kilometers)

Major Cities: Apia, Asau, Mulifanua

Population: 218,764

Bordering Countries: No direct borders

Languages: Samoan, English

Major Landmarks: To Sua Ocean Trench, Papase'ea Sliding Rocks, Lalomanu Beach, Piula Cave Pool

Famous Samoans: Nuufolau Joel Seanoa (wrestler), David Tua (boxer)

Find the Words

```
T V U L J H T U G X X W
T T F P T A A J G H N L
T P C U O S R G P A E A
M V O E A L W Q O A C L
V S Z G D F U M M U A O
M M U L I F A N U A V M
Z A V E N S H H C L E A
X D N P B E A C H F P N
L H Z U O U G H H A O U
V N B P M R N D X P O I
F S X H K E N G T I L Y
C K J T N B A V C A K J
```

APIA	MANUMEA
ASAU	MULIFANUA
BEACH	SAMOAN
CAVE POOL	SOUTH
LALOMANU	UPOLU

National Symbol

Manumea

SAN MARINO

National Motto: Liberty

ITALY

Falciano
Dogana
Serravalle
Acquaviva
Domagnano
Borgo Maggiore
SAN MARINO
SAN MARINO
Faetano
Poggio Chiesanuova
Fiorentino
Montegiardino
ITALY

Capital: San Marino
Area: 24 square miles (61 square kilometers)
Major Cities: Borgo Maggiore, Serravalle, Domagnano
Population: 33,931
Bordering Countries: Italy
Language: Italian
Major Landmarks: Rocca Guaita, Monte Titano, Basilica di San Marino
Famous Sammarinese: Massimo Bonini (soccer player)

National Symbol

Horse

Find the Words

T	H	R	E	E	T	O	W	E	R	S	I
S	M	M	E	D	I	E	V	A	L	O	F
E	T	I	O	M	X	W	G	C	N	A	O
R	S	U	C	V	I	O	N	A	S	O	R
R	G	A	W	R	R	T	T	L	T	O	T
A	U	S	N	H	O	I	A	S	P	Q	R
V	A	R	X	M	T	S	E	L	K	R	E
A	I	V	S	E	A	T	T	I	P	S	S
L	T	O	T	H	A	R	M	A	Y	A	S
L	A	N	R	L	H	L	I	R	T	X	N
E	O	D	A	S	G	T	D	N	K	E	M
M	B	M	D	X	B	N	Z	K	O	S	Q

FORTRESS   MICROSTATE
GUAITA   MONTE TITANO
ITALIAN   SAN MARINO
MALATESTO   SERRAVALLE
MEDIEVAL   THREE TOWERS

SÃO TOMÉ AND PRÍNCIPE

National Motto: Unity, Discipline, Work

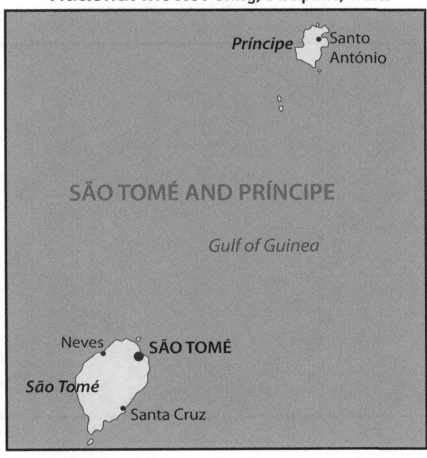

SÃO TOMÉ AND PRÍNCIPE

Gulf of Guinea

Príncipe · Santo António

Neves · **SÃO TOMÉ**

São Tomé

Santa Cruz

Capital: São Tomé

Area: 372 square miles (964 square kilometers)

Major Cities: São Tomé, Santo Antonio

Population: 223,107

Bordering Countries: Maritime borders with Equatorial Guinea, Gabon, and Nigeria

Language: Portuguese

Major Landmarks: Boca do Inferno, Obo National Park, Rolas Island

Famous Santomeans: Francisco Fortunato Pires (politician), Aurélio Martins (journalist), Naide Gomes (athlete)

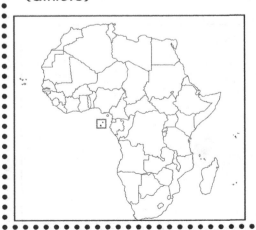

Find the Words

O	Z	O	S	G	G	N	E	V	E	S	D
I	A	I	L	E	M	A	A	O	G	A	L
N	U	R	S	N	Y	L	Y	S	Z	T	D
O	Y	P	I	A	Y	G	X	R	A	O	A
T	P	E	D	G	O	J	D	N	W	F	M
N	R	D	R	P	M	T	A	J	N	A	O
A	I	N	O	U	I	T	O	D	B	M	T
O	N	A	F	C	N	C	D	M	B	Z	T
T	C	R	V	A	U	M	O	R	E	O	A
N	I	G	S	R	Z	X	F	C	L	E	Y
A	P	S	A	N	T	O	M	E	A	N	S
S	E	O	V	I	F	Z	T	A	I	O	P

DA MOTTA   PRINCIPE
GRANDE   SANTANA
LAGOA AMELIA   SANTO ANTONIO
NEVES   SANTOMEANS
PICO CAO   SAO TOME

National Symbol

African Grey Parrot

SAUDI ARABIA

National Motto: There Is no God other than God and Muhammad Is His Prophet

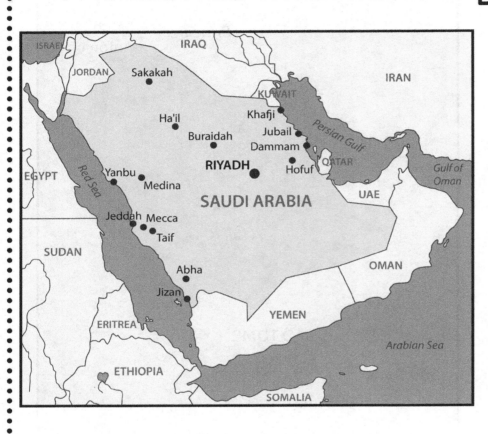

Capital: Riyadh
Area: 830,000 square miles (2,149,690 square kilometers)
Major Cities: Jeddah, Medina, Mecca, Dammam
Population: 35.95 million
Bordering Countries: United Arab Emirates, Qatar, Kuwait, Iraq, Jordan, Yemen, Oman
Language: Arabic
Major Landmarks: Masjid al-Haram and Kaaba, Madinah's Prophet's Mosque, Diriyah Historical City, Edge of the World, Masmak Fortress
Famous Saudi's: King Salman bin Abdulaziz Al Saud (politician), Mohammed bin Salman (politician), Ghazi Al-Gosaibi (writer, diplomat)

National Symbol

Arabian Camel

Find the Words

P	I	X	C	K	K	I	B	N	A	I
L	D	M	R	I	A	I	Q	A	B	A
H	H	A	L	I	Q	A	N	D	U	R
I	A	M	F	K	Y	I	B	E	B	A
E	F	M	K	A	D	A	Y	A	A	B
Y	G	A	A	E	W	J	D	J	K	I
P	N	D	M	Y	E	Z	M	H	R	C
A	I	B	A	R	A	I	D	U	A	S
E	K	H	C	O	R	N	I	C	H	E
Z	J	E	D	D	A	H	V	I	Y	P

ABU BAKR   KAABA
ARABIC   KING FAHD
CORNICHE   MEDINA
DAMMAM   RIYADH
JEDDAH   SAUDI ARABIA

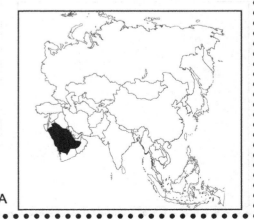

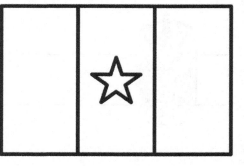

SENEGAL

National Motto: One People, One Goal, One Faith

Capital: Dakar

Area: 75,955 square miles (196,723 square kilometers)

Major Cities: Dakar, Touba, Thiès

Population: 16.88 million

Bordering Countries: Mauritania, Mali, Guinea, Guinea-Bissau

Languages: French, Wolof

Major Landmarks: Gorée Island, African Renaissance Monument, Djoudj National Bird Sanctuary

Famous Senegalese: Youssou N'Dour (singer), Akon (singer), Sadio Mané (soccer player)

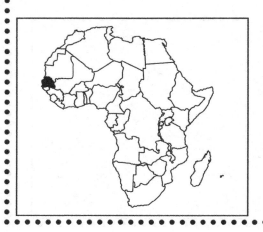

Find the Words

D	C	C	K	G	O	R	E	E	A	F	R
D	A	X	J	O	U	S	P	H	B	T	J
A	S	Y	W	U	S	I	A	M	S	B	U
K	A	B	T	R	J	A	C	L	A	I	U
A	M	A	Z	W	U	K	L	G	O	G	A
R	A	Z	Y	P	C	F	T	Y	R	U	Q
G	N	L	R	A	F	Z	I	R	A	X	M
T	C	H	L	Z	J	L	U	S	C	W	I
K	E	O	B	A	A	O	F	H	Q	F	D
W	A	Z	V	O	B	V	R	R	I	U	S
K	B	W	J	M	L	H	D	V	S	E	E
J	M	T	O	U	B	A	C	O	U	T	A

CASAMANCE   MBOUR
DAKAR   RUFISQUE
GOREE   SALOUM
JOAL   SALY
KAOLACK   TOUBACOUTA

National Symbol

Lion

SERBIA

National Motto: Only Unity Saves the Serbs

Capital: Belgrade
Area: 29,905 square miles (77,453 square kilometers)
Major Cities: Niš, Subotica, Kragujevac
Population: 8,737,371
Bordering Countries: Hungary, Romania, Bulgaria, North Macedonia, Kosovo, Croatia, Bosnia and Herzegovina, Montenegro
Language: Serbian
Major Landmarks: Vratna Gates, The Belgrade Fortress, Skadarlija
Famous Serbians: Novak Djokovic (tennis player), Constantine the Great (emperor)

National Symbol

Grey Wolf

Find the Words

```
Z R N R V O K D B J S S
V Z A V F E O X L E B K
Z E A S B B L S T M E A
V U P U P V O A H N L D
T A N D N B G S N Q G A
T A M L N A E A G N R R
D G X P N W I R G Q A L
B O Q T I B Y Y R Y D I
R W A G R R P Y C I E J
C R D E M U E G A W E A
V X S Q B A L K A N S S
D E R D A P G O R G E P
```

BALKANS	RASPBERRIES
BELGRADE	SERBIAN
DANUBE	SKADARLIJA
DERDAP GORGE	VAMPIRE
KOLO	VRATNA GATES

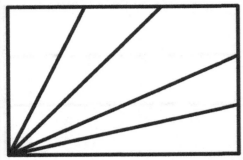

SEYCHELLES

National Motto: The End Crowns the Work

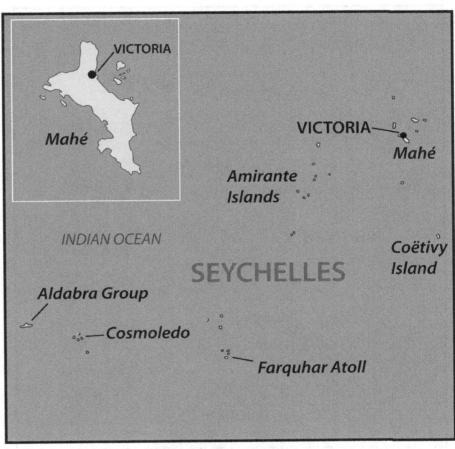

Capital: Victoria

Area: 174 square miles (451 square kilometers)

Major Cities: Victoria

Population: 99,258

Bordering Countries: Martime borders with Kenya and Madagascar

Languages: Seychellois Creole, French, English

Major Landmarks: Anse Source d'Argent, Vallée de Mai Nature Reserve, Aldabra Atoll

Famous Seychellois: James Michel (politician), France-Albert René (politician)

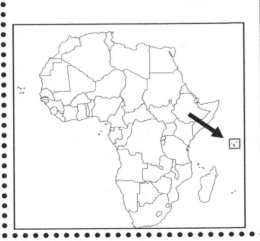

Find the Words

T	B	C	E	I	B	M	E	E	G	Z	S
A	E	C	M	O	D	V	G	S	Z	Z	E
I	A	R	M	N	A	I	D	G	I	A	Y
R	U	C	A	E	T	L	O	O	O	K	C
O	V	E	R	M	U	P	L	E	L	A	H
T	A	F	K	F	L	L	N	K	L	M	E
C	L	V	E	S	E	C	O	F	K	A	L
I	L	L	T	H	R	W	I	K	J	K	L
V	O	V	C	O	I	R	S	U	U	A	E
A	N	Y	A	W	L	E	S	E	S	T	S
T	E	M	P	I	O	H	I	N	D	U	S
S	L	E	H	C	I	M	M	G	M	L	S

BEAU VALLON   SEYCHELLES
MARKET   SEYCHELLOIS
MICHEL   TAKAMAKA
MISSION LODGE   TEMPIO HINDU
SESELWA   VICTORIA

National Symbol

Black Parrot

SIERRA LEONE

National Motto: Unity, Freedom, Justice

GUINEA

Kabala

Kambia

Makeni

Lungi
Pepel
Lunsar

Koidu Town

FREETOWN

SIERRA LEONE

Kailahun

Shenge

Bo

Kenema

Momaligi

Bonthe

LIBERIA

ATLANTIC OCEAN

Sulima

Capital: Algiers
Area: 919,595 square miles (2,381,741 square kilometers)
Major Cities: Algiers, Oran, Constantine, Annaba
Population: 44.6 million
Bordering Countries: Tunisia, Libya, Niger, Mali, Mauritania, Morocco, Western Sahara
Languages: Arabic, French, Tamazight (Berber)
Major Landmarks: Kasbah of Algiers, Djemila, Fort Santa Cruz, Pic des Singes, Ahaggar National Park
Famous Algerians: Albert Camus (author), Rachid Boudjedra (author), Yves Saint Laurent (fashion designer)

National Symbol

Chimpanzee

Find the Words

F	K	D	H	C	K	V	N	G	O	U	N
G	U	D	I	O	K	W	I	Z	L	G	E
U	A	E	I	T	O	L	N	N	W	D	F
I	L	W	F	T	R	Y	E	E	Q	O	T
N	T	C	E	O	J	T	K	E	F	O	O
E	M	E	F	N	C	V	A	D	K	I	V
A	R	V	Q	T	Y	O	M	R	V	W	I
F	S	I	E	R	R	A	L	E	O	N	E
E	K	E	N	E	M	A	H	B	K	H	D
N	B	X	C	E	K	U	Y	A	I	U	A
O	V	N	S	E	G	R	O	E	G	T	S
A	I	R	E	B	I	L	R	F	T	M	S

ABERDEEN   KOIDU
COTTON TREE   LIBERIA
FREETOWN   MAKENI
GUINEA   SIERRA LEONE
KENEMA   ST GEORGES

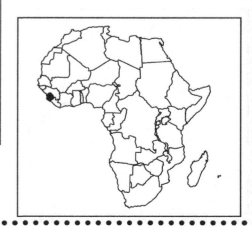

SINGAPORE

National Motto: Onward Singapore

Capital: Singapore

Area: 280 square miles (725 square kilometers)

Major Cities: Singapore, Woodlands

Population: 5.45 million

Bordering Countries: Malaysia, Indonesia

Languages: Chinese, Malay, Tamil, English

Major Landmarks: Marina Bay Sands, Gardens by the Bay, Sentosa Island, Merlion Park, Orchard Road

Famous Singaporeans: Lee Kuan Yew (politician), Tan Swie Hian (artist), Joseph Schooling (athlete), Stefanie Sun (singer)

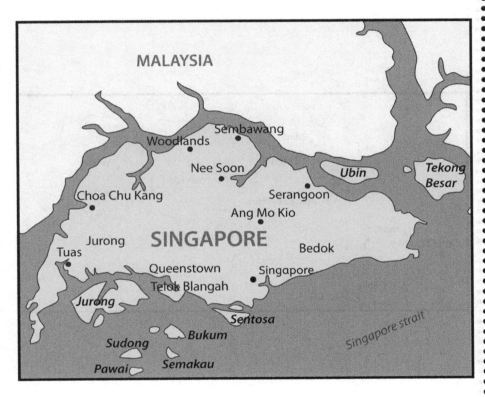

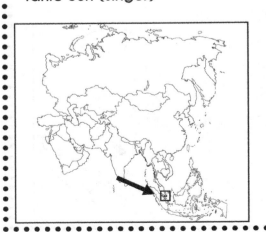

Find the Words

```
K W O O D L A N D S D K
M D M T U O F L Q A E E
Y E J A Y Q J W O F T S
M U R U R X T R M A I I
A V N L J I D Z T F S N
L A Q Z I R N S R B L G
A C E L A O Y A F M A A
Y Q F H P T N T B L N P
Z V C E I O S P A A D O
R R G C O Z A N A M Y R
O B S E N T O S A R I E
Q O N H W N V H U Q K L
```

CITY STATE   ORCHARD ROAD
ISLAND   SENTOSA
MALAY   SINGAPORE
MARINA BAY   TAMIL
MERLION PARK   WOODLANDS

National Symbol

Lion

SLOVAKIA

National Motto: No official motto

Capital: Bratislava

Area: 18,933 square miles (49,036 square kilometers)

Major Cities: Košice, Nitra, Prešov

Population: 5,459,642

Bordering Countries: Poland, Ukraine, Hungary, Austria, Czech Republic

Language: Slovak

Major Landmarks: Spis Castle, Slovak Radio, Grassalkovich Palace, Bratislava Castle

Famous Slovaks: Martina Hingis (tennis player), Peter Sagan (cyclist)

Map

POLAND

CZECH REPUBLIC

Žilina

Martin

Trenčín

SLOVAKIA

Prešov

Banská Bystrica

Košice

UKRAINE

Trnava

BRATISLAVA

Nitra

Lučenec

AUSTRIA

Danube

Gabčíkovo

Komárno

HUNGARY

National Symbol

Brown Bear

Find the Words

```
N I T R A T P Q G O O P
L L S J M E C A D A M F
J W V P Y L X A V Q K O
Z A T X I Y L A V A Z L
T R V A M S L O V E P K
K H W P T S C O K T S D
C O M N I R L A U W N A
J L Q T K S A E S L Y N
E Z A F X J E S M T B C
B R Y Y L R C G D U L E
B A M O U N T A I N S E
J A W C A S T L E S Y D
```

BRATISLAVA

CASTLES

CAVES

FOLK DANCE

MOUNTAINS

NITRA

SLOVAK

SPIS CASTLE

TATRAS

WARHOL

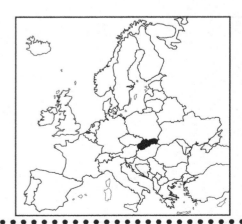

SLOVENIA

National Motto: No official motto

Capital: Ljubljana

Area: 7,827 square miles (20,273 square kilometers)

Major Cities: Maribor, Koper, Piran

Population: 2,079,303

Bordering Countries: Austria, Hungary, Croatia

Language: Slovenian

Major Landmarks: Predjama Castle, Lake Bled, Lipica Stud Farm, Postojna Cave, Triglav National Park

Famous Slovenians: Slavoj Žižek (philosopher), Tina Maze (skier)

Find the Words

```
S F P R E D J A M A L E
L L H B P U A N E B G X
O N J X M L V O J D Q O
V M T U F C I C I X M O
E A N C B A A R G A D E
N R V K Y L B S V S R X
I I J T O E J N T R Y T
A B A G L P N A H L B H
N O O P Q A E S N K E V
F R I H R E H R R A Y Y
A R M I M J R M M S G M
T Y P L A K E B L E D E
```

CASTLE	PIRAN
KOPER	PREDJAMA
LAKE BLED	SLOVENIAN
LJUBLJANA	TRIPLE BRIDGE
MARIBOR	

National Symbol

Lipizzan Horse

SOLOMON ISLANDS

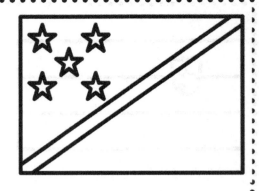

National Motto: To Lead Is to Serve

Capital: Honiara

Area: 11,157 square miles (28,896 square kilometers)

Major Cities: Honiara, Gizo, Auki, Kirakira

Population: 707,851

Bordering Countries: No direct borders

Languages: English, Solomons' Pijin

Major Landmarks: Kennedy Island, Honiara Solomon Peace Memorial Park, Marovo Lagoon, Mount Popomanaseu

Famous Solomon Islanders: Peter Kenilorea (prime minister), Ellison Pogo (bishop), Jeniifer Wate (singer)

National Symbol

Frogmouth

Find the Words

```
F H P T I O Y A L L M J
T S W E V Y R E F O O N
T V A O I I L B R K F Q
H S R U K N Q A O R X C
J A O A K Y H P G M W B
M U R L F I O I M O H E
U I Y P O Z H J O N O T
K L H E I M D I U J Y N
J Y M G K Z O N T L J A
W I Q U Q I Z N H S O C
P O P O M A N A S E U G
H O N I A R A B U Z M F
```

AUKI	LAGOON
FROGMOUTH	MAROVO
GIZO	PIJIN
HONIARA	POPOMANASEU
KIRAKIRA	SOLOMON

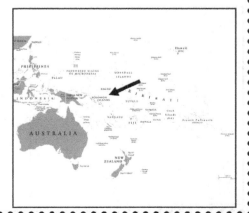

SOMALIA

National Motto: No official motto

Capital: Mogadishu

Area: 246,201 square miles (637,657 square kilometers)

Major Cities: Mogadishu, Hargeisa, Galkayo

Population: 17.07 million

Bordering Countries: Kenya, Ethiopia, Djibouti

Languages: Somali, Arabic

Major Landmarks: Laas Geel, Ruins of the Adal Sultanate, Mogadishu Lighthouse

Famous Somalis: Ayaan Hirsi Ali (author), K'naan (singer), Iman (model)

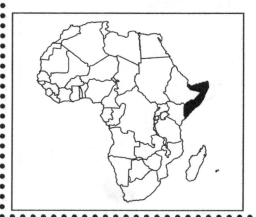

Find the Words

```
H S O M A L I L A N D S
A O H A R G E I S A N O
P D R K G K W D E A X M
U M J N N A Q A E W V A
N J O E O L L C G D K L
T U J G W F O M N B O I
L Z H E A N A A U Y B S
A W T P A D L F A D P E
N T Q I L A I M R X U A
D E D Q B V S S D I U G
I N V U B I N O H N C P
I V J U K Q B K D U P A
```

GALMUDUG   KISMAYO
HARGEISA   MOGADISHU
HORN OF AFRICA   PUNTLAND
INDIAN OCEAN   SOMALI SEA
JUBALAND   SOMALILAND

National Symbol

Leopard

SOUTH AFRICA

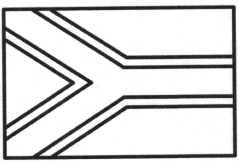

National Motto: Unity in Diversity

Capitals: Cape Town, Pretoria & Bloemfontein

Area: 471,455 square miles (1,221,037 square kilometers)

Major Cities: Johannesburg, Cape Town, Durban, Pretoria

Population: 59.39 million

Bordering Countries: Nambia, Botswana, Zimbabwe, Eswatini, Mozambique

Languages: Zulu, Afrikaans, English, Xhosa, Pedi, Venda, Soho, Tswana, Tsonga, Swati, Ndebele

Major Landmarks: Table Mountain, Robben Island, Kruger National Park

Famous South Africans: Nelson Mandela (activist and president), Desmond Tutu (bishop), Charlize Theron (actress)

National Symbol

Springbok

Find the Words

T	Z	C	P	E	Z	W	W	K	Z	H	Z
J	O	H	A	N	N	E	S	B	U	R	G
R	H	A	I	M	I	C	P	Z	L	R	G
E	Y	V	X	M	A	N	D	E	L	A	P
R	O	B	B	E	N	I	S	L	A	N	D
H	K	D	A	F	R	I	K	A	A	N	S
B	U	V	E	H	O	O	C	J	S	D	P
Y	P	R	E	T	O	R	I	A	O	U	T
H	Q	R	B	F	C	Q	D	Z	W	R	Z
C	A	P	E	T	O	W	N	K	E	B	U
N	A	B	O	E	R	W	A	R	T	A	L
E	A	D	M	J	X	G	G	L	O	N	U

AFRIKAANS
BOER WAR
CAPE TOWN
DURBAN
JOHANNESBURG

MANDELA
PRETORIA
ROBBEN ISLAND
SOWETO
ZULU

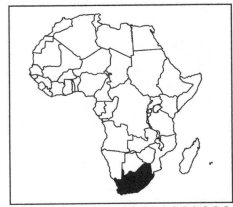

SOUTH SUDAN

National Motto: Justice, Liberty, Prosperity

Capital: Juba

Area: 248,777 square miles (644,329 square kilometers)

Major Cities: Juba, Malakal, Wau, Aweil

Population: 10.75 million

Bordering Countries: Sudan, Ethiopia, Kenya, Uganda, Democratic Republic of the Congo, Central African Republic

Languages: English, Arabic, Luo, Dinka, Nuer, Murle, Bari, Zande

Major Landmarks: Boma National Park, Nimule National Park, John Garang Mausoleum

Famous South Sudanese: John Garang de Mabior (politician), Alek Wek (model)

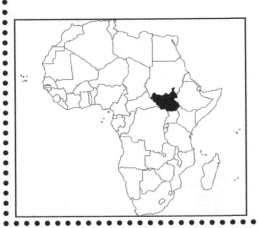

Find the Words

```
B O M A P L A T E A U L
F Z B A H X Q H Z Q A T
D U D R K O I N Q N B Y
I Y S Q O I Y B A L W K
N P E F L I X C O L H W
K I B I I O I X A R I A
A Q N U R E Y K H R T U
O B Z J L I A K L I E K
N L U G U L V J K J N W
J F N D A B K E K Y I F
S O H M W P A I R N L J
J X A Q N I M U L E E E
```

BOMA PLATEAU   MALAKAL
BOR   NIMULE
DINKA   WAU
JONGLEI CANAL   WHITE NILE
JUBA   YEI RIVER

National Symbol

African Fish Eagle

SPAIN

National Motto: Further Beyond

Capital: Madrid
Area: 192,476 square miles (498,511 square kilometers)
Major Cities: Barcelona, Seville, Granada
Population: 46,754,778
Bordering Countries: Portugal, France, Andorra
Language: Spanish
Major Landmarks: Camp Nou, Templo del Sagrado Corazon de Jesus, La Sagrada Familia
Famous Spanish: Pablo Picasso (painter), Fernando Torres (soccer player), Francisco Franco (politician)

National Symbol

Bull

Find the Words

```
E B A R C E L O N A R W
V G I B E R I A N H O Q
E W R M A D R I D F Y S
P S U A J N O Y Q W A O
I C H X N D H E Q N L Q
C Z W S A A L N U C P M
A X P R P L D O P E A R
S W P G I A N A F I L K
S L U V X P N U P D A T
O J E Y M B V I B C C X
E S V A N W R J S K E V
X E C D N V A Z T H W J
```

BARCELONA   PICASSO
CAMP NOU   PRADO
GRANADA   ROYAL PALACE
IBERIAN   SEVILLE
MADRID   SPANISH

SRI LANKA

National Motto: No official motto

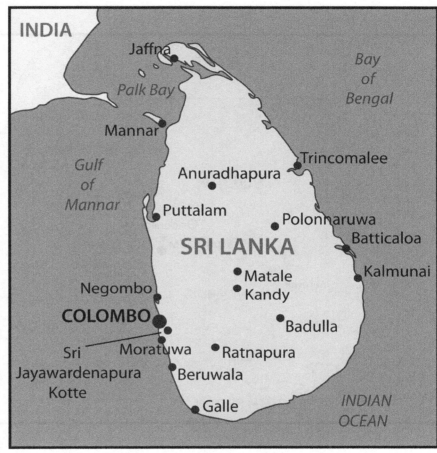

Capital: Sri Jayawardena-pura Kotte, Colombo

Area: 25,330 square miles (65,610 square kilometers)

Major Cities: Colombo, Kandy, Galle

Population: 22.16 million

Bordering Countries: Maritime borders with Maldives, India

Languages: Sinhala, Tamil

Major Landmarks: Sigiriya Rock Fortress, Temple of the Sacred Tooth Relic, Galle Fort, Adam's Peak, Yala National Park

Famous Sri Lankans: Mahinda Rajapaksa (politician), Muttiah Muralitharan (athlete), A. T. Ariyaratne (activist)

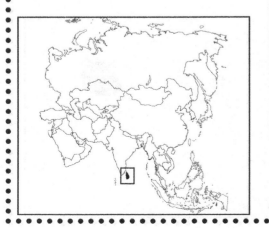

Find the Words

```
E H K P F O R T R E S S
X S G T B O M W A L F S
W J A A H Y R Y X B G I
S D Y C N X I T C M O N
L H G O R R K G R B Q H
B W P A I E A A M V N A
T G X G L L D O N A P L
A J I L A L L T P D A A
M S Z Y U O E Z O E Y B
I V F U C Z P T C O J C
L J A N G F O I T U T Z
B T E M P L E I D U Y H
```

COLOMBO   SIGIRIYA
FORTRESS   SINHALA
GALLE   TAMIL
KANDY   TEMPLE
SACRED TOOTH   YALA

National Symbol

Junglefowl

SUDAN

National Motto: Victory Is Ours

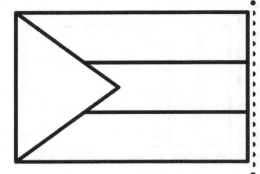

Map showing Sudan and bordering countries: LIBYA, EGYPT, SAUDI ARABIA, Red Sea, CHAD, ERITREA, ETHIOPIA, SOUTH SUDAN, CENTRAL AFRICAN REPUBLIC. Cities: Port Sudan, Ad-Damir, Omdurman, KHARTOUM, Kassala, Wad Madani, Al Qadarif, Geneina, Al-Fashir, Al-Ubayyid, Sennar, Nyala, Ad-Damazin, Kaduqli

Capital: Khartoum

Area: 718,723 square miles (1,861,484 square kilometers)

Major Cities: Khartoum, Omdurman, Port Sudan, Nyala

Population: 45.66 million

Bordering Countries: Egypt, Eritrea, Ethiopia, South Sudan, Central African Republic, Chad, Libya

Languages: Arabic, English, Beja

Major Landmarks: Pyramids of Meroë, Temple of Amun at Jebel Barkal, Old Dongola

Famous Sudanese: Mo Ibrahim (businessman), Leila Aboulela (writer), Manute Bol (basketball player)

National Symbol

Secretary Bird

Find the Words

X	B	A	H	R	I	D	F	Z	L	K	T
H	N	J	K	V	Y	A	G	V	O	R	X
M	E	I	W	H	E	I	I	O	E	P	P
E	D	G	L	S	A	N	L	S	N	C	O
R	S	A	D	E	Z	R	E	Z	G	A	R
O	V	E	R	R	R	D	T	E	X	X	T
W	R	F	Y	F	N	I	T	O	L	O	S
E	L	C	A	A	U	L	V	V	U	R	U
D	W	I	I	I	K	R	J	E	Q	M	D
A	W	B	W	X	U	T	Y	O	R	Y	A
M	U	S	O	M	D	U	R	M	A	N	N
N	R	J	E	B	E	L	M	A	R	R	A

BAHRI
DARFUR
JEBEL MARRA
KHARTOUM
MEROWE DAM

NILE RIVER
NUBIAN DESERT
OMDURMAN
PORT SUDAN
RED SEA

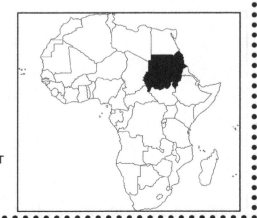

SURINAME

National Motto: Justice, Piety, Loyalty

Capital: Paramaribo

Area: 63,251 sq mi (163,821 sq km)

Major Cities: Paramaribo, Lelydorp, Nieuw Nickerie, Moengo

Population: 586,632

Bordering Countries: Brazil, French Guiana (France), Guyana

Languages: Dutch, Sranan Tongo, Surinamese Hindi, Javanese

Major Landmarks: Central Suriname Nature Reserve, Fort Zeelandia, Jodensavanne

Famous Surinamese: Ronnie Brunswijk (politician, ex-rebel leader), Dési Bouterse (former President), Clarence Seedorf (footballer)

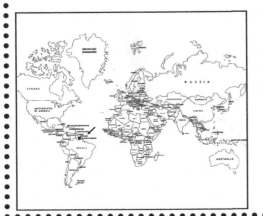

Find the Words

```
K S U R I N A M E X F Q
V Q B R O K O P O N D O
C R E O L E P D U T C H
S M R I C E A E D R J Z
A A C B J T R H Q X A A
R R J A S D A T J Q V J
A O A U L E M H X Y A S
M O O X S K A A H A N I
A N C I Z W R U Q U E B
C S Q T S J I U F N S T
C M F E X Q N S O Q E L
A Q A J D Q O L N Y D P
```

BAUXITE   MAROONS
BROKOPONDO   PARAMARINO
CREOLE   RICE
DUTCH   SARAMACCA
JAVANESE   SURINAME

National Symbol

Scarlet Ibis

SWEDEN

National Motto: No official motto

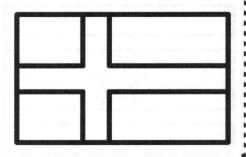

Capital: Stockholm
Area: 173,860 square miles (450,295 square kilometers)
Major Cities: Gothenburg, Malmo, Uppsala
Population: 10,099,265
Bordering Countries: Finland, Norway
Language: Swedish
Major Landmarks: Turning Torso, Svettekörka, Stockholm Cathedral, Drottningholm Palace
Famous Swedish: Ingrid Bergman (actress), Carl Linnaeus (botanist), Björn Borg (tennis player), Alfred Nobel (chemist)

National Symbol

Elk

Find the Words

```
S Y A M E A T B A L L S
F C G B E R G M A N S M
W W A M O O S E E E T J
P G U N Y G D O S Y O S
F K O P D C T I G A C W
V R P T R I A O S R K E
I O P E H K N T P K H D
T N X Q E E S A I Z O I
I A U N W E B K V G L S
Y Y B M R Y Q U Z I M H
Y E Y O X X K R R P A P
K M F Z P Z D W A G D F
```

BERGMAN   MEATBALLS
FORESTS   MOOSE
GOTHEBURG   SCANDINAVIA
KEBNEKAISE   STOCKHOLM
KRONA   SWEDISH

SWITZERLAND

National Motto: One for All, All for One

Capital: Bern

Area: 15,940 square miles (41,290 square kilometers)

Major Cities: Geneva, Lucerne, Basel

Population: 8,654,622

Bordering Countries: Italy, France, Germany, Austria

Language: German, French, Italian

Major Landmarks: Lake Geneva, The Matterhorn, Titlis, Rhine Falls

Famous Swiss: Jean-Jacques Rousseau (philosopher), Carl Jung (psychologist), Leonhard Euler (mathematician)

Find the Words

```
C C C F I E M R F R D A
C H J I A L P S C N I S
O O T I T L I S A M V Q
E C G B L I D L F W M J
G O K E F U R R M D L S
F L E U N E C N W E M K
D A V R Z E L E S W T I
U T T T N T V A R N O I
T E I H U G B A R N H N
Q W I B T H H E G Q E G
S N I Y N X B H K S U K
J K M A T T E R H O R N
```

ALPS LUCERNE
BASEL MATTERHORN
BERN SKIING
CHOCOLATE SWITZERLAND
GENEVA TITLIS

National Symbol

Saint Bernard Dog

SYRIA

National Motto: Unity, Freedom, Socialism

Capital: Damascus
Area: 71,500 square miles (185,180 square kilometers)
Major Cities: Aleppo, Homs, Latakia
Population: 21.32 million
Bordering Countries: Turkey, Iraq, Jordan, Lebanon, Israel
Language: Arabic
Major Landmarks: Palmyra Archaeological Site, Aleppo Citadel Umayyad Mosque, Krak des Chevaliers, Dead Cities
Famous Syrians: Bashar al-Assad (politician), Rafik Schami (writer)

National Symbol

Brown Bear

Find the Words

Q	C	H	E	X	A	B	X	M	F	S	H
H	A	L	E	P	P	O	T	S	E	I	O
U	D	B	W	Z	Z	V	N	I	V	E	M
B	U	A	Y	A	P	Z	T	H	U	Q	S
R	L	E	M	W	S	I	Y	Q	C	B	H
L	F	A	O	A	C	S	S	T	I	U	F
F	D	J	T	D	S	O	A	A	T	M	L
X	F	B	A	A	M	C	N	D	A	A	X
G	E	E	G	Y	K	R	U	B	D	Y	L
J	D	D	D	Y	S	I	Q	S	E	Y	B
R	N	K	U	X	J	C	A	Y	L	A	R
R	H	Z	P	A	L	M	Y	R	A	D	F

ALEPPO	HOMS
ASSAD	LATAKIA
CITADEL	MOSQUE
DAMASCUS	PALMYRA
DEAD CITIES	UMAYYAD

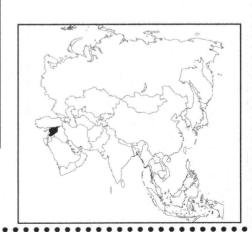

TAIWAN

National Motto: No official motto

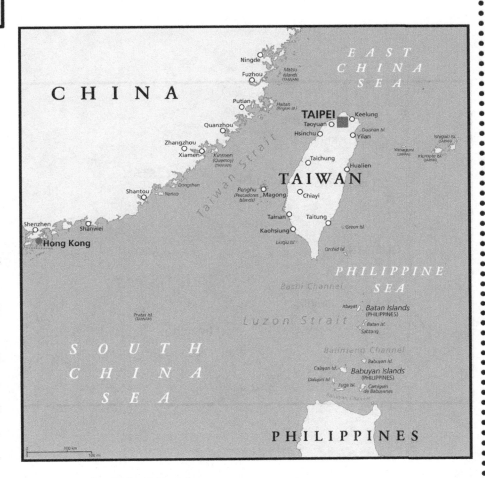

Capital: Taipei

Area: 13,974 square miles (36,193 square kilometers)

Major Cities: Tainan City, Hsinchu

Population: 23.57 million

Bordering Countries: Maritime borders with China, Japan, Philippines

Language: Mandarin Chinese

Major Landmarks: Taroko Gorge, Sun Moon Lake, Alishan National Scenic Area, Jiufen Old Street

Famous Taiwanese: Tsai Ing-wen (politician), Ang Lee (filmmaker), Teresa Teng (singer), Chiang Kai-shek (politician)

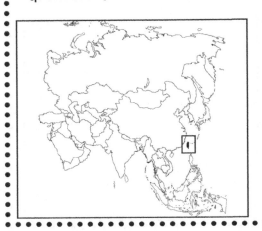

Find the Words

```
T S L M W D T T Y G T M
A U F M J O A R P H O L
I N V A V R R V L S H D
N M L N Z A O C A I X Q
A O A D I V K G L N P T
N O U A G V A X I C A M
C N C R Q N G Z S H N Z
I H U I Q B O V H U G A
T C O N M K R S A A L M
Y C H I N A G S N A E G
T A I P E I E B P O E H
L N I G H T M A R K E T
```

ALISHAN	NIGHT MARKET
ANG LEE	SUN MOON
CHINA	TAINAN CITY
HSINCHU	TAIPEI
MANDARIN	TAROKA GORGE

National Symbol

Formosan Blue Magpie

TAJIKISTAN

National Motto: Independence, Freedom, Homeland!

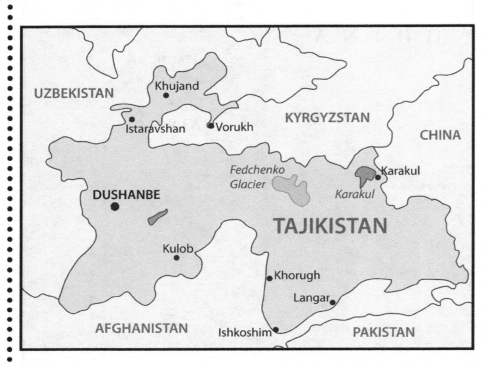

Capital: Dushanbe
Area: 55,300 square miles (143,100 square kilometers)
Major Cities: Khujand, Kulob
Population: 9.75 million
Bordering Countries: Kyrgyzstan, China, Afghanistan, Uzbekistan
Languages: Tajik, Russian
Major Landmarks: Pamir Mountains, Iskanderkul Lake, Khujand, Fann Mountains and Seven Lakes, Rudaki Park
Famous Tajik: Emomali Rahmon (politician), Abdujalil Samadov (artist), Sohibqironi Abduxoliqov (poet), Sharifjon Yoqubov (singer)

National Symbol

Marco Polo Sheep

Find the Words

```
K Y N V K T S Q G U F K S P D
N M W Z D K A P K R B G M C N
O W J B U K U J W Q F I O G A
P Y Z S S I W L I F Y Z S A J
D Q R Y H J W K O K R G Q D U
X H L S A A U V K B I D U P H
F U K I N T K Y A O M S E V K
Y R A R B I L L A N O I T A N
F S S G E I V L S F J I G A H
K I Q U R G O N T E P P A F N
W K E M O M A L I R A H M O N
I V I N O M O S L I O M S I L
```

DUSHANBE	MOSQUE
EMOMALI RAHMON	NATIONAL LIBRARY
ISMOIL SOMONI	QURGONTEPPA
KHUJAND	TAJIK
KULOB	TAJIKISTAN

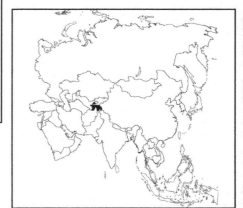

TANZANIA

National Motto: Freedom and Unity

Capital: Dodoma
Area: 364,945 square miles (945,203 square kilometers)
Major Cities: Dar es Salaam, Mwanza, Dodoma
Population: 63.59 million
Bordering Countries: Kenya, Uganda, Rwanda, Burundi, Democratic Republic of the Congo, Zambia, Malawi, Mozambique
Languages: Swahili, English, Arabic, Chaga, Makonde, Sukama, Datooga
Major Landmarks: Mount Kilimanjaro, Serengeti National Park, Ngorongoro Conservation Area
Famous Tanzanians: Julius Nyerere (founding father), Freddie Mercury (singer), Reginald Mengi (businessman)

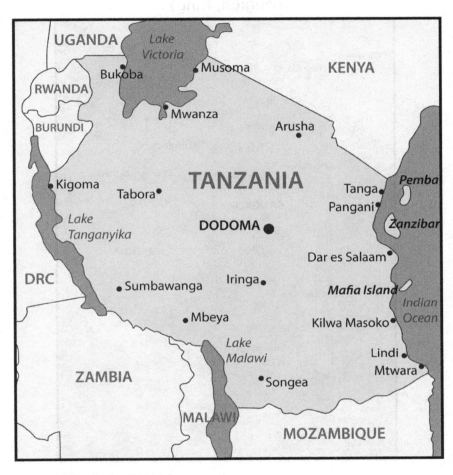

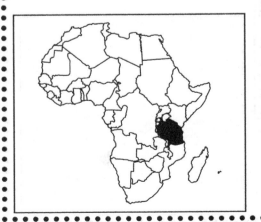

Find the Words

```
R A I N A Z N A T P T O
M D M A Z N A W M Y R C
M S A M O U N T F A A A
T W O R W E A B J Y M T
E A R M E Y T N K D O D
R H I S E S A G I C D Q
E I C B Y M S L B H O Y
R L M U I X K A O J D P
E I R L G O Q E L O U P
Y I I W J A U X S A Z W
N K D Q F I J H E D A Y
I T A N Z A N I A N S M
```

DAR ES SALAAM	MWANZA
DODOMA	NYERERE
KILIMANJARO	SWAHILI
MBEYA	TANZANIA
MOUNT	TANZANIANS

National Symbol

Masai Giraffe

THAILAND

National Motto: No official motto (unofficial: Nation, Religion, King)

Capital: Bangkok

Area: 198,120 square miles (513,120 square kilometers)

Major Cities: Chiang Mai, Pattaya, Phuket

Population: 71.6 million

Bordering Countries: Cambodia, Laos, Malaysia, Myanmar

Language: Thai

Major Landmarks: Wat Arun, Ayutthaya Historical Park, Wat Phra Kaew, Phang Nga Bay, James Bond Island, Sukhothai Historical Park

Famous Thai: Bhumibol Adulyadej (politician), King Rama IX (politician), Apichatpong Weerasethakul (filmmaker)

National Symbol

Thai Elephant

Find the Words

```
J K O K G N A B V J D L K
E J L G B B R P P N L V U
E M E R A L D L A G O O N
N N H E M R C L T V R C M
C U H K E Q I Y T E J C I
H R B D C A A T A O A A A
I A Z P H O V I Y V M D D
A T A T G A N C A G P A M
N A E C A L A P D N A R G
G W D E F V P H U K E T Z
```

BANGKOK
CHIANG
CITY
EMERALD LAGOON
GRAND PALACE
MAI
PATTAYA
PHUKET
THAILAND
WAT ARUN

TOGO

National Motto: Work, Liberty, Homeland

Capital: Lomé

Area: 21,925 square miles (56,785 square kilometers)

Major Cities: Lomé, Sokodé, Kara, Atakpamé

Population: 8.645 million

Bordering Countries: Benin, Burkina Faso, Ghana

Languages: French, Ewé, Kabiyé

Major Landmarks: Koutammakou, Togoville, Lomé Grand Market

Famous Togolese: Emmanuel Adebayor (soccer player), Edem Kodjo (politician), King Mensah (singer)

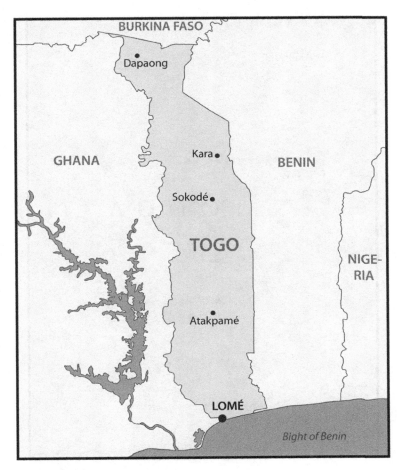

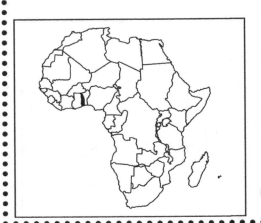

Find the Words

```
Y M O N O R I V E R Y T
T H M S O K O D E K U F
O Y A A U M R G Q O J E
G A Y E N E Q G K C M C
O N T C V A M A Z I S A
L K D A R I M F L R U N
E A Y C K M L A Q G X E
S R P U A P P L D H F H
E A Y T R K A S A F V O
W F U D Q S D M G G L H
A O B L O M E Z E O E M
K D E O M W W E K Z N S
```

ANEHO
ATAKPAME
KARA
KOUTAMMAKOU
KPALIME

LOME
MONO RIVER
SOKODE
TOGOLESE
VILLAGES

National Symbol

Lion

TONGA

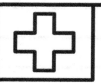

National Motto: God and Tonga Are My Inheritance

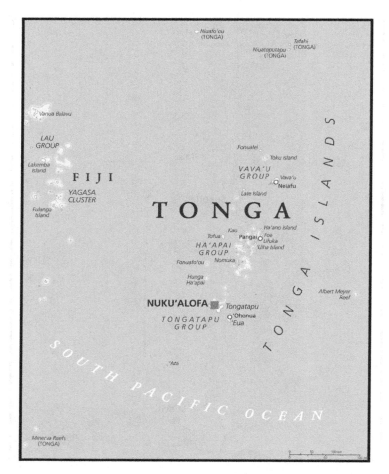

Capital: Nuku'Alofa

Area: 289 square miles (750 square kilometers)

Major Cities: Nuku'Alofa, Neiafu

Population: 106, 017

Bordering Countries: No direct borders

Languages: Tongan, English

Major Landmarks: Ha'amonga 'a Maui, Mapu'a 'a Vaea Blowholes, Eua National Park, Tongatapu Lagoon

Famous Tongans: Pita Taufatofua (Olympian), 'Akilisi Pohiva (politician), George Tupou V (king), Taniela Tupou (rugby)

National Symbol

Tongan Megapode

Find the Words

```
W H A L E S M T N K J O
X U M B R W E O C H P O
P D Q Y K N G N B R V J
K A P U A K A G I T P P
P S C E K H P A K I S S
R N C I Y W O N J W D E
D O E J F N D E Y N T T
B B T I O I E T A Y L J
R Y U O A D C L U M Q M
M X G V I F S Q Q P O E
M A T V A I U X I J O W
L N U K U A L O F A R U
```

ISLANDS	OCEAN
LAGOON	PACIFIC
MEGAPODE	TONGAN
NEIAFU	TUPOU
NUKU ALOFA	WHALES

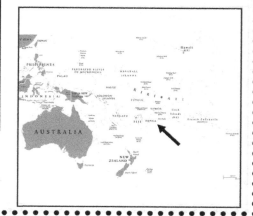

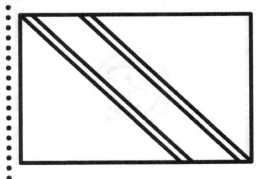

TRINIDAD AND TOBAGO

National Motto: Together We Aspire, Together We Achieve

Capital: Port of Spain

Area: 1,981 sq mi (5,131 sq km)

Major Cities: Port of Spain, San Fernando, Arima

Population: 1.399 million

Bordering Countries: Maritime borders with Grenada, Venezuela

Languages: English, Creole

Major Landmarks: Maracas Bay, Caroni Bird Sanctuary, Pigeon Point, Port of Spain's Queen's Park Savannah

Famous Trinidadians/Tobagonains: Brian Lara (cricketer), V. S. Naipaul (author), Nicki Minaj (rapper)

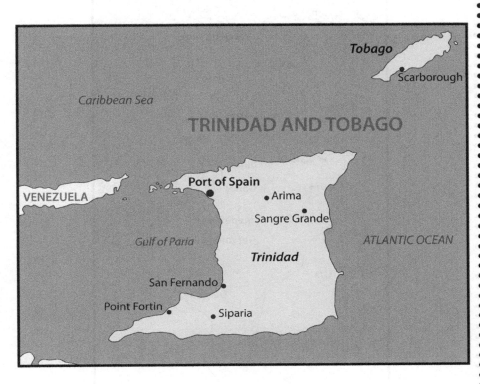

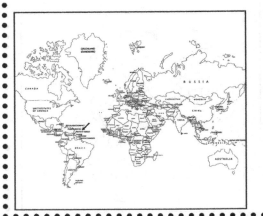

Find the Words

G	C	S	O	T	U	H	D	K	K	H	I
N	H	C	V	O	S	U	B	Q	H	T	B
F	U	A	P	B	S	M	Y	Q	O	H	G
Z	T	L	I	A	T	M	X	R	W	N	O
Y	N	Y	T	G	E	I	R	D	C	T	A
R	E	P	C	O	E	N	C	E	H	C	O
X	Y	S	H	B	L	G	S	O	O	H	A
O	U	O	L	Q	P	B	B	S	U	Z	V
Q	B	F	A	Y	A	I	L	C	L	V	P
L	O	V	K	O	N	R	I	R	C	U	A
Z	Y	O	E	F	D	D	V	D	Y	O	M
P	O	R	T	O	F	S	P	A	I	N	R

CALYPSO   PORT OF SPAIN
CHUTNEY   ROTI
COUVA   SOCA
HUMMINGBIRD   STEELPAN
PITCH LAKE   TOBAGO

National Symbol

Scarlet Ibis

TUNISIA

National Motto: Freedom, Order, Justice

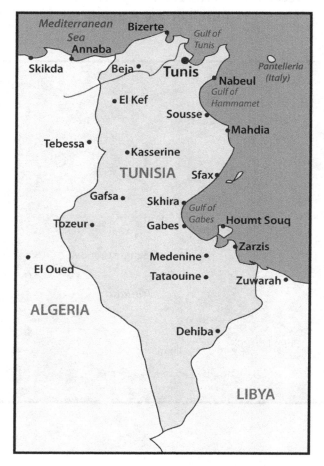

Capital: Tunis

Area: 63,170 square miles (163,610 square kilometers)

Major Cities: Tunis, Sousse, Sfax, Gabes

Population: 12.26 million

Bordering Countries: Algeria, Libya

Language: Arabic

Major Landmarks: El Djem Amphitheater, Sidi Bou Said, Carthage, Great Mosque of Kairouan

Famous Tunisians: Hannibal Barca (general), Habib Bourguiba (politician), Oussama Mellouli (swimmer)

National Symbol

Dromedary

Find the Words

```
C K T N S A G G U O D Z
A A H U E F Y D D V U Z
R Q B T N D A H T M M B
T X K L P I F X Q G B U
H R T J S S S F F L Q L
A N A N U O R I A K A A
G W S O U S S E A B D I
E Q Y J P F T F I N D S
A R A B I C U N Y C S I
J V K P D U N A W Y J N
H Y Q X C A I X S D C U
L Q R J H Y S Y U N L T
```

ARABIC	SFAX
CARTHAGE	SOUSSE
DOUGGA	TUNIS
HANNIBAL	TUNISIA
KAIROUNAN	TUNISIANS

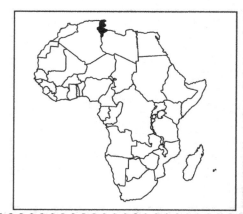

TURKEY

National Motto: No official motto

Capital: Ankara

Area: 293,280 square miles (759,592 square kilometers)

Major Cities: Izmir, Istanbul, Antalya

Population: 84.78 million

Bordering Countries: Georgia, Armenia, Azerbaijan, Iran, Iraq, Syria, Greece, Bulgaria

Language: Turkish

Major Landmarks: Hagia Sophia, Cappadocia's Fairy Chimneys and Hot Air Ballooning, Ephesu, Pamukkale's Travertine Terraces, Topkapi Palace

Famous Turks: Mustafa Kemal Atatürk (politician), Recep Tayyip Erdoğan (politician), Orhan Pamuk (writer), Hakan Şükür (athlete)

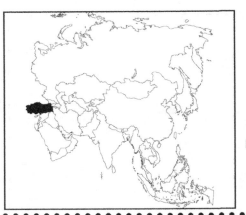

Find the Words

```
G A S R U B I O M A G
T L K C X K P P J F G
A I H P O S A I G A H
J Y X B U E K Y S T Q
A N K A R A P L G S U
H B L U E M O S Q U E
L I Z M I R T R Q M P
I S T A N B U L F R L
W Y E K R U T E Z Y H
L B O G H S I K R U T
```

ANKARA
BLUE MOSQUE
BURSA
HAGIA SOPHIA
ISTANBUL

IZMIR
MUSTAFA
TOPKAPI
TURKEY
TURKISH

National Symbol

Grey Wolf

TURKMENISTAN

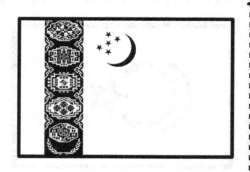

National Motto: Independence, Neutrality, Stability!

Capital: Ashgabat
Area: 188,500 square miles (488,100 square kilometers)
Major Cities: Turkmenabat, Mary
Population: 6.342 million
Bordering Countries: Kazakhstan, Uzbekistan, Afghanistan, Iran
Language: Turkmen
Major Landmarks: Darvaza Gas Crater (Door to Hell), Ancient City of Merv, Ashgabat's White Marble Buildings, Kow Ata Underground Lake, Nisa Archaeological Site
Famous Turkmen: Saparmurat Niyazov (politician), Kurban Berdyev (athlete)

National Symbol

Akhal-Teke Horse

Find the Words

J	V	X	D	A	R	V	A	Z	A	F	S
N	E	J	E	T	Y	H	A	A	M	X	D
G	Y	P	J	A	K	M	O	S	Q	U	E
G	B	A	L	K	A	N	A	B	A	T	W
A	F	L	R	R	V	X	R	F	J	S	C
S	M	U	S	L	U	R	G	U	T	R	E
A	S	H	G	A	B	O	T	J	G	L	V
N	A	T	S	I	N	E	M	K	R	U	T
O	Z	N	N	E	M	K	R	U	T	P	N
U	Y	G	Y	R	A	M	P	R	U	Y	U

ASHGABOT
BALKANABAT
DARVAZA
ERTUGRUL
GAS
GYPJAK MOSQUE
MARY
TEJEN
TURKMEN
TURKMENISTAN

TUVALU

National Motto: Tuvalu for the Almighty

Capital: Funafuti

Area: 10.04 square miles (26 square kilometers)

Major Cities: Funafuti

Population: 11,204

Bordering Countries: No direct borders

Languages: Tuvaluan and English

Major Landmarks: Funafuti Atoll, Funafuti Conservation Area, Te Namo Lagoon

Famous Tuvaluans: Iakoba Italeli (governor-general), Kamuta Latasi (prime minister), Alesana Kleist (writer)

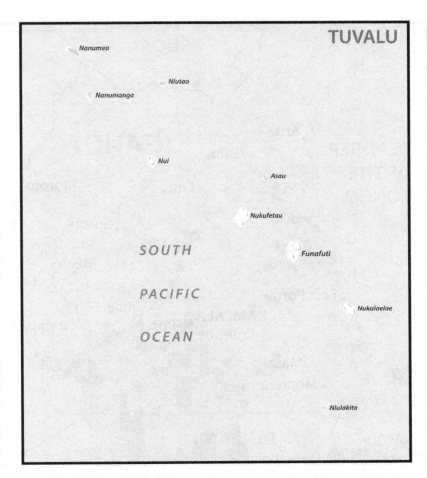

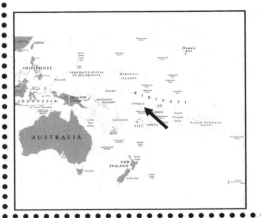

Find the Words

Y	R	P	P	F	W	T	I	Y	L	X	N
E	X	O	T	N	U	Q	A	L	Y	O	Y
W	V	L	J	G	R	N	A	G	I	F	S
O	C	Y	L	B	S	M	A	T	R	B	K
T	L	N	P	V	S	T	A	F	Y	G	I
A	S	E	A	L	E	V	E	L	U	N	P
W	L	S	T	S	R	I	O	N	I	T	G
B	A	I	P	E	S	S	A	H	A	V	I
G	G	A	S	R	F	Z	P	Y	I	M	L
R	O	N	S	M	W	L	X	J	X	I	O
B	O	K	L	C	O	U	A	T	O	L	L
C	N	B	X	D	Y	T	U	V	A	L	U

ATOLL
CONSERVATION
DOLPHIN
FUNAFUTI
LAGOON
POLYNESIA
SEA LEVEL
SMALL
TE NAMO
TUVALU

National Symbol

Pantropical Spotted Dolphin

UGANDA

National Motto: For God and My Country

Capital: Kampala

Area: 93,065 square miles (241,037 square kilometers)

Major Cities: Kampala, Gulu, Lira

Population: 45.85 million

Bordering Countries: Kenya, South Sudan, Democratic Republic of the Congo, Rwanda, Tanzania

Languages: Swahili, English, Luganda

Major Landmarks: Bwindi Impenetrable National Park, Murchison Falls National Park, Kasubi Tombs

Famous Ugandans: Idi Amin (leader), Kiprotich (runner)

National Symbol

Grey Crowned Crane

Find the Words

```
L P W U E M N E E I R K
B U L B A I B O E Z I A
Y U G J W B S Y W M L M
G J N A E I K H Y B I P
W I D T N M N Z J A R A
J K N U G D D D N L A L
U E F Q I U A Z I E I A
K A S U B I T O M B S E
N X P U I U G K L M Q U
K F K M Y Z I S B Y Y R
T Y E D P B F O P O X J
V G M A S A K A Y W E B
```

BWINDI
ENTEBBE
GULU
JINJA
KAMPALA

KASUBI TOMBS
LIRA
LUGANDA
MASAKA
MBALE

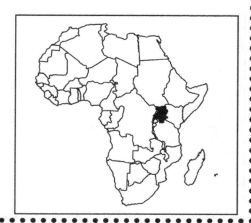

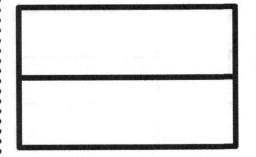

UKRAINE

National Motto: Glory to Ukraine! Glory to the HAeroes!

Capital: Kyiv

Area: 233,062 square miles (603,628 square kilometers)

Major Cities: Odesa, Lviv, Kharkiv

Population: 43,733,762

Bordering Countries: Belarus, Russia, Moldova, Romania, Hungary, Slovakia, Poland

Language: Ukrainian

Major Landmarks: Lake Svityaz, Askania-Nova, Probiy Waterfall, Livadia Palace

Famous Ukrainians: Leon Trotsky (revolutionary), Wladimir Klitschko (boxer)

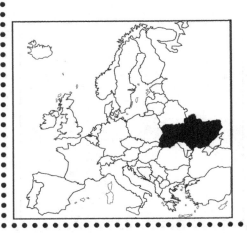

Find the Words

```
B L A C K S E A P L C L
L T K U H L N W U I L A
C A D Y J D P M L T D R
O I K Y I F V B Y J X G
S K N E M V U G E P C E
S L H J S P W K J V O S
A L D A E V Q M L S A T
C V Y R R L I S G S G B
K I T U V K J T E O I E
S V R Q Z C I D Y K U O
C E W D J G O V O A K P
U K R A I N I A N A Z Q
```

BLACK SEA   LARGEST
COSSACKS   LVIV
KHARKIV   ODESA
KYIV   REPUBLIC
LAKE SVITYAZ UKRAINIAN

National Symbol

Nightingale

UNITED ARAB EMIRATES

National Motto: God, Nation, PresidentA

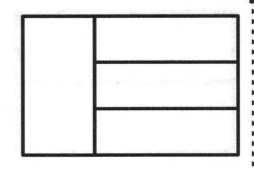

Capital: Abu Dhabi

Area: 32,300 square miles (83,600 square kilometers)

Major Cities: Dubai, Sharjah, Al Ain, Ajman

Population: 9.365 million

Bordering Countries: Saudi Arabia, Oman

Language: Arabic

Major Landmarks: Burj Khalifa, Sheikh Zayed Grand Mosque, Palm Jumeirah, Dubai Mall and Fountain Show, Sharjah

Famous Emiratis: Mohammed bin Rashid Al Maktoum (politician), Khalifa bin Zayed Al Nahyan (politician)

National Symbol

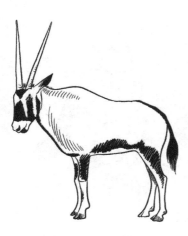

Arabian Oryx

Find the Words

```
B O S T D E S E R T Z E
U M U H G N O I L T U D
R Y W F A B L Z I Q L U
J A S R J R H E S X U B
K N B T P K J O P A B A
H Y A U I X M A V K C I
A S D E D D Q H H G Q L
L P H A N H C Q W W O J
I S Q A Y E A F C K U M
F K R X A M J B O K Z Q
A G U U N Y K O I G E X
F O U N T A I N S H O W
```

ABU DHABI   GRAND MOSQUE
BURJ KHALIFA   OIL
DESERT   SHARJAH
DUBAI   SHEIKH
FOUNTAIN SHOW   UAE

UNITED KINGDOM

National Motto: No official motto

Capital: London

Area: 93,628 square miles (242,495 square kilometers)

Major Cities: Edinburgh, Glasgow, Birmingham

Population: 67,886,011

Bordering Countries: Ireland

Language: English

Major Landmarks: Blackpool Tower, Sherwood Forest, Big Ben, River Thames, Tower of London, Buckingham Palace

Famous British: Victoria (monarch), William Shakespeare (author), Winston Churchill (statesman), Charles Darwin (biologist)

Find the Words

```
N S T O N E H E N G E H
M U W A L E S B N Q N E
B B F E L B I G O P R W
S R N X L P W N K A C E
V I U S L O E O E D W D
W T T E C B N P N N I I
C I L Z G O S D E G C N
U S I I U E T E O V L B
N H B S K Y U L C N Y U
H R X A G Q M V A J S R
A B H C J K M N K N L G
A S J E N G L A N D D H
```

BIG BEN
BRITISH
EDINBURGH
ENGLAND
LONDON
QUEEN
SCOTLAND
SHAKESPEARE
STONEHENGE
WALES

National Symbol

Lion

UNITED STATES

National Motto: In God We Trust

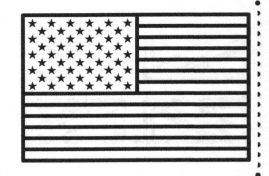

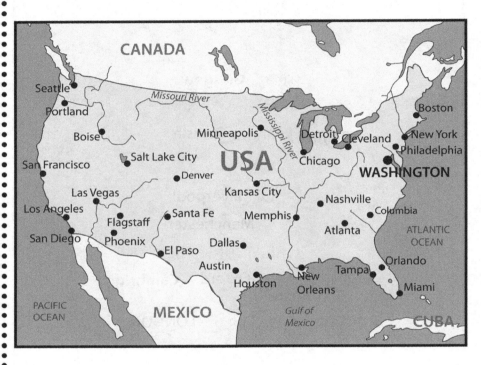

Capital: Washington, D. C.

Area: 3,796,742 sq mi (9,833,517 sq km)

Major Cities: New York City, Los Angeles, Chicago, Houston

Population: 331.002 million

Bordering Countries: Canada, Mexico

Languages: English, Spanish

Major Landmarks: Statue of Liberty, Grand Canyon, Yellowstone National Park, Mount Rushmore

Famous Americans: Martin Luther King Jr. (civil rights leader), Serena Williams (tennis player), Bill Gates (business magnate)

National Symbol

Bald Eagle

Find the Words

```
L I B E R T Y A F R U G
Z H E A G L E S H L X G
H O L L Y W O O D M J R
Y E L L O W S T O N E E
B J Q Y O G C X R Y A A
A X X P R S F O Z Q S T
S W A S H I N G T O N P
E J D C O W B O Y G K L
B A A Q P K E C C U X A
A Z K Z H M C X B B D I
L E F J Z K B E S A M N
L E S T S T A T U E C S
```

BASEBALL	JAZZ
COWBOY	LIBERTY
EAGLES	STATUE
GREAT PLAINS	WASHINGTON
HOLLYWOOD	YELLOWSTONE

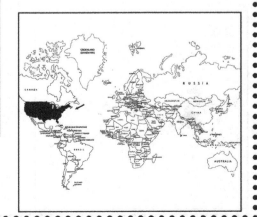

URUGUAY

National Motto: Liberty or Death

Capital: Montevideo

Area: 68,037 sq mi (176,215 sq km)

Major Cities: Montevideo, Salto, Ciudad de la Costa, Paysandú

Population: 3.473 million

Bordering Countries: Argentina, Brazil

Language: Spanish

Major Landmarks: Montevideo's Ciudad Vieja, Punta del Este, Casapueblo, Colonia del Sacramento

Famous Uruguayans: Luis Suárez (footballer), José Mujica (former President), Jorge Drexler (musician)

Find the Words

```
S U A M A T E I O W C F
E E A T A N G O V M L C
S F P W L W W N O L Y A
T G E S E O N S E J D U
A M O N T E V I D E O E
N C M O L C O L Y O B P
C E P A C O H O N M G L
I L A A C B H A O R A A
A E C A M C H D R F P T
S S P G U P N B P R V A
W T P A S A A S U G U Q
R E G Q C L Z S J Z B A
```

CANDOMBE
CELESTE
CHARRUA
ESTANCIAS
GAUCHO

MATE
MONTEVIDEO
PAMPAS
PLATA
TANGO

National Symbol

Southern Lapwing

UZBEKISTAN

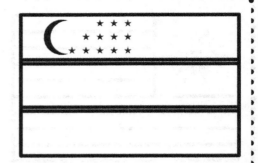

National Motto: The Strength Is In Justice

Capital: Tashkent

Area: 172,700 square miles (447,400 square kilometers)

Major Cities: Samarkand, Namangan, Andijan

Population: 34.92 million

Bordering Countries: Kazakhstan, Kyrgyzstan, Tajikistan, Afghanistan, Turkmenistan

Language: Uzbek

Major Landmarks: Registan Square, Bukhara Old City, Khiva's Historic Center, Shah-i-Zinda, Ayaz Kala and Toprak Kala

Famous Uzbeks: Islam Karimov (politician), Mirziyoyev Shavkat (politician), Abdulla Oripov (writer), Salim Abduvaliev (businessperson)

National Symbol

Turkestan Sand Cat

Find the Words

L T T B K K H A S T I M A M
Z D A V I H K T F E N Q I I
X N V K Z R B U K H A R A T
K A L T A M I N O R T U L E
V K L S J Y S P E O S E K B
E R A U Q S N A T S I G E R
P A H J K O A D B H K F B Z
Q M T N E K H S A T E Q Z T
F A I J P F C K B W B A U W
X S H Q X F G T U Q Z A C E
F B F L V Y B R R C U E U X

BABUR   REGISTAN SQUARE
BUKHARA   SAMARKAND
KALTA MINOR   TASHKENT
KHAST IMAM   UZBEK
KHIVA   UZBEKISTAN

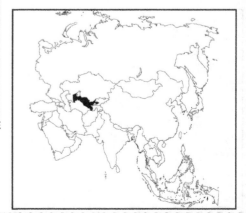

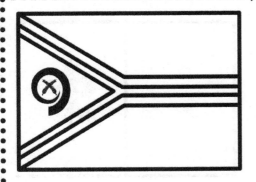

VANUATU

National Motto: In God We Stand

Capital: Port Vila

Area: 4,707 square miles (12, 190 square kilometers)

Major Cities: Port Vila, Luganville, Saratamata

Population: 319,137

Bordering Countries: No direct borders

Languages: Bislama, English, French

Major Landmarks: Mount Yasur, Millennium Cave, Mele Cascades

Famous Vanuatuans: Father Walter Lini (prime minister), Sethy Regenvanu (cultural influencer), Ralph Regenvanu (politician), Vanessa Quai (singer)

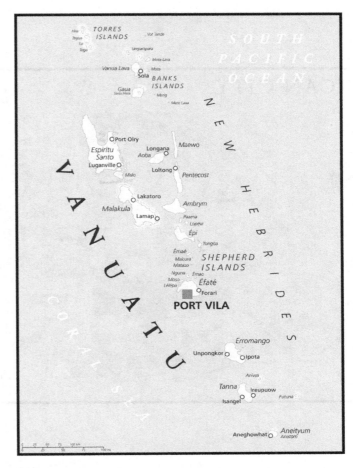

Find the Words

R	I	C	A	N	N	I	B	A	L	S	T
Y	P	B	U	N	G	E	E	J	U	M	P
A	V	V	V	D	W	I	T	A	N	R	A
P	G	O	R	A	Q	I	M	Y	U	M	E
O	B	P	L	R	N	A	G	S	S	E	U
R	R	B	Y	C	L	U	A	U	W	L	E
T	O	B	U	S	A	Y	A	M	A	A	C
V	B	T	I	Y	T	N	C	T	P	N	Y
I	F	B	S	N	K	Y	O	J	U	E	A
L	M	O	U	N	Y	X	W	E	D	S	W
A	V	O	V	Y	M	U	L	R	S	I	A
I	M	V	X	Q	H	A	P	P	Y	A	Y

BISLAMA
BUNGEE JUMP
CANNIBALS
HAPPY
IGUANA

MELANESIA
MOUNT YASUR
PORT VILA
VANUATU
VOLCANOES

National Symbol

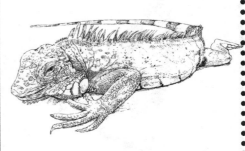

Iguana

VATICAN CITY

National Motto: No official motto

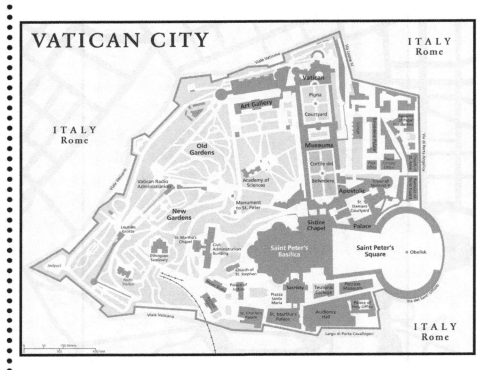

Capital: Vatican City

Area: 109 Acres

Major Cities: Vatican City

Population: 801

Bordering Countries: Italy

Language: Latin, Italian

Major Landmarks: Sistine Chapel, St. Peter's Basilica, Saint Peter's Square

Famous Vaticans: Pope Francis

National Symbol

Dove

Find the Words

M	X	B	F	S	M	A	L	L	E	S	T
T	I	Y	H	N	H	O	L	Y	S	E	E
S	L	C	X	P	Z	V	Z	B	N	I	C
I	A	X	H	Y	M	X	Z	A	O	B	I
L	T	B	G	E	K	U	I	I	N	Q	T
P	I	A	B	B	L	L	S	A	G	F	Y
A	N	S	E	L	A	A	C	E	H	S	H
Y	A	I	X	T	J	I	N	D	U	P	R
P	A	L	I	C	T	E	C	G	J	M	H
V	I	I	M	A	P	Z	V	A	E	K	S
F	I	C	V	O	F	B	V	N	U	L	U
L	V	A	P	N	M	B	L	B	T	P	O

BASILICA   MICHELANGELO

CITY   MUSEUMS

HOLY SEE   POPE

ITALIAN   SMALLEST

LATIN   VATICAN

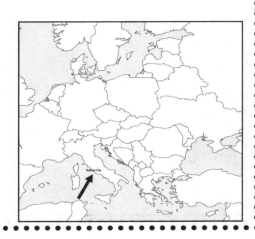

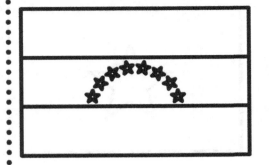

VENEZUELA

National Motto: No official motto (unofficial: God and Federation)

Capital: Caracas

Area: 353,841 sq mi (916,445 sq km)

Major Cities: Caracas, Maracaibo, Valencia, Barquisimeto

Population: 28.435 million

Bordering Countries: Brazil, Colombia, Guyana

Language: Spanish

Major Landmarks: Angel Falls, Canaima National Park, Los Roques Archipelago, Caracas' Birthplace of Simón Bolívar

Famous Venezuelans: Simón Bolívar (military leader), Gustavo Dudamel (conductor), Carolina Herrera (fashion designer)

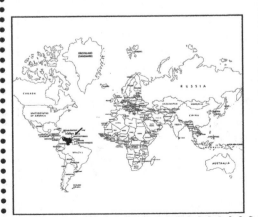

Find the Words

```
A M F C U P L O C M K E
J N U B L I R G H A V I
M Y G O O A N R V R J O
N D D E V N K C O A Y Q
K Z C I L K S C T C P S
R O L A E F O A X A M M
Z O A M C N A U G I E D
B N B R I A E L D B R Z
V H W R E R O Z L O I A
V I O T S P F R L S D G
J O R O P O A M N W A F
C A R A C A S F F N D J
```

ANGEL FALLS   JOROPO
AREPA   MARACAIBO
BOLIVAR   MERIDA
CACAO   OIL
CARACAS   ORINOCO

National Symbol

Venezuelan Troupial

VIETNAM

National Motto: Independence, Freedom and Happiness

Capital: Hanoi
Area: 127,882 square miles (331,212 square kilometers)
Major Cities: Ho Chi-Minh City, Haiphong, Da Nang
Population: 97.47 million
Bordering Countries: China, Laos, Cambodia
Language: Vietnamese
Major Landmarks: Ha Long Bay, Hoi An Ancient Town, Ho Chi Minh City's Cu Chi Tunnels, Hue's Imperial City, My Son Sanctuary
Famous Vietnamese: Ho Chi Minh (politician), Nguyen Van Thieu (politician), Nguyen Du (poet), Pham Thi Hue (athlete)

National Symbol

Water Buffalo

Find the Words

I	B	D	J	F	Y	F	V	P	Y	E	S
O	M	M	A	G	V	S	F	A	E	L	W
H	S	P	P	N	W	J	B	Y	E	G	H
O	L	G	E	I	A	G	Z	N	D	T	P
C	Z	J	G	R	N	N	J	B	O	I	I
H	D	A	G	O	I	U	G	Z	X	N	H
I	H	P	L	U	T	A	M	T	C	K	B
M	R	A	V	I	L	Z	L	Y	Y	I	Z
I	H	Y	H	X	S	F	K	C	Q	N	R
N	J	C	B	H	A	N	O	I	I	C	O
H	U	M	E	K	O	N	G	M	V	T	M
C	V	I	E	T	N	A	M	E	S	E	Y

CU CHI TUNNELS   HO CHI MINH
DA NANG   IMPERIAL CITY
GULF   MEKONG
HA LONG BAY   TONKIN
HANOI   VIETNAMESE

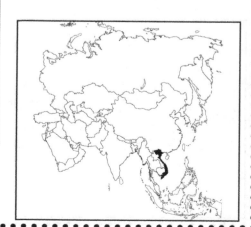

YEMEN

National Motto: God, Homeland, Revolution, Unity

Capital: Sana'a

Area: 203,850 square miles (527,968 square kilometers)

Major Cities: Taizz, Al Hudaydah, Aden

Population: 32.98 million

Bordering Countries: Saudi Arabia, Oman

Language: Arabic

Major Landmarks: Old City of Sana'a, Socotra Island, Shibam Hadramawt (The Manhattan of the Desert), Al-Mahwit Palace, Marib Dam and Archaeological Site

Famous Yemeni: Ali Abdullah Saleh (politician), Tawakkol Karman (activist), Abdu Rabu Mansour Hadi (politician)

Find the Words

```
N M A R I B D A M Q E K
G U A I M M U K A L L A
T Z D S L V Y U E Y B L
S T S T J T X H P E E I
D O I D I O L A F M N K
K K C C S R V D V E J Y
X I D O A J Z R O N U I
Z L J A T Z Q A Z I R R
O A N F I R M M R G X S
L A B A N E A A S O D Y
S L T I R O X U A D E N
O R O I D Z R T U Q M N
```

ADEN   SANAA
HADRAMAUT   SOCOTRA
MARIB DAM   TAIZZ
MUKALLA   YEMENI
OLD CITY   ZABID

National Symbol

Arabian Leopard

ZAMBIA

National Motto: One Zambia, One Nation

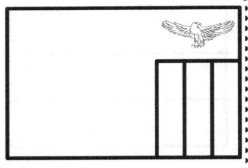

Capital: Lusaka
Area: 290,586 square miles (752,614 square kilometers)
Major Cities: Lusaka, Ndola, Kitwe, Chipata
Population: 19.47 million
Bordering Countries: Angola, Bostwana, Democratic Republic of the Congo, Mozambique, Malawi, Tanzania, Zimbabwe
Languages: English, Bemba, Nyanja, Tonga, Lozi
Major Landmarks: Victoria Falls, South Luangwa National Park, Lower Zambezi National Park
Famous Zambians: Kenneth Kaunda (president), Dambisa Moyo (economist), Kalusha Bwalya (soccer player)

National Symbol

African Fish Eagle

Find the Words

L	X	F	S	T	Q	D	Z	F	K	A	Z
I	A	V	I	N	J	R	A	D	A	T	B
V	V	Q	A	L	S	F	M	O	R	C	E
I	Q	M	V	B	U	I	B	K	I	H	M
N	A	Q	O	P	H	Q	E	B	B	I	B
G	Y	J	N	F	I	D	Z	V	A	P	A
S	V	X	G	W	U	C	I	K	D	A	E
T	M	F	A	Q	N	Z	R	Z	A	T	Q
O	N	D	O	L	A	S	I	H	M	A	B
N	K	A	F	U	E	Y	V	U	G	I	S
E	L	U	S	A	K	A	E	F	C	T	Z
K	A	S	A	N	K	A	R	J	W	E	Y

BEMBA
CHIPATA
KAFUE
KARIBA DAM
KASANKA

LIVINGSTONE
LUSAKA
NDOLA
SIAVONGA
ZAMBEZI RIVER

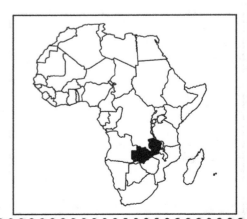

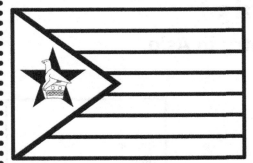

ZIMBABWE

National Motto: Unity, Freedom, Work

Capital: Harare
Area: 150,872 square miles
(390,757 square kilometers)
Major Cities: Harare, Bulawayo, Mutare, Chitungwiza
Population: 15.99 million
Bordering Countries:
South Africa, Botswana,
Zambia, Mozambique
Language: Chewa, Chibarwe, English, Kalanga, Koisan,
Nambya, Ndau, Ndebele,
Shangani, Shona, Sotho, Tonga, Tswana, Venda, Xhosa
Major Landmarks: Victoria Falls, Great Zimbabwe,
Hwange National Park
Famous Zimbabweans:
Robert Mugabe (politician),
Tsitsi Dangarembga (author), Kirsty Coventry (swimmer)

MOZAMBIQUE
ZAMBIA
Kariba
Lake Kariba
Chinhoyi
HARARE
Chitungwiza
Binga
Kadoma
Hwange
ZIMBABWE
Mutare
Gweru
Bulawayo
Masvingo
BOTSWANA
Beitbridge
SOUTH AFRICA

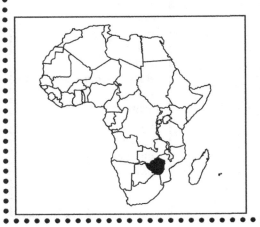

Find the Words

```
M A W B U L A W A Y O R
C T L L X L Q K B I O D
O H W V C L E Q N E A M
N X S U R E W G W Z P A
S N A E W B A B M I Z I
S E S H N B A K T W P R
S R L U A B L P P E M O
K S W V M R V F G L U T
C W H I P J A D I I T C
O Y Z O B E I R E A A I
R L V V N R N K E V R V
P Q Y T B A P W H R E I
```

BRIDGE	ROCKS
BULAWAYO	SHONA
GWERU	VICTORIA
HARARE	ZIMBABWE
MUTARE	ZIMBABWEANS

National Symbol

Sable Antelope

Country Capitals
Write the capital for each country in Asia

1 Afghanistan _____
2 Armenia _____
3 Azerbaijan _____
4 Bahrain _____
5 Bangladesh _____
6 Bhutan _____
7 Brunei _____
8 Cambodia _____
9 China _____
10 Cyprus _____
11 Georgia _____
12 India _____
13 Indonesia _____
14 Iran _____
15 Iraq _____
16 Israel _____
17 Japan _____
18 Jordan _____
19 Kazakhstan _____
20 Kuwait _____
21 Kyrgyzstan _____
22 Laos _____
23 Lebanon _____
24 Malaysia _____
25 Maldives _____
26 Mongolia _____
27 Myanmar _____
28 Nepal _____
29 North Korea _____
30 Oman _____
31 Pakistan _____

32 Palestine _____
33 Philippines _____
34 Qatar _____
35 Russia _____
36 Saudi Arabia _____
37 Singapore _____
38 South Korea _____
39 Sri Lanka _____
40 Syria _____
41 Taiwan _____
42 Tajikistan _____
43 Thailand _____
44 Timor-Leste _____
45 Turkey _____
46 Turkmenistan _____
47 United Arab Emirates _____
48 Uzbekistan _____
49 Vietnam _____
50 Yemen _____

Abu Dhabi
Amman
Ankara
Ashgabat
Astana
Baghdad
Baku
Bandar Seri Begawan
Bangkok
Beijing
Beirut
Bishkek
Colombo
Damascus
Dhaka
Dili
Doha
Dushanbe
Hanoi
Islamabad
Jakarta
Jerusalem
Kabul
Kathmandu
Kuwait City
Kuala Lumpur
Malé
Manila
Manama
Moscow
Muscat
Naypyidaw
New Delhi
Nicosia
Phnom Penh
Pyongyang
Ramallah
Riyadh
Seoul
Sana'a
Singapore
Sri Jayawardenepura Kotte
Taipei
Tashkent
Tbilisi
Tehran
Thimphu
Tokyo

Color the Countries!

Color the map of Europe below and then
use the map to answer the questions

1. How many countries are also islands? _____

2. Which is the largest country in Europe? _____

3. How many countries are landlocked? _____

4. Which countries begin with the letter F? _____

5. Which is the northern most country? _____

Use the numbered map to fill in the names of the African countries below.

1. _____
2. _____
3. _____
4. _____
5. _____
6. _____
7. _____
8. _____
9. _____
10. _____
11. _____
12. _____
13. _____
14. _____
15. _____
16. _____
17. _____
18. _____
19. _____
20. _____
21. _____
22. _____
23. _____
24. _____
25. _____
26. _____
27. _____
28. _____

29. _____
30. _____
31. _____
32. _____
33. _____
34. _____
35. _____
36. _____
37. _____
38. _____
39. _____
40. _____
41. _____
42. _____
43. _____
44. _____
45. _____
46. _____
47. _____
48. _____
49. _____
50. _____
51. _____
52. _____
53. _____
54. _____
55. _____

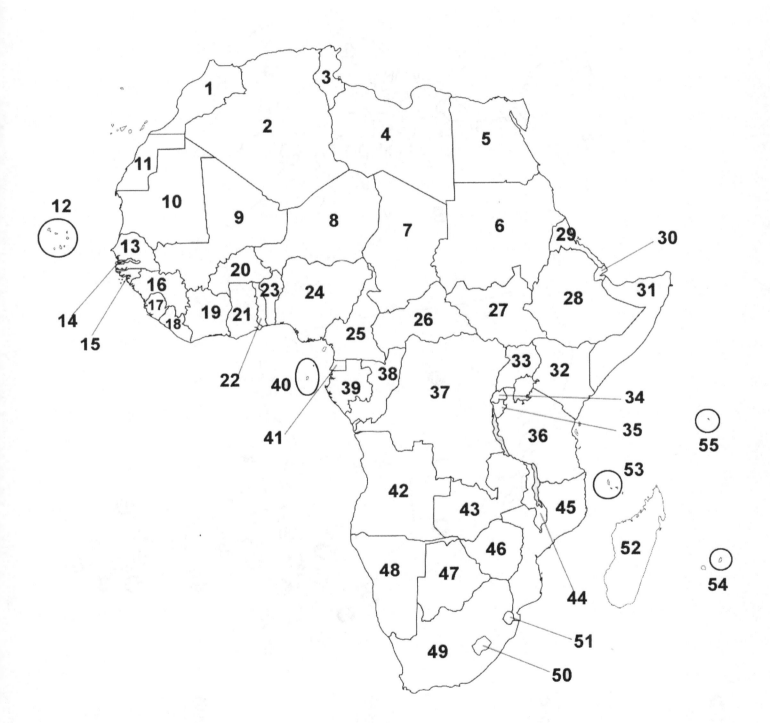

Use the numbered maps to fill in the names of the countries of North and South America.

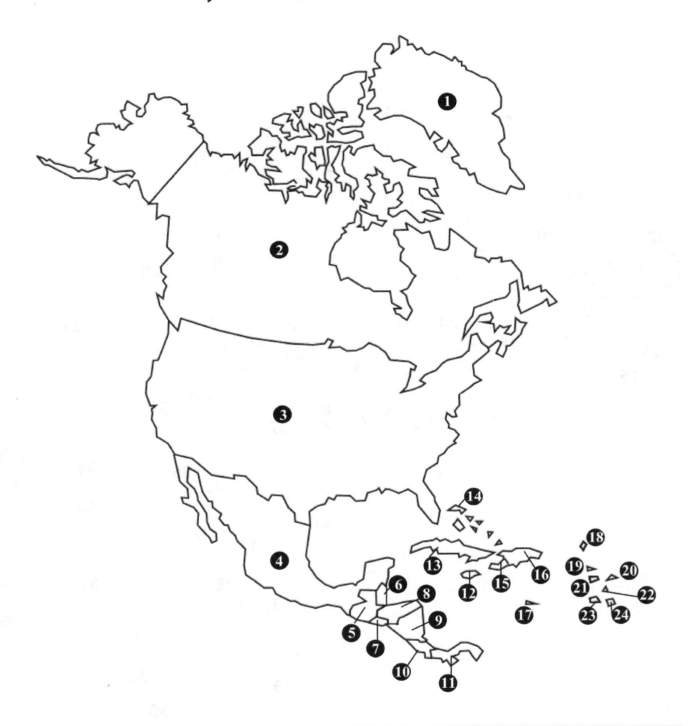

❶		❼		⓭		⓳	
❷		❽		⓮		⓴	
❸		❾		⓯		㉑	
❹		❿		⓰		㉒	
❺		⓫		⓱		㉓	
❻		⓬		⓲		㉔	

❶		❻		⑪	
❷		❼		⑫	
❸		❽		⑬	
❹		❾			
❺		⑩			

Complete the Crossword Puzzle about Oceania

Across

1. Capital of Fiji
3. Number of stars in Australia's flag
7. Australia's capital city
8. Small island nation known for its coral atolls
9. Native Polynesian people of New Zealand
11. Jellyfish Lake is located here
12. Large Australian marsupial with a pouch
13. New Zealand's native bird, known for being flightless

Down

1. Australia's largest city
2. Country Christmas Island is located in
4. Wellington is its capital
5. Tiny island country in Oceania; starts with 'N'
6. Solomon Islands national bird
10. Ocean surrounding many of the Oceania islands

Answers

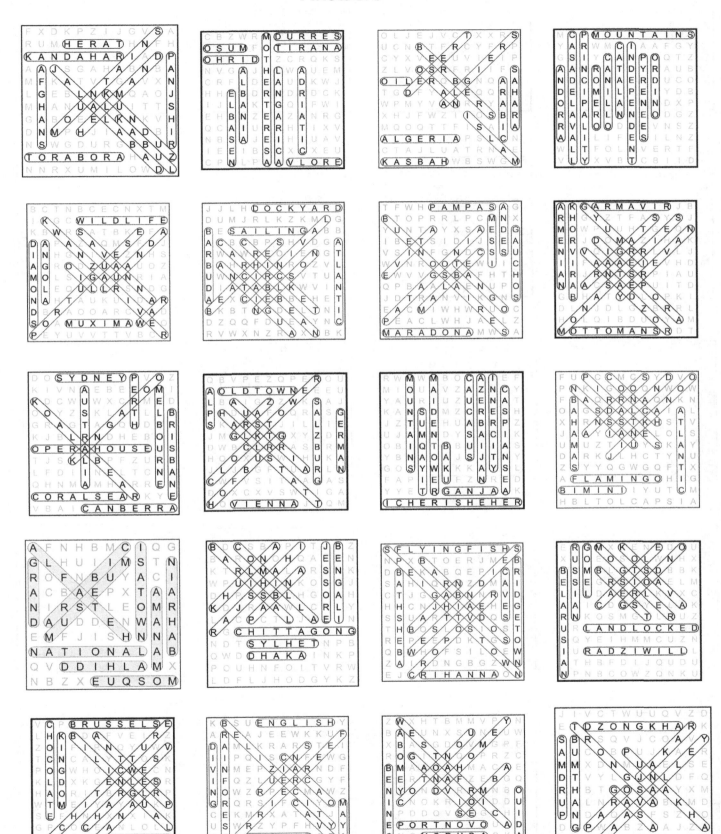

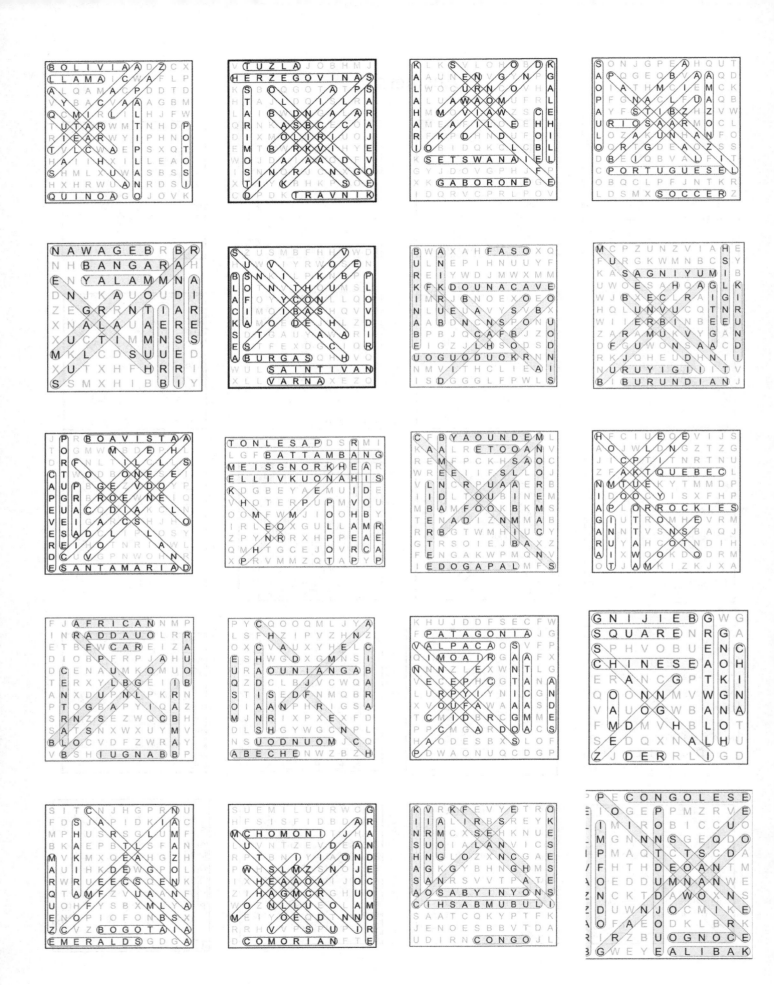

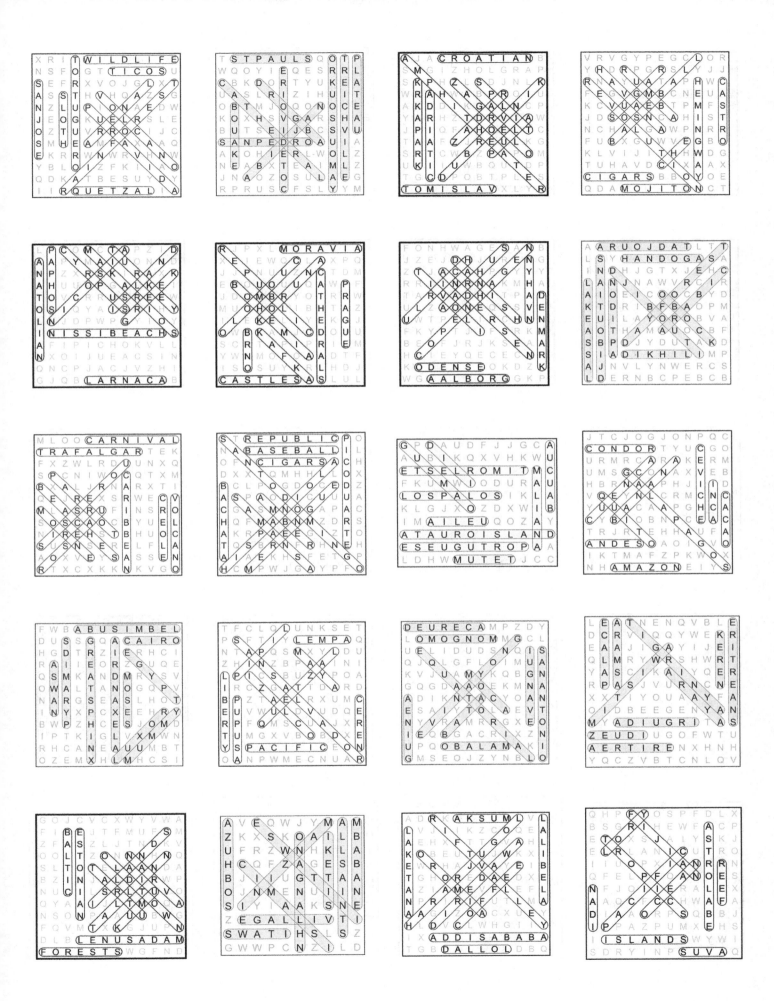

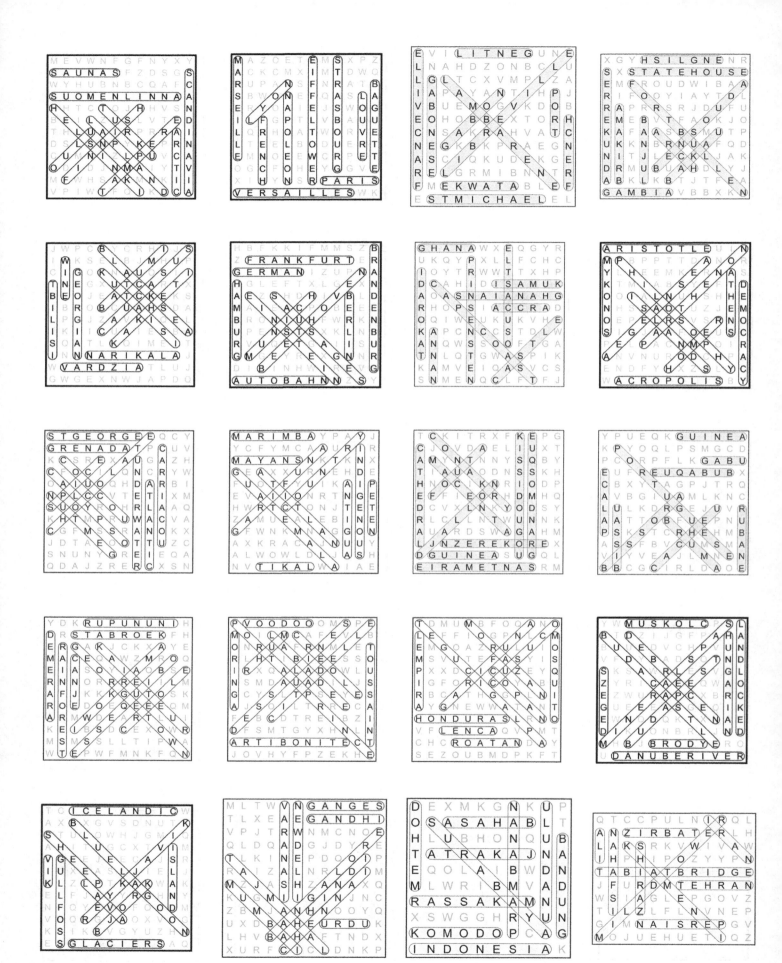

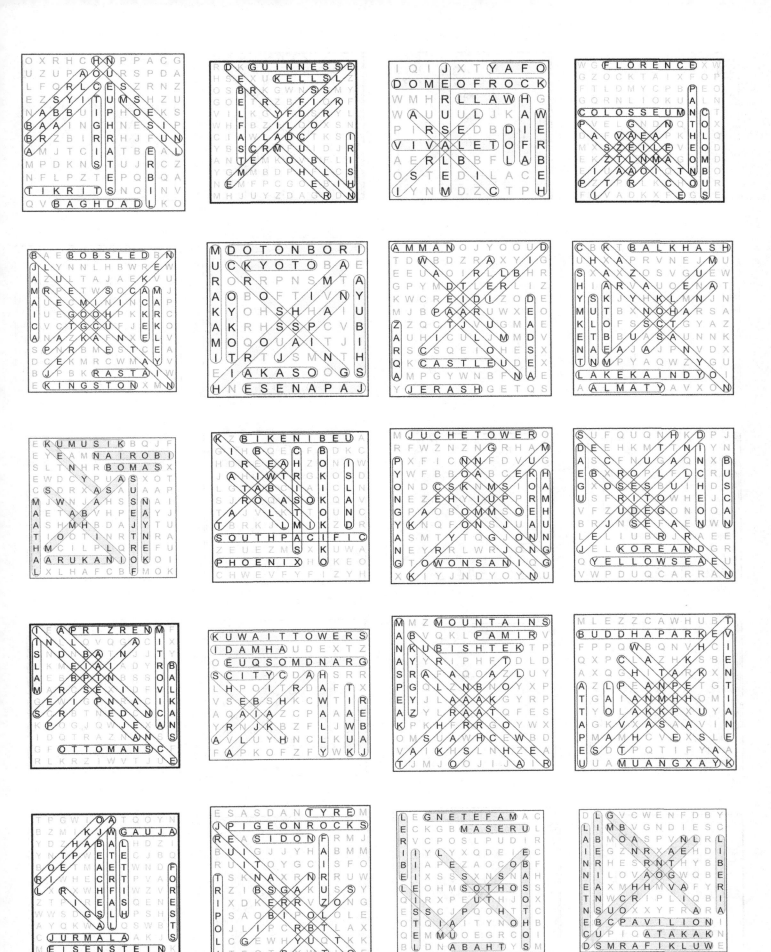

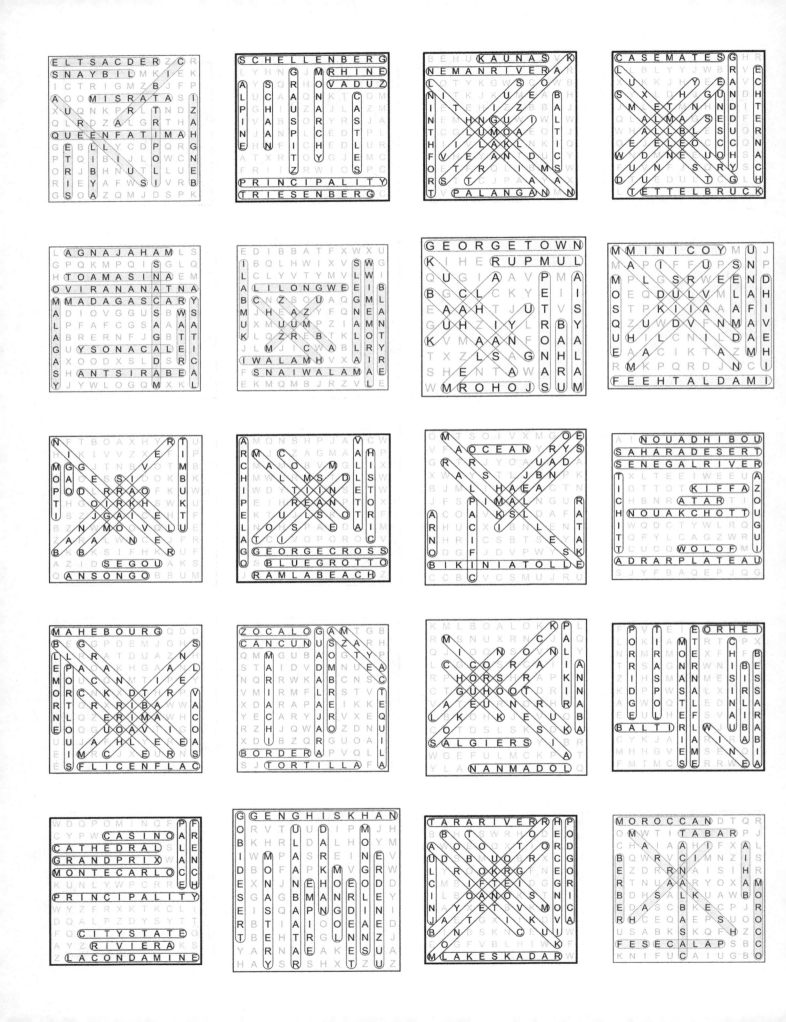

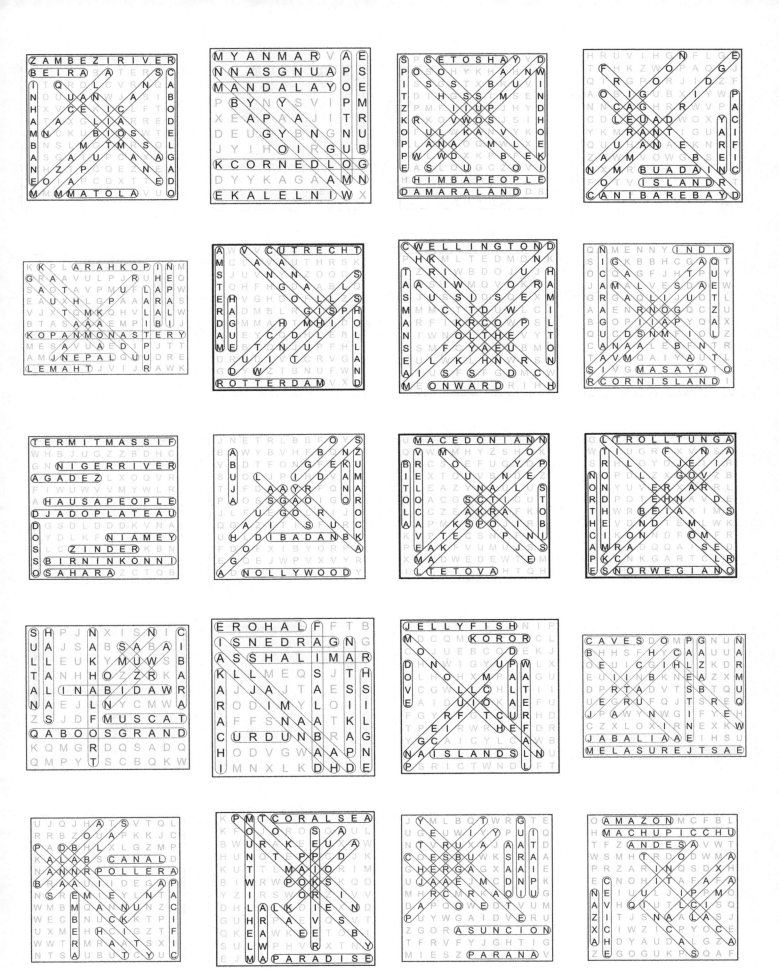

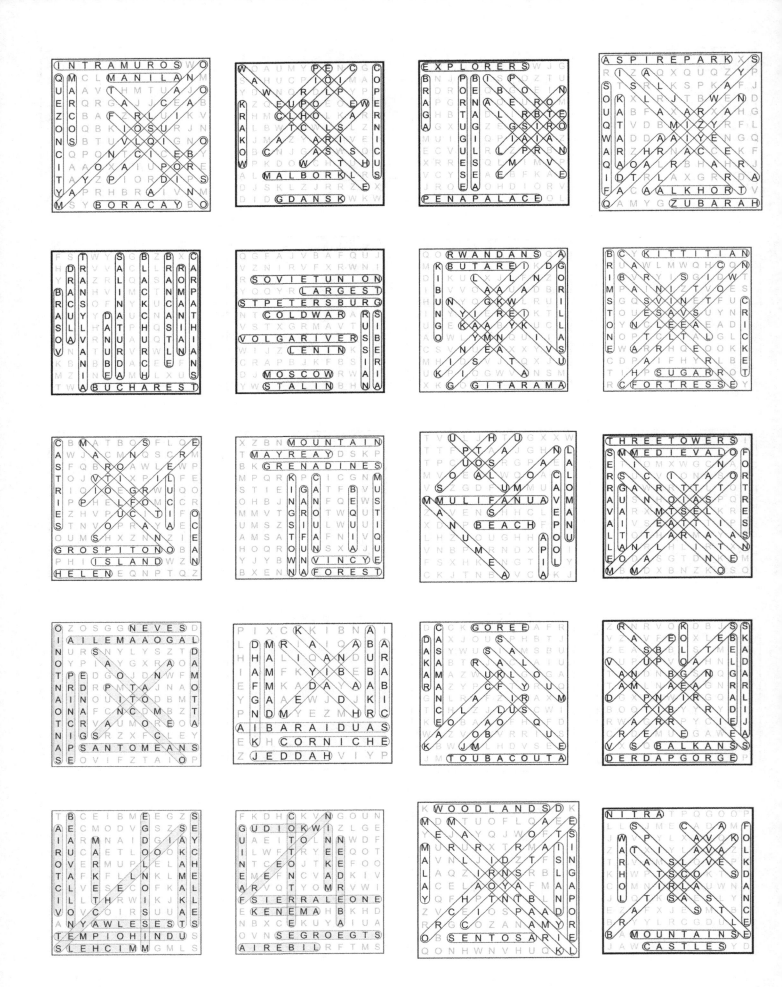

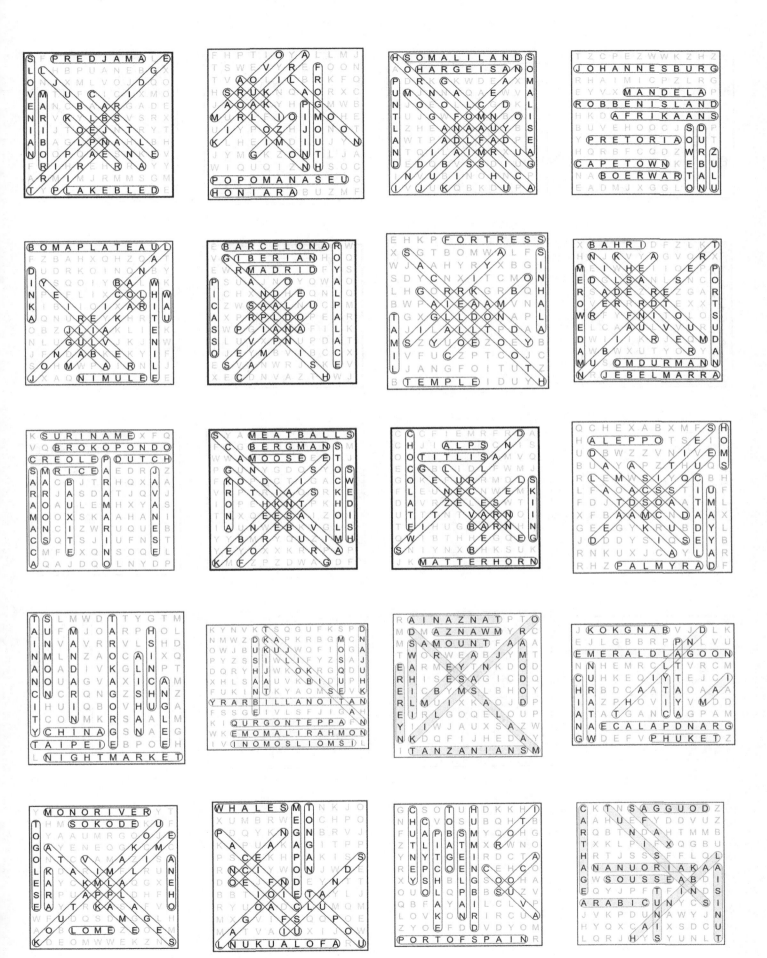

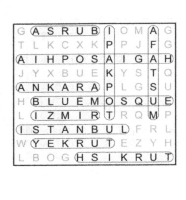
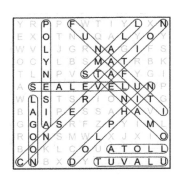
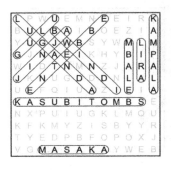
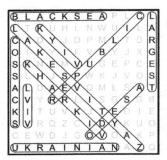

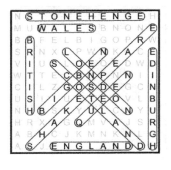

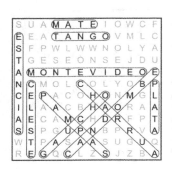
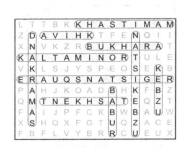
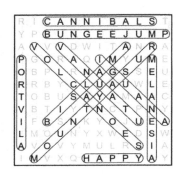
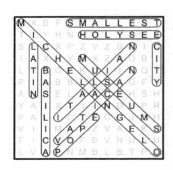

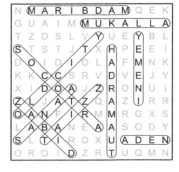

Asia Capitals

1. Georgia
2. Azerbaijan
3. Armenia
4. Turkey
5. Syria
6. Cyprus
7. Lebanon
8. Palestine
9. Israel
10. Jordan
11. Saudi Arabia
12. Yemen
13. Oman
14. United Arab Emirates
15. Qatar
16. Bahrain
17. Kuwait
18. Iraq
19. Iran
20. Turkmenistan
21. Uzbekistan
22. Kazakhstan
23. Kyrgyzstan
24. Tajikistan
25. Afghanistan
26. Pakistan
27. India
28. Sri Lanka
29. Maldives
30. Nepal
31. Bhutan
32. Bangladesh
33. Myanmar
34. Thailand
35. Malaysia
36. Singapore
37. Indonesia
38. Timor-Leste
39. Brunei
40. Philippines
41. Vietnam
42. Cambodia
43. Laos
44. China
45. Taiwan
46. South Korea
47. North Korea
48. Japan
49. Mongolia
50. Russia

Europe Map

1. Five (Iceland, UK, Ireland, Malta, Cyprus)
2. Ukraine
3. Fourteen
4. Finland, France
5. Norway

Africa Map

1. Morocco
2. Algeria
3. Tunisia
4. Libya
5. Egypt
6. Sudan
7. Chad
8. Niger
9. Mali
10. Mauritania
11. Western Sahara
12. Cabo Verde (Cape Verde)
13. Senegal
14. The Gambia
15. Guinea-Bissau
16. Guinea
17. Sierra Leone
18. Liberia
19. Côte d'Ivoire (Ivory Coast)
20. Burkina Faso
21. Ghana
22. Togo
23. Benin
24. Nigeria
25. Cameroon
26. Central African Republic
27. South Sudan
28. Ethiopia
29. Eritrea
30. Djibouti
31. Somalia
32. Kenya
33. Uganda
34. Rwanda
35. Burundi
36. Tanzania
37. Democratic Republic of the Congo
38. Republic of the Congo
39. Gabon
40. São Tomé & Príncipe
41. Equatorial Guinea
42. Angola
43. Zambia
44. Malawi
45. Mozambique
46. Zimbabwe
47. Botswana
48. Namibia
49. South Africa
50. Lesotho
51. Eswatini (Swaziland)
52. Madagascar
53. Comoros
54. Mauritius
55. Seychelles

North America Map

1. Greenland
2. Canada
3. United States
4. Mexico
5. Guatemala
6. Belize
7. El Salvador
8. Hondoras
9. Nicaragua
10. Costa Rica
11. Panama
12. Jamaica
13. Cuba
14. Bahamas
15. Haiti
16. Dominican Republic
17. Dominica
18. Antigua and Barbuda
19. St. Kitts and Nevis
20. St. Lucia
21. St. Vincent and the Grenadines
22. Barbados
23. Grenada
24. Trinidad and Tobago

South America Map

1. Venezuela
2. Guyana
3. Colombia
4. Suriname
5. French Guiana
6. Brazil
7. Ecuador
8. Peru
9. Bolivia
10. Chile
11. Paraguay
12. Argentina
13. Uruguay

Oceania Crossword

Across:
1. Suva
3. Six
7. Canberra
8. Tuvalu
9. Maori
11. Palau
12. Kangaroo
13. Kiwi

Down:
1. Sydney
2. Kiribati
4. New Zealand
5. Nauru
6. Frogmouth
10. Pacific

Made in the USA
Monee, IL
02 March 2024

54157476R00125